ORIGINAL WRITING

from

IRELAND'S OWN

ORIGINAL WRITING

978-1-907179-62-4

A CIP catalogue for this book is available from the National Library.

Published by ORIGINAL WRITING LTD., Dublin, 2010.

Printed by CAHILL PRINTERS LIMITED, Dublin.

INTRODUCTION

There has been an explosion of interest in writing in Ireland in recent years, despite the arrival on the scene of so many electronic and other distractions. Ireland's Own has always tried to encourage the idea of writing among ordinary people and we are one of the few outlets for budding writers of both factual articles and fiction. We have a regular corps of professional and part-time contributors, and we also receive a great many unsolicited submissions every week, many of them are of a high standard. We are only able to use a small portion of them, but we do try to be sympathetic and encouraging rather than abruptly rejecting.

In furtherance of this same aim, we have run our Annual Short Stories and Memories Writing Competitions for many years, and they attract a great many entries, some of them extremely good. We publish the winners in our Winning Writers Annual every May. For the past three years we have been sponsored by the self-publishing company, Original Writing, from Dublin, and their support is greatly appreciated.

This year for the first time we are publishing an anthology, and it contains over fifty winners and highly recommended entries. This has been made possible by our partnership with Original Writing. We congratulate the three overall category winners, the other nine prizewinners and the forty other writers included in this inaugural volume; we thank them all for their help and co-operation with this project. We also compliment everybody else who took the time and trouble to submit entries.

Maeve Binchy has always been a great friend to Ireland's Own; we thank her for her generous foreword to this book; we also thank former Ireland's Own editors, Gerry Breen and Margaret Galvin, for all their help, and a special word of thanks to Martin Delany, Garrett Bonner, Steven Weekes and all the crew at Original Writing for their patience and assistance.

As Maeve Binchy says in her foreword, this is a significant day for all the authors in this collection, especially those never before published in a book. Perhaps for some it will be a springboard to greater literary success in the future. This first anthology is also a special occasion for Ireland's Own, another milestone in our own story which has continued without a break in service since 1902. It is our sincere hope that this will be the first of many such publications.

> Phil Murphy, *Monthly Editor*
> Sean Nolan, *Weekly Editor*
> *Ireland's Own.*

FOREWORD *by Maeve Binchy*

It is an honour to be invited to introduce this collection of original writing and short stories.

Ireland's Own has been like a good kindly Fairy Godmother for all of us, publishing our first works, giving us encouragement, always answering our letters. The magazine has been like a friend, a great cushion against the tough world out there.

While I know some of those appearing in this book are quite experienced, there will be others reading their very first work in print between the covers of a book. It's a heady experience, it's marvellous. You want to stop passers-by and ask them have they seen it, read it, studied it. You will get several copies so that they can be shown around. It's the proof that you have had something to say and that you said it.

This is why collections like this are so important to us. As Irish people, or as anyone living in Ireland will know, we think it's good to talk. We never believe that keeping yourself to yourself is a good way of life. We are open and interested and curious about life, our own and other peoples.

And in terms of writing this is good. Very good.

We notice things and remember them; we have memories that can be called up, we have nostalgia for times gone by, or hopes for the future. This is the stuff of writing, the wish to share your thoughts with others, and the discipline to sit down and write them out, with a beginning, a middle and an end.

It's not easy to submit a story or a memory and give it to someone else for judgement. We all hate putting that work out there. While it's safe at home in the drawer nobody can hurt us or reject it. But you were lucky people, you sent your work to the kindly, generous Ireland's Own who know how hard it is to make that step and who will often write to you an encouraging note even if they cannot accept your work.

And now in this joint venture with Original Writing from Dublin your work is appearing in an Anthology. You have made it. You have begun your journey in some cases, continued it in others, and the world lies ahead.

Congratulations to you all, especially those who are now Published Authors for the first time!

I am greatly looking forward to sitting down and reading these pages and to knowing that you will feel like me . . . that it is great to be part of a nation of story tellers and we must keep it all going.

Warmest wishes from Maeve Binchy

ORIGINAL WRITING

For the past three years it has been Original Writing's great pleasure to sponsor Ireland's Own Annual Short Stories and Memories Writing Competitions. Over these years there have been many wonderful entries and it was with this in mind that we came up with the idea for this anthology.

We would like to take this opportunity to congratulate all of the winners and other authors whose writings are contained in this anthology.

ABOUT ORIGINAL WRITING

Original Writing Limited (www.originalwriting.ie) is Ireland's premier self publishing company. Founded in late 2006, we have published over 180 authors to date. While each wrote and published for different reasons, one requirement dictated the choice of Original Writing as publisher - the author, in every case, wanted ultimate control over the design, editorial and publishing process.

Original Writing is committed to publishing books affordably and to a high standard. We offer guidance to authors but unlike traditional publishers, our authors make all the key decisions about their work. Providing an array of tools and services Original Writing allows authors to make their own choices throughout the publishing process. Authors retain all the rights, maintain editorial control and choose the exact selection of services that best suits their needs and goals.

We have a great team ready to work with each author. Our mission is to ensure every author has a clear understanding of how our programme will help them achieve their publishing goals. Whether you want to get your work published for family and friends or to sell at a profit we can help you realise your dream.

We handle Autobiography, Memoirs, Poetry, Fiction - both Novel and Short Stories - Philosophical and Religious Studies, Travel Writing and many other genres.

You make all the decisions about your book with regard to content, appearance and price. We will work closely with you to turn your book into a beautifully designed and professionally printed reality. The author retains full copyright of the work throughout.

Once your book is published we will give you the tools to publish and promote your work online in front of a global audience. Your book is automatically made available for sale online and is produced on a print-on-demand basis. There is absolutely no inventory risk for the author. Copies are printed and shipped worldwide as needed.

WWW.WRITING4ALL.IE

Writing4all is an online writers' resource where you can share your creative writing - from poetry to short stories and from memoirs to novels - get feedback and comment on other writers' work. There is also news, events, competition information and listings for creative writing courses, writing groups, workshops and many more writing resources. Check out the site at: www.writing4all.ie

CONTENTS

Open Short Story First Prize Winner

Maiden Flight

by Pauline O'Hare
Balbriggan, Co. Dublin

A farmer and his daughter cope with the pain of parting as she heads off to London

She waited until the dessert was served before slipping the words into the conversation. They were celebrating her exam results. "I've applied for a teaching job in London, Da. I've an interview next week."

The words seemed to hang in the air, like a black cloud blocking the sun, chilling the atmosphere between them. She heard her father gasp before he bent his head, fixing his attention on the bowl of ice-cream that he rhythmically stirred into a smooth pink liquid.

Fiona put a hand on his arm saying, "It's time for me to stand on my own feet, Da." He shrugged it off as one would a bothersome fly.

His chair scraped on the tiled floor as he stood up. "I think I've eaten enough. I need a smoke. I'll wait for you outside."

At home he refused to discuss the issue. Almost overnight he began to walk with his back arched and his shoulders hunched up into his neck, as if carrying an invisible load. He looked old and defeated, not the fit middle-aged man she knew. One morning she found him in the granary, sitting on the heap of grain with a map of the British Isles spread open on his knee.

"London's only an hour"s flight from Dublin, Da. You could come and visit."

"Huh! And bring the cows in a hold-all and milk them mid-flight!" he snorted. He drizzled a handful of corn through his cupped fist onto the map, where it bounced like falling hailstones. "Your mother must be turning in her grave. We promised her we'd look after each other."

Brandy the old sheepdog, lying at his feet, suddenly lifted his head and whined. Fiona, annoyed her mother was being dragged into their emotional battle, replied angrily,

"That's unfair, Da. You know she encouraged me to be independent. Remember what she always said. 'Make sure you stick it out at your studies, girlie. Education's easy carried'."

He idly scratched Brandy's ears. "I never understood what that meant. But if she'd known you'd abandon your home and country she wouldn't have said it."

Fiona's instinct was to contradict him again. Her mother had constantly urged her not to bury her ambitions ankle-deep in cow dung and gutters, as she, herself, had done: "Never marry a farmer. Not even if you love him like I love your father; for the farm will always be number one and come between you and him. And worse still, between you and yourself. Education's the key to freedom, and don't you forget it, girlie, and it's as light and portable as a passport."

But it would have been cruel to tell him, now that she was dead, that his wife had yearned for something more than farm life could give her, when he hadn't seen it for himself when she was alive. How she lifted a guidebook at every snatched moment; fed hungrily on travel documentaries; tilted her head to listen to the oddest of news items someone running away to a circus; go ing up in a space shuttle; shooting the rapids – and sigh, "That's another way of escaping."

How, when the cancer took hold, she fought it by seeing the positive, how she fingered her St Christopher medal at her neck and pointed to her stack of travel books and atlases: "All the time in the world now to explore."

And, when her eyesight went, how that was the end of her journeying and she was gone in a week. Her father, not being a reader, hadn't seen that either. Not that it mattered anymore, when the result was the same heartbreaking desolation for both of them.

Her eyes blurred with tears. "She'd have given me her blessing."

Whether or not he heard the whispered rebuke she didn't know, but he scrunched the map into a ball and threw it at the wall, before pushing past her and stomping off. Brandy limped out behind him. Fiona sat in the still-warm hollow in the corn and cried. If she changed her mind and stayed to please him, she knew she would end up hating him.

When she returned from the interview, the rift between them grew. He rarely spoke. When he did, it was in sharp reproach-laden sentences that Fiona determined to ignore. At mealtimes she turned the radio volume up to drown out the silence. It was he who took the letter from the postman, when it arrived a few weeks later. He placed it on the table and walked out, banging the door so hard that the cups rattled on their hooks on the dresser.

Half an hour later he returned, a blood-soaked rag wrapped around his left hand. "I caught it on a bit of wire. I wasn't paying attention. I had too many things on my mind."

"Let me see," Fiona said, but he turned his back on her. The rag was dripping red onto the yellow quarry tiles.

"I'll drive you to the doctor."

"I'll drive myself. I have to get used to doing things for myself." The barb was as sharp as the wire that had sliced into him.

"And killing yourself driving one-handed is a great way to start, I suppose," she said, grabbing the keys from him.

"Three stitches and a tetanus jab," he said grumpily, settling himself into the front seat.

"Did he give you pain killers?" Fiona asked

"There are some aches tablets can't ease," he gibed, under his breath. She refused to be baited. She switched on the engine.

"Doc Bradley wanted to know when you were leaving, but I couldn't tell him seeing as I don"t know myself?"

This was the moment to tell him she hadn't got the job; she was too inexperienced for a school in Inner London; they wished her luck in finding a suitable position elsewhere. It was raining. The only sound was the swish and whoosh of the wipers. He took out his pipe and began to bite the end of it, a sign he was agitated.

"You mark my words," he said finally, "some day, when the flame of the Big Smoke burns out, you'll be happy to crawl home and slum it here in the bog-hole of nowhere."

She recognised his anguish in the unkindness of the words, but the sting of the verbal slap prevented her from reassuring him. She kept her eyes steadfastly on the road, wondering what it was about the twisted logic of pride that persuaded them both that theirs was the greater hurt, when all the while they were feeding into and off each other's, like spinning magnets, creating one dynamo of resentment.

By the time they reached home she had made up her mind not to tell him at all. He'd only get his hopes up that she would stay. He would never understand the need within her for this new adventure. Her friend Sarah had a spare room in her flat in Battersea. She'd get a job somewhere, in McDonald's if all else failed. He'd never know.

"I'll be leaving at the end of August," she told him, as she unbuckled her seat belt, her mood as black as the sky.

On the morning of her departure, he stood at the window staring out onto the farmyard. He looked gaunt and vulnerable. Fiona sat at the table, feigning a stoicism she didn't feel. She heard the taxi changing gears as it slowed down at the top of the lane. He heard it too, for he turned and said "I could have driven you."

"No, it's better like this. You've the cattle to see to."

He moved to lift her luggage. This was her last chance to make things right, before the suitcases erected a final barricade between them. She threw her arms around him. She had not hugged him since the day of her exam results in the middle of June. She was sure his body had diminished. She wished she could bi-locate, like Padre Pio, and go and stay at the same time.

"Look after yourself, I'll miss you." She willed him to say something in reply, to wish her luck, to say he'd write; anything at all that meant he still loved her. Did his arms tighten around her for a second, or did she just imagine it?

He did not speak.

They went outside.

Fiona stood looking at the familiar landmarks; the farmhouses dotted along the valley; the sheep grazing on the dew-soaked slopes; the rising sun catching the dormer window of the bungalow on the crest of the opposite hill. A blot on the horizon, the old people said when it was built, and Fiona had agreed at the time. But as she stood, her gut knotting with sorrow at the thought of saying goodbye to her father, she felt that the bouncing shaft of light was shining straight at her, like a beckoning finger urging her to follow her star, just like her mother had always told her to do.

"Time to be going," her father said and, as though he had caught her mood, he swept his arm expansively towards the verdant fields, saying gruffly "It's not natural to abandon all you were brought up to love."

The tell-tale catch in his voice brought a lump to her throat. She tried to lighten the mood. "Sure, I'll be back in no time at all Da. I'll be home for Christmas."

"A few months; that's all it'll take and you'll be looking down your nose on the likes of me and mine."

There it was again, the wrong words at the wrong time. Was this the way it would always be; he picking at the scab of his hurt to show her the rawness beneath and she pretending she didn't feel his pain? She could not leave him on a sour note. She waited until the suitcases were loaded into the boot of the taxi.

"Ma meant that education didn't have to be packed. It's something you carry inside yourself... like love Da. Tell me I'm taking yours with me. Tell me it's all right to go."

"Aye, well, yes...yes, well..." he was fumbling in his pocket. If he took out his pipe, and started chomping on it, she'd be gone before he said the words she wanted to hear. He opened his hand; a golden olive branch - her mother's Saint Christopher medal and chain. He held it out to her. His voice, when he spoke, was thick with emotion, "To keep you safe."

He rubbed his eyes with the heels of his hands. "She told me there'd come a time when I'd have to let go; *don't cage her butterfly*, she said. But she didn't tell me how hard it would be."

5

She felt the wetness of his tears on her cheeks as he pulled her to him and held her close. He mussed her hair with his rough farmer-hands, as he used to do when she was a child. "Be happy, girlie," he said, as he kissed her.

Over his shoulder she saw that the sun had risen higher to flash fiery orangey-red on the bungalow's large front window. "Look Da, look," she said, her smile wide in her tear- streaked face. "If that's the glow from the bog-hole of nowhere, then the flame of the Big Smoke hasn't a snowball's chance in hell of keeping me."

He was laughing when she slipped out of his arms and into the taxi. At the end of the laneway she stuck her head out the window and waved.

Her father waved back.

Beginners Short Story Winner

DICK DROOGAN'S
DREADFUL DECEPTION

By SEÁN Ó CEALLAIGH
Phibsboro, Dublin

A law clerk pretends to be a solicitor to impress his girlfriend but an old lady is the one to really make an impression!

Dick Droogan nearly got a heart seizure when his boss, Mr Mathew Mulcahy of McEntagart and Mulcahy Solicitors, asked him to accompany him to make a will for a Miss Nagle in St Martin's Hospital.

To discover why he was so upset we must go back three days and out six miles to the previous Sunday at Killiney Beach where he first met Betty – she and another girl were sunning themselves on the sand and Mulligan and himself were tipping about with a ball. When it accidentally finished up where the girls were lying, Dick went over to retrieve it and to apologise to them; and a few seconds later the four of them were gassing away goodo.

He made a date with her for the pictures on the following Tuesday night and afterwards as they sipped their coffee in the 'Blue Lagoon' she told him that she worked at reception in St Martin's Hospital and they arranged to meet again on the Thursday.

So shouldn't Dick be delighted with himself that he would be seeing Betty a day sooner than planned? Wouldn't it be a great surprise for her too? No – because he had told her the night before as he was taking the paper off his second chocolate biscuit that he was a solicitor, that he would be a partner in the firm in a few years, if you don't mind – and he knowing darn well that he was only a poor law clerk with no prospects whatever!

What kind of an ass was he to spin that cock and bull story to her anyway? Sure she wouldn't have the respect of a dog for him when she saw him traipsing in like a small boy behind old

Mulcahy. And sure she was bound to see him; didn't she tell him that nobody could get in or out of the joint unknown to her. There were a dozen hospitals in Dublin, how was he to foresee that Mulcahy would drag him off to the one where she was working, and so soon after his meeting her? God, but he was in trouble!

He thought again of their talk in the café on the previous night. She had told him about her job in the hospital and asked him laughing "And what about yourself? A big job in the Civil Service is what you have I bet."

"No bedad," he replied airily "but a poor solicitor whose heart is broken from unreasonable clients; that's what I am now."

"Oh you're one of those rascals," she cried excitedly. "They say that none of ye ever get to Heaven."

And later when they were talking about summer holidays and she had told him that she would be getting a fortnight off in August. "You're a lucky colleen, I'll be lucky if I get a bare week myself and things will be a hell of a sight worse in a few years time."

"How's that?" she asked obviously intrigued.

"Well it's, it's like this" he said with mock hesitation as if he was too modest to talk too much about himself. "When they promote a junior solicitor on to the staff and make him a partner in our firm, they expect him to work without any holidays for a few years - to do with a few long weekends instead."

She looked at him with interest and affection. She was clearly impressed; what would she think when she found out the truth about him? He wouldn't have the guts to look at her straight in the face, and she had a lovely face, had Betty, with whom he had been looking forward to spending another pleasant night on the morrow; Betty who was probably thinking of him that very moment and longing for the company of her ambitious young solicitor soon again! What kind of a blinking idiot was he anyway?

But, says you, wouldn't she have found out anyway in due course; that he was only a clerk and not a solicitor? Ah yes, but by then she would have been captivated by his charm and personality and would be unlikely to drop him because of his poor job. After all law clerks were important people in the legal profession and a few of them even went ahead and qualified as solicitors, as he might well do himself some day. Yes, Betty wouldn't reject him then on account of his job but she was sure to run a mile from him now when she found out that he was nothing but a low down, good-for-nothing liar and cheat!

They arrived outside the hospital and parked the car. Mr. Mulcahy strode majestically in front while Dick slouched along behind carrying the brief case; he dreaded going in that big front door and seeing Betty perched behind the reception desk. She would not have to be very smart to realize that ould Mulcahy was the master and that he was only an employee. She would size up everything before he had gone ten feet.

A porter opened the door for them and they both entered a spacious hall and to Dick's surprise and delight there was no reception desk in sight. He gave a sigh of relief. He was sure she would be there inside the front door. They turned to their right and began to walk along the corridor to St Gabriel's Ward, and a short distance down at the front of the stairs was a sort of open office with a counter and a lassie seated on a stool behind. The lassie behind the counter on the stool was not Betty! She was red haired and ordinary looking. Dick left Mr. Mulcahy's name with her and also the name of the client they were about to visit. But where was Betty? Hopefully she had taken the day off.

Miss Nagle was in the fourth bed down the ward. The nurse brought them a second chair and drew the curtains around the bed.

"Thank you young lady," said Mr. Mulcahy magnanimously. "If we need anything, my law clerk here will be on to you." Dick got as red as a turkey cock. That capped it altogether. "My law clerk!"

"Well my good woman," said Mr Mulcahy patronizing the patient, "what can we do for you?"

"Not much Sir thank you," the old lady managed a feeble smile, "but I would like to make some arrangements about my little house at home. Someone told me that the Corporation could take back the house if I hadn't made some definite arrangements about it."

"Yes, yes, that could well be," he agreed betraying a little impatience. "Anyway, everyone should make a will. Well, let's get down to business. Tell us now please of what do your assets consist?"

"Wisha sir, all I have is the little house and the pension," she wheezed.

"Hum I see, alright Droogan start writing". Dick clutched his black biro unwillingly. Yes, he was only the small boy after all. His boss continued to interrogate the patient and to dictate to him in turn. She had neither brother nor sister. She just had number of cousins. However, it wasn't to any of them that she wished to leave her little home but to a man to who was not related to her at all – a man who came to live with her when he was a left a young orphan and who was reared along with her. John was his name; he was living and married in London.

"I remember well," she gasped "though I was only three years at the time – I remember well the day my father carried him home in his arms to be a little playmate for me. He was reared on the same floor with me. We were ever and always very great with one another; we were so".

"Yes yes" said the solicitor looking at his watch. "But tell me now, supposing you were to come into some money, supposing you drew a ticket in the sweepstake or a prize bond – to whom would you like to leave that?"

"To John, sir."

"All of it?"

"Yes sir, every single penny of it; I would leave him my heart if I could."

The old lady's remarks made a deep impression on Dick as he wrote out her will. She certainly thought an awful lot of this fellow who had been reared on the same floor with her! Had she been in love with him long ago and had he rejected her love? Or maybe it was that he had never shown her more than a brotherly affection and she had never revealed her feelings for him but had gone on adoring him in secret. And that even now, and she at death's door, she would leave her heart to him if she could.

What material for a short story by Gogal or Turgenev! He had recently begun to read those Russian masters.

It was with great difficulty that Miss Nagle managed to sign her name to the will. Dick had to guide the pen for her. He and his boss then subscribed their names as witnesses and took their leave.

They had almost reached the front hall and Dick was still thinking about Miss Nagle when he heard someone call his name. He looked around and there was Betty seated on the stool behind the counter in the office at the foot of the stairs. The foxy one was gone! He excused himself to Mr. Mulcahy and stopped to talk to her for a minute, though his heart was thumping violently with anxiety. His boss kept walking on.

"What mischief are ye up to?" she mocked. "Trying to cod some poor creature or other I bet!"

He laughed but it was a dry forced laugh. "No, we got an urgent call here a while ago. Little did I think last night that I would be seeing you here today. Well business is business," he added pointedly consulting his watch. "See you tomorrow night; be a good girl."

"Bye" she called gaily after him

He caught up with Mr Mulcahy at the front door. He hadn't been able to dodge Betty after all. By now she would have seen old Mulcahy's name on the records and wouldn't waste much time in finding out all about himself – "my law clerk here" would surely be recalled by the nurse in Miss Nagle's Ward.

Sure she wouldn't have the respect of a dog for him now. He'd never have the neck to face her the next night. He'd drop her a note when he got back to the office – that he had go do down the country on important business for a few days, that he was sorry he couldn't keep the date with her but that he'd ring her again when he got back to town. He would in his hat!

But when they came out on the street the sun was shining, a group of carefree children were playing on the footpath, a lovely brunette passed him and smiled at him! All of a sudden his heavy load was lifted from his heart and he felt happy again. If Miss Nagle could still experience the wonders of love and she a crippled old woman in the throes of death, what pity was he in need of and he in the full bloom of his youth and health. Even if Betty did give him up for good now, there were still many beautiful young lassies knocking around in dear old Dublin town!

POCKET PEOPLE

By PADDY REID

Fairview, Dublin

*Remembering Granddad Pat who had a job as a night watchman
in the hard winter of 1963 when he befriended a sick dog*

For me, childhood memories remain among the strongest.
One incident in particular will stay forever in my memory.
During the bitter winter of 1963/64, the huge complex of
old tenements just behind Temple Street Children's Hospital in
Dublin, were demolished. All I ever saw of George's Pocket
were countless piles of bulldozed, snow-covered rubble, sheared
floorboards jabbing into the frosty sky like rusted bayonets.

Pat, my Granddad, got a job in the winter of 1963 as a temporary night watchman for Dublin Corporation. For most of his life,
he had found any work hard to get, having been badly wounded
in the Great War. While in a Belgian hospital he'd learned that his
young wife, Margaret, had died in Dublin of the Spanish flu, an
epidemic that had killed hundreds in the city.

Granddad had spent years in and out of Leopardstown Mili-
tary Hospital in Stillorgan. One piece of shrapnel had lodged so
near his heart that the doctors considered it too risky to remove
it. Any chance of working back as a labourer on Dublin docks,
as he did before the war, was ruled out as soon as he returned to
Dublin. One of his cousins had given him a job feeding pigs in
the docklands but that, like all other jobs he attempted, didn't
last long. He'd only got the night watchman job because the site
foreman had served with the same Royal Dublin Fusiliers unit
decimated by German artillery at the battle of Ypres (or 'Wipers', as he called it).

That seemingly endless winter, my mother sometimes sent
me to the Pocket with food for her dad, as he often 'forgot' to

12

eat. Her instructions never changed. "Make sure he eats it, not you." I mostly obeyed.

One night I stood at the watchman's brazier, warming myself and watching people in the distance, like an army of ants, scouring the mounds, sons helping fathers to drag out rafters and floorboards, while sisters and mothers stacked and tied up the wood with twine.

As Granddad took a bite from his sandwich a large black dog silently appeared beside him. It was barely skin and bone with black, watery eyes. Its fur was caked in mud. I asked him where it came from. He told me it had probably been left behind by its owner.

"Here, Maggie!" Granddad tossed his sandwich to the dog. He then placed four sausages on a bent metal grille and quickly cooked them on the brazier. I asked where they came from and he pointed to an elderly woman struggling with a pile of wood that kept sliding off a lopsided old pram. "She said thanks for giving her a few sticks. She'll chop them into bundles and sell them for a penny each."

He let everyone else around Temple Street take home firewood too, or so it seemed. Doors, window frames, floorboards and rafters seemingly drifted by us on the snow covered ground in the dark of the Pocket. Few people spoke, as if saving all their energy for the hard haul homewards. Granddad said that anything that would burn would have a pair of legs to carry it away in such weather.

I know I resented people taking our wood. He said it was better used to keep people warm than being dumped in a Corporation landfill just to rot away.

When the sausages were cooked he tossed one to me, then another. "Here Maggie!" He dropped one at the dog's feet. She devoured it. He took a small bite from the last one, and gave it to Maggie. She looked at me, but I wasn't feeling so generous.

"All gone, Maggie." I reached out to pat her.

"Leave her be." Something in his voice stopped my hand in mid-air. I asked what was wrong. "She has distemper," he pointed to bald patches of fur. "She hasn't long to go either."

I didn't like the sound of that.

"Do dogs go to heaven?" My ten-year old mind was curious about such things.

"I don't know, Paddy."

"It's only fair," I insisted, "if people go, then why not dogs?"

"True," he smiled, "why not?"

The dog moved off to rest under a broken doorway. Granddad thought she must have lived there before it was bulldozed around her. "Maggie's just waiting, son."

"For what?" I asked.

"Her owner," he said, "she will mind the house until he returns." His voice sounded tired and faraway. I looked at him hard. No one was coming back to this heap of icy rubble.

The next night I came, I brought some bones from home, and well-chewed ones at that. As I neared the watch box, I tossed them all towards the dog's 'home' just across from where Granddad sat warming his hands.

"Paddy, don't give her any bones!" He jumped up, calling urgently.

Too late. Maggie was devouring the bones. I saw them move visibly down her gullet into her belly. The dog then came over and lay down beside the old man. Snow began to fall and all was peaceful. We three watched the long line of people going home with their overloaded bicycles, handcarts, trolleys and prams.

The whole scene reminded me of a film I'd recently seen at the New Electric Cinema in Talbot Street. A long trail of ragged French civilians wearily dragging all their belongings on carts, prams, anything that had wheels, down rubble-strewn roads to escape German dive-bombers in 1940.

Suddenly Maggie began to shake and rose unsteadily to her feet. All the food she had eaten was coughed up, steaming on the white ground.

"Granddad. . ."

"It's okay, Paddy. I'll take care of her. You go on home now."

"But. . ."

"Go!" He said sharply, then sighed and smiled. "It's getting late, son." He pulled some coins out of his trouser pocket. "Here, buy yourself something in Mister Mac's on the way home."

I nodded, squeezing the warm coins in my hand as I moved away.

Granddad stood still until he thought I was gone. Instead I made a wide circle around the watchbox and knelt behind some rubble, where I could see everything. I saw Granddad rummage around inside the box. He held out a small heart-shaped shovel he used to pile up coke for the fire. Slowly he moved to where Maggie lay on her side on the ground. He knelt beside her.

As he patted the dog, I heard him softly sing a favourite song of his. 'The city we knew is long gone, Maggie. . .'

As the old man raised the shovel, Maggie raised her head slightly then lay back down. I thought I heard a whimper, but I'm not sure of that. He brought the shovel down with all the strength he could muster. I jumped at the sound of steel against flesh. Maggie made no sound at all. Dark drops seeped into the white snow.

The old man returned to his seat and sat down heavily. He pulled out a hankie and held it to his face as he began to shake. As my own eyes were getting blurry, I crept away quietly and, once out of the Pocket, ran home, not even stopping at Mister Mac's shop to spend my money.

The next, and last, night I visited the Pocket, I saw a small mound where Maggie had once lived. The heart-shaped shovel was standing like a cross atop the mound. I never spoke about the dog and neither did he. What was there to say?

Granddad only lasted for two months as a night watchman before he had to give up the job. He survived through the winter, only to slip away as the flowers began to bloom in May. That tiny piece of Krupp's steel, long close to his heart, had, after so many years, finally found its target. His life ended, as much of it had been spent, in Leopardstown Hospital. Surrounded by other old soldiers from the Great War, who were also fading away.

THE INNOCENT

By VINCENT MCDONNELL
Newmarket, Co. Cork

Two sisters live totally different lives, one forging her way in the world, the other locked forever in a child's mind, and now bad news comes calling

Whent the grey, limestone walls of the building loom before me, I slow my footsteps. Uncertainty once more grips me. There is still time to change my mind. I don't have to go through with this. I am obligated to no one. But I know, too, that I will have no peace until this is done. I must not falter now.

The main gates are closed and I enter through an adjacent gate intended for pedestrians. The security guard in his box pays me no heed and I walk up the footpath to the entrance, my high heels click-clacking on the paving. The doors are locked and I ring to gain admittance. When I inform the nurse, who answers my ring, of who I am and why I'm here, she smiles sympathetically and asks me to take a seat in the waiting room.

There are two other people waiting – an elderly man and a youngish woman who is about my own age. They do not acknowledge my presence and when I sit, I studiously avoid them, staring instead at the scuffed, vinyl floor tiles and the grey-green institutional walls. There are a few posters dealing with health related matters and a calendar which is set to the wrong month. I assume that nobody here cares about time or dates.

The elderly man is summoned, and he walks stiffly from the room – probably a combination of arthritis and an effort to maintain his dignity. A few minutes later I am summoned by a nurse who looks competent and officious, and who makes no allowances for why I've come here.

There are doors to be unlocked with jangling keys and then relocked behind us. I follow the nurse into a large ward lined on either side with iron beds. Tall, narrow windows, that are fitted with steel grills, fail to lighten the room. There is a pervasive sense of gloom, even though it is still early afternoon and I can glimpse blue sky beyond the small, grimed panes of glass.

I do not recognise my sister among the women who sit by their beds, or those seated at a table in the centre of the floor. It's been fifteen years since I last saw her and I know that I too have changed appearance in that time. Yet, when the nurse stops at a bed halfway down and speaks to the grossly obese woman sitting on a chair by the bedside, I sense a tiny click of recognition.

"Maire," the nurse says in a forced, cheerful voice. "Your sister Julie has come to visit you. Now, I'll leave you two to get on with it. When you're ready to leave," she adds, turning to me, "just come to the nurses' station and someone'll see you out."

I feel panic rising, and there is the old anger and resentment too, and I have to fight to control them. I tell myself that it is not my sister's fault that I feel like this. The blame lies elsewhere. But blame and anger need a focus, and it is easier to lay the blame here than where it really belongs.

I have come here to tell Maire that our mother is dead, but I do not even know how to greet her, never mind impart such news. It is she who seems to understand the norms of greeting. She rises ponderously and holds out her arms to me. Her embrace crushes me against her flabby, yet powerful body, and I instinctively put my arms about her massive shoulders and hold her.

She releases me and sits again and stares up at me. She does not speak and her silence disconcerts me. I am the sane one, the normal one, the one who isn't crazy, the one with the degree and the career and a husband and children. But now none of that matters here. I am a child again, the youngest daughter, the one who must always defer to her older sister, God's chosen little one, special to Him and to everyone else.

***

"Why can't you be like your sister?" My mother's voice echoes accusingly in my head and I am a child once more. It is an old refrain and I have heard it many times, yet it still has the power to hurt as only words can.

17

We are all in the kitchen. My mother is baking Maire's favourite Madeira cake and I have just come running in and knocked the mixing spoon from the table. It splatters cake mixture on the vinyl floor covering and before I, or my mother, can react, Maire has picked it up and wiped it clean on the front of her candy-striped dress.

I do not speak. I do not ask my mother if this is what she wants me to be like – the Maire who does such stupid things, who throws tantrums, who cannot spell such simple words as cat or dog, or even recite her two times tables.

She is already showing signs of the obesity that will plague her with the onset of puberty, and later still will give her the strength to overpower our mother when the tantrums erupt into episodes of violence. The seeds are all there but my mother refuses to see them. I am too young to understand that she sees her daughter with a mother's love, and thus sees perfection where I can see none. She wants her daughter to be normal, but instead of wanting her to be more like me, she wants me to be more like her.

We do everything together – music, Irish dancing and elocution. I know the major scales on the piano and can play *Twinkle, Twinkle, Little Star*, while Maire just bashes the bass keys with her fists. Yet our music teacher gives her the allotted amount of time and smiles at her and calls her a good girl, while she berates me for a discordant note and scolds me for not practising enough.

I tried to explain once that I cannot practise because of Maire – she always wants to join in and bash the keys – but the teacher said I should not carry tales. No one ever reprimands Maire and my mother just laughs and, like the teacher, calls her a good girl. No one ever calls me a good girl, or hugs me, or praises my dancing of the hornpipe, which my teacher describes as excellent.

She wants me to enter competitions but my mother refuses to allow this. As Maire does not know how to dance, my mother does not wish her to be made to feel inferior. She cannot see that Maire is inferior - that she will never be able to play the piano or dance. It is through my mother's attitude and indulgence that she is creating a person that one day she will not be able to control anymore.

**

Somewhere in the ward there is a metallic clang and I'm startled out of my reverie to find Maire watching me. She seems wary, and I know that within that head of hers her brain is trying to come to terms with my presence here after such a long time. Perhaps she is wondering where our mother is. I know she visited three times each week in the years Maire has been locked up here. Now that those visits will cease, I wonder how Maire will cope with the void in her life.

I search for the right words but there is no easy way to impart the news I have to convey. "I've got some bad news," I say eventually. "I'm afraid mother is dead. She had a massive stroke yesterday and didn't recover."

It is the language of the adult. There is obviously a way to impart such knowledge to a child, but I do not know how. Of course, one could take a child onto their knee and hold them tight while telling them the news – that their mother has gone to heaven and is now with God – while at the same time imparting some comfort through physical contact and taking some in return.

I wait, and for a few moments there is no reaction. Maire keeps on staring at me, her eyes devoid of expression. I realise that she is drugged – that even a normal person in such circumstances would take some moments to assimilate what they'd just been told. Maire, I assume will have no reaction.

So I am startled when that massive body begins to heave with emotion, folds of flesh quivering as she shakes. Tears come freely and they roll down the bulging flesh of her cheeks and drip from the tip of her treble chins. It has been a long time since I've seen her cry, and I do not know how to react. Some primitive instinct urges me to go to her and comfort her, but I cannot do so.

She sobs silently, only the heaving and the tears betraying her emotion. She draws the attention of some of the other women at the table and they approach the foot of the bed. I stand awkwardly, wishing now that I'd worn sensible shoes. Why have I dressed so carefully to come here and why have I worn such ridiculous high heels? Who was I trying to impress? I have not taken the trouble to find a chair and sit – not even bothered to perch on the edge of the bed. I didn't even take my sister's hand while I told her the terrible news.

It's too late now for recriminations and I want to get away. But I cannot walk out and leave her crying like the child she really is – a big, helpless child who does not understand. I have never thought of her like that before – that she is just a child and now is just as frightened as my four year old daughter would be if she were told that I was dead and she would never see me again.

A woman breaks away from the group gathered at the foot of the bed. She is probably in her sixties, grey haired, frail and unsteady on her feet. She edges past me in the gap between the two beds, bends down and puts her arms about Maire's shoulders and they begin to rock backwards and forwards. Behind me the other women also begin to rock. They, too, are crying.

Fear grips me. I have a terrible urge to run. I swing about seeking the presence of a nurse, but there is only the group of women staring at me. I seek for accusation in their eyes, but there is none. Instead there are just their tears and bewilderment and collective sadness. If I close my eyes I can imagine that they are children. They have always been, and always will be children, as innocent as they were on the day they were born.

One of them moves toward me and puts her arms about me. She is Maire's age – maybe a little older – and she holds me gently and begins to rock backwards and forwards. I rock with her, getting into the rhythm. My fear eases and as grief threatens to overwhelm me, for the first time ever I want to be like my sister. I want to be a child again like her, wrapped safe from the world, from all its hurt and pain and the knowledge of death. But I can never have that, and though I would not swap her life for mine – not for all the riches in the world – yet for the first time ever, I envy her.

RETURN TO SENDER

by E.M. BARRETT
Goatstown, Dublin

Jim is getting old and thinking more often about his estranged brother in America, to whom he had sent some family photos as a step towards reconciliation

The postman was leaning on the gate, calling his name. Jim left his work and crossed the field to join him, his Wicklow collie Patch running along beside him, "Ah Mick I see you have something for me."

"That I have," Mick replied, holding out a small packet, "and it looks as if you sent it to yourself via America!"

Jim froze for a moment and then smiling faintly he took the packet from Mick. The address had been crossed out and 'return to sender' was written beside Jim's own address. "I must be getting back to work now Mick," Jim said, "so much rain this summer, half the crops have been ruined."

"Same story everywhere I go," nodded Mick and added, "that young nephew of yours is doing fine I hear."

Jim's face lit up, "Best thing I ever did bringing him here to join me. And young ones about the place again, that's as it should be." He paused for a moment before adding, "It was Mary who persuaded me to do it, of course. Bless her memory."

"How long since they moved in?" asked Mick.

"Five years," Jim replied, with a sigh. "A quick five years, so busy at first when Denis moved in and converted the outhouses to living quarters. He did a great job, you know, dividing and modernising the farm. Patch here and myself were left with the sheep and a few fields, enough for us, quite enough." He smiled down at Patch resting quietly at his feet.

Then suddenly he laid the packet on the ground at the gatepost and without another word headed back across the field.

He walked with a heavy heart as a few tears of sadness and humiliation ran down his cheeks. He didn't make any effort to check them.

He thought about the packet containing his precious family photos and how they hadn't even bothered to get fresh paper to wrap them up in. He wondered if they had even opened the packet. Then another thought struck him, it must surely have been sent back by return of post. How else could it have crossed the Atlantic and back so quickly? He knew he had to stop dwelling on the packet. 'I must think of the work,' he told himself.

Autumn was a busy time on the farm with the last of the harvesting and general maintenance to be done. Even in his small portion of the farm there was still a lot to be done in preparation for the winter: crops to be harvested, fences to be repaired, gates to be checked and if needs be painted.

But he couldn't concentrate. He needed comfort and he needed comfort now. He decided to call on Mrs O'Sullivan – there were two more hours of light and work left in the day but he realised there would be no more work for him today. He needed to talk to somebody, about anything. He needed to be distracted.

He had an unwritten agreement with his nephew Denis that he would not call on them except at weekends or on special days and of course in emergencies. Sunday lunch with them was the highlight of Jim's week. The little ones were around him all the time, but Sunday was different.

He picked up the packet as he closed the gate and walked back to the farmhouse. He brought it into the kitchen, laying it reverently on the table. Then he collected some potatoes and a cabbage and went down the road to spend a couple of hours with Molly O'Sullivan in her warm kitchen.

Pushing the ginger cat out of the armchair to let him sit down, Molly remarked, "At last we're having a dry spell of weather."

"At last indeed," Jim agreed.

She gave him tea and soda bread scones with farm butter and homemade blackcurrant jam. He blessed her silently for the hospitality and her unquestioning welcome. He had made some silly excuse about the bottom field being too muddy to work in and the others had already been harvested. But being a farmer's widow, Molly would have known that this was no time for an ordinary social call. She remembered how it was a crucial time on the farm, to get the work done before the days got too short and winter and the frost set in. She would have guessed that there was something very wrong for him to have called at that time, but she didn't ask any questions. He would tell he if he needed to.

They chatted in general, mostly about the locals and of course about Denis of whom she thought the world. "It must be about five years now since Denis moved in?"

"Yes," he agreed, "he came at Christmas 2004. Do you remember I was Santa to the little ones. Michael was three then, Clare just two and Connor wasn't even born."

Jim did not mention his trouble. Inside though, he dreaded going home. Even though he had lit his fire and damped it down earlier in the day, so at least the house would be warm when he returned, he knew he was going back to pain and rejection, the small packet of photos on the kitchen table.

As he walked home, he remembered the day of the row, now so long ago, with all its details. He remembered his beloved older brother, Tom, running down the stairs. Their father shouting after him, 'Never come back.' And Tom never did come back. Instead he went to a near neighbour, to a family whose daughter Eileen he was courting and two weeks later they both left for America. Jim had never been told what that row was about. But seldom a day passed that he did not miss his elder brother – as he knew his mother and father had too, although they never mentioned it.

He had been a fool to imagine anything would come of his gesture. But he had to try before it was too late. After all, Tom must be in his early eighties now. Jim's own eyesight was deteriorating and his body was slowing down. He needed to hear from his brother. He needed it very badly.

The light shone from his nephew's house, brightening up the yard as he crossed it to his own door. Patch rose to greet him, wagging his tail as he pushed the door open and turned the light on. The first thing he saw was the packet on the table.

As he sat by the fire, looking out on the yard, he could faintly hear noises and laughter coming from an open window. For once, it did not cheer him up. His nephew's family were the greatest comfort to him in his old age. But could find no comfort tonight. Nothing could lift the sadness, loneliness and dejection that he felt.

Why had he sent the photos? Why had he even done it, sentimental fool that he was, opening up old wounds, exposing himself to pain and rejection all over again?

He knew the answer. He needed some communication, some sign of affection after all the years.

Eileen had returned to Ireland on a few occasions but Tom never came with her and never made contact. He knew Eileen and her young children had stayed once or twice with her parents down the road. Maybe his mother had slipped out to see her grandchildren, and maybe his father knew about it, but neither of them said a word. He knew their oldest boy was called Jim after him and that they had three children, the two boys and a girl called Kitty after his mother.

He took the packet up in his hands and, trembling, he examined it closely. It had been opened and resealed and, of course, re-stamped. He slit it open gingerly and shook the photos out over the table. There was no sign of the letter he had written so carefully and so painstakingly – at least they had not returned that. He collected the old photo albums from the cupboard, tossing a sod on to the fire as he passed by.

Patch wagged his tail, so he bent down to pat his head gently. Straightening up he looked out again at the yard. He knew that the farm would be in safe hands with Denis. He would not be held back by sentiment like himself, he would always move with the times, diversify if needs be. Change is the way of the future and he knew that it made no sense to live in the past. But just for tonight he would reminisce and grieve.

Returning to the table, he set the old albums down beside the pile of photos. It was time to replace them in the gaps. He put the large family photo back in its frame and placed it on the mantelpiece beside his wife's picture. He was glad to have the photo of his mother and father back on display, sitting proudly with their four children: Tom, Una, Eithne and himself.

He began to spread the photos out on the table and then suddenly his heart skipped a beat. There was a note. He opened it up and started to read:

Dear Jim

We are sending back your photos by return post in case you're missing them. We've made copies of them and will also send you photos of our family. We plan to come to Ireland in the spring and will email Denis soon to confirm the dates. Long letter to follow. Looking forward to seeing you on our visit.

All our love

Eileen and Tom

Tom's signature was very shaky – an old man's signature. Jim held the letter in his hand for a long time, long after the lights in the yard had gone out.

MUSTARD

by NORA BRENNAN
Kilkenny

A jar of mustard on a friend's table stirs happy childhood memories

When I saw the jar of mustard on a friend's dining table, the memory of it hit me: the way the taste shot down my nose and out through my eardrums all those years before. I pictured the yellow covered tin box of my childhood with a fat chuckling Buddha on the front saying 'Welcome to our community. You have been christened with the powder of the orient, orange and saffron that will lift the dead slice of your life and send you into the heavens'.

I was five years old. My mother would not have bacon in the house if the yellow box of mustard powder wasn't already in the cupboard. My job was to mix it. Add a few drops of water into the centre and stir from inside out the way I saw her make dough in the kitchen, or my father mix cement in the yard.

I barely reached the large kitchen table back then. My mother sat me down on the old leather sofa that ran beneath the kitchen window. I kept on stirring until I had a creamy pool of mustard on the corner of the enamel plate. It was the one occasion where I didn't let a stray finger into the cooking mix.

'You're a good girl' she'd say taking away the plate. I'd watch her spoon the mustard into a small ceramic dish the shape of a beehive, with a scooped out lid for the handle of the spoon. That dish was as much part of the dining table in our house as the bowl of sugar in front of my father. And a box of mustard powder lasted several months.

Then came Coleman's jars where someone else had done the mixing. I was devastated. For those moments had been snatched away from me, that time with my mother in the kitchen, being close to the large moving backside of her navy apron that I pulled on regularly just to feel safe in the world. And each time I would hear her say those words: 'Ah sure you're a good girl'. As if she came back from somewhere in herself and suddenly saw me, her words a confirmation that I was alive, I had not faded before her eyes like my two sisters years before. I never knew their ages, knew nothing beyond the inscription on the headstone that read: *Pray for Margaret and Anna who died young.*

I wonder now if my mother ever really saw me, so clouded was the lens of her world after the loss of those two girls. I trailed at the end of her brood and found ways to ease and please her, always yearning to be near. But I see her still, dipping a thick slice of bacon into a large yellow dollop on the side of her plate. No matter what the weekly food supplies, there was always the breaded cooked ham, a stopgap for the leaner times. She would take a slice in her hand as if it was a hearthrug she was rolling, and wipe the plate clean of that tangy lake of mustard.

I saw so much mustard growing up that I never bought it when I moved away from home. I didn't know if Coleman's had gone down the plughole long before the current recession or the arrival of oriental spices to this country. Until that day recently in a friend's house, when it was a bull's head I saw on the yellow label of a Coleman's jar and not the happy chuckling face as I had imagined. My guess is that in the Ireland of the fifties, Coleman's mustard was one of the few guilt-free pleasures to spice up a woman's life in those dreary years.

THE STUDENT

by NOLLAIG ROWAN
Ranelagh, Dublin

Anybony has just finished his Leaving Cert and he is dreaming of September and escape from his island farm home

The weather was fine and still. It had rained earlier so now the air had that fresh, clean smell of countryside after a downpour. A lone curlew chanted from the stand of trees above the pier. A chevron of swallows swooped low and rose again ... a sure sign that summer was here.

Anthony Collins was on his way home from his final Leaving Cert paper. He disembarked from the ferry and walked west on the asphalt road that split the island. The sun, still high in the sky at four o'clock on this June day, burnt his face and drops of sweat hung from his eyebrows. The exams had gone well, despite the mix-up over the leaked English Paper 2. There was a week or so to consider changing his college application. Arts, (taking English and History), in Galway university was top of his list and he saw no reason to change it. The 'Change-of-mind' form was for losers. Anthony looked back at the road. Much as he liked the island, he couldn't wait for September, to be away from it. He would be nineteen next week, had recently passed his driving test and was saving hard for a second-hand car. The future couldn't come too soon.

As he rounded the bend, turning north towards his home, he heard men's voices. "What's up?" said Anthony as he reached the edge of the huddled group.

"Ah, there you are" said one of the labourers from a nearby farm. "Your mother will be glad to see you." The other men, neighbours, fell silent. Anthony walked by. They frequently made jibes at him about who would take over the farm after the old man was gone. He couldn't give a damn who took over the farm. All he knew was that he was not going to be stuck here for life, like Padraic Coyne over on Carraig Mór – twenty-four and farming his life away.

Anthony looked ahead towards the farmhouse and beyond. Cattle were dotted around the fields like in a Constable painting. It was mostly dry stock but he was surprised that his dad had not brought the milking cows into the farmyard by this time of evening. Dismissing the thought, he looked forward to catching up on Facebook which he had neglected during his exams.

"Dad's had a fall." His mother ran out to meet him wiping her hands over and over on her bottle-green apron. "Go in and see him" she said, ushering Anthony into the large kitchen where his father, Tom, sat by the Aga stove.

"What happened Da?" He had never heard the grandfather clock tick before, although it must have done so every minute of his nineteen years. The clock ticked now, the air was heavy, his father wheezed.

"A heifer ... beyond in the top field ..." He paused for breath. "She was calving ..." Anthony had seen his father so many times help deliver a calf by attaching a rope to the calf's hooves and gently easing the animal into the world. "The rope got entangled somehow ... pulled me along ... " Tom closed his eyes and lay back in the armchair.

"D'you think you've broken a bone, or is it just bruising?" said Anthony itching to get to his laptop to check out how many 'friends' he had accumulated.

"We'll go to the hospital on the first ferry in the morning" said his mother. "I've given him pain relievers for the moment – You'll be able to drive us? Oh, by the way, how'd the exam go?"

"OK, I suppose." Anthony was becoming used to being relied upon to drive his mother on errands in the car they kept on the mainland. His two sisters had done it, before they escaped to the city. Now his father couldn't drive, with the injury. Roll on September, he thought, I'm out of here. He looked out the window. Down the lane the neighbours were still gossiping. He knew that not one of them would lift a finger to help. None of the locals had spoken to his father since he had refused to sell land to a developer for holiday homes on the island – a project in which they had shares. That was six years ago. Islanders did not shed grudges easily.

The X-ray showed a broken collar bone on the right side and Tom was put in a sling for six weeks. Anthony and his parents knew what this meant. End of June was silage time. Extra hands had already been hired and were due to start next week, but the fields had to be cut before the hired machines could bale the hay and wrap it in black plastic. Anthony knew he was the only one to do it. He shifted from one foot to the other in the hospital foyer, pushing in his earphones and turning up his ipod. The Killers – great band. His mother was mouthing something. He removed one earphone.

"Let's go home" she said.

Driving his parents up from the ferry, along the road he had walked yesterday, he heard the long grasses hiss, ready to be cut. The window of the old Corolla was jammed open and he felt the breeze warm and tingling on his sunburnt face. He swung the car into the farmyard.

"I'll do it ... OK?" he said to his father.

"Thanks. Can you ..."

"I can't work Friday ... Goin' to Robbie's party. Y'know, after the Leaving an' all." He'd seen Amanda Sweeney's 'profile' on Facebook and guessed she'd be there. His heart skipped a beat. She'd probably be at Oxegen music festival too.

Two weeks saw the silage work completed. Lying on the short grass in the top field, Anthony inhaled the heavy aroma of the silage bales, sickly sweet as molasses. The black plastic mounds of moulting grass were like hulking dinosaurs in the corners of each field. He had loved hay bales as a child ... climbing up them, tumbling over them, hiding behind them. But progress, or some perversity on his father's part, had deemed that haystacks were out, silage bales were in.

From the far side of the field came a low moan, like an old man sighing. A cow, heavy with calf, stood swaying slightly. She spread her hind legs and even from where he lay, Anthony knew that she was about to deliver. He walked quietly towards her, making the soothing sounds he had heard his father make.

"That's the girl. Easy does it. That's my girl." She glanced at him, but returned to her purpose. "That's it ... Whoa ... Gently does it." He crouched near her, watching. The cow groaned and with one final effort the calf slid from its mother. She bent down and, oblivious to any human presence, began licking her newborn.

Sensing that she would prefer to be alone, Anthony moved away. The earth warmed his body and supported his back. Pulling a handful of daisies, he laid them on his chest. He thought of his grandfather who had farmed this land and his great-grandfather. He had never met these men but he knew them from the stories his father told, from trees they had planted, from channels they had dug. They were still here on this land. Everything that had happened to them related to him in some way.

The cow made a low sound like a contented lover. Her young one was lying still, but even at a distance Anthony could see that it was breathing. All was well. He fingered the rock festival ticket in his pocket. He'd go there next week-end – maybe with Amanda - see The Killers. Then there'd be the post-Leaving Cert holiday to Greece, already booked, with the lads, then the 12th of August – results day – and before he knew it, it'd be September and college and freedom.

There was a slight smell of blood, the cow shuddered and in a gush the placenta tumbled onto the muddy grass. Anthony crawled to the calf, still caught in its own thick membrane, its curled coat slippery. Froth streaming into the grass, it bucked at Anthony's slap and the cow at last made her long drawn-out moo to call and claim it, while the hills all around spun slower with Anthony, the cow and the calf at its centre.

There was a calmness now about the island that often descended in the late afternoon while the sun was still warm and the wind had died. A mist was approaching from the west, seesawing its way across the Atlantic, gobbling islands as it went. Soon the temperature would drop. The new family at Anthony's feet should be back in the farmyard close to the house. But he was reluctant to move the mother, now lying on the grass, her newborn alongside her nuzzling an udder. The two getting to know each other, finding out how this life works. Encouraging and leading, the cow made herself comfortable while the calf, although only newly born, knew exactly where his rightful place was. Things would work out well for these two, thought Anthony, there's give and take.

And when he was walking down to the farmhouse where the mist had done a U-turn and was receding from the island, he realised that truth and beauty which had been a guiding star through the generations, and continued to do so until the present day, constituted the most important elements in human life and on earth in general. Life seemed full of sublime meaning, as in a Chekov story. Maybe change-of-mind options were not for losers. And September was not a fixed star.

Maybe it was possible to follow two dreams ... to go away and still feel rooted to the land that would always be there for him. He waved to his dad who stood leaning on the farmyard gate and, running to tell him the news of the calf, he felt a lightness in his soul that had never been there before but which he knew was here to stay.

One Hundred Strokes

By Mary O'Gorman
Ballyvaughan, Co. Tipperary

The Major and Mrs. Bridgewater had come from England to settle in Ireland but they seemed to have a rather unusual relationship as she endured constant humiliation

Of course, if I had normal parents, I'd never have heard of the Bridgewaters. Other girls didn't live over a bar and grocery. Other girls didn't have a dad who lugged crates of bottles or a mother who weighed quarters of tea for customers while the apples for Eve's pudding turned brown in the kitchen. I knew of no other girl who did her homework behind a grocery counter, stopping half-way through her English composition to sell a packet of Rinso or give Nora Doyle ten Woodbines on tick.

I spent from seven o'clock until nine o'clock every night that winter in the grocery, legs tucked in beside a crate of oranges, saluting various male customers like Big Jerh or Dancer Doyle on their way through the grocery to the door that led into the bar. This was where dad or mam filled pints or half-ones, washed glasses and made sure everyone was spoken to. Sometimes, I pictured my friends doing homework in comfy chairs, being handed lemonade and sticky buns by mothers who had time to bake. Worse still, my two pals Helen and Maura had talked about going to the new picture *From Russia with Love.*

"It's not fair," I wailed to my parents.

"Too bad!" was Dad's reply.

About half past seven each night, Mrs. Bridgewater would sweep in. She was tall with greying hair coiled into a loose, but carefully pinned, bun at the back of her head and she wore perfume that transported me to Paris, though I had never been outside of Ireland.

Her long wool coat was pale-coloured and she always carried matching gloves and handbag. A short pearl necklace finished off the outfit.

"Eileen dear," she nodded at me, "how are you?"

"I'm great, Mrs. Bridgewater and yourself?"

"One could only be splendid on an evening like this. Enjoy each moment, dear. Remember Shakespeare's wonderful words, *"Summer's lease hath all too short a date."*

I wanted to remind her that summer had finished weeks ago but remembered dad's frequent words – "The customer is always right."

"Please Eileen, pop through to the bar and tell the Major I'm here to drive him home for dinner. Though I say so myself, it's a culinary delight."

So I would go to the bar and give the Major her message. "Tell her I shall be there anon," was his inevitable dismissive reply.

She would retreat to their Morris Minor, having bought a small box of Black Magic. I retreated, in turn, to the excesses of the French Revolution or the endurance test that was *Peig*. Occasionally, I would keep an Agatha Christie under the schoolbooks and read a few pages just for a treat. Most of the time, I wanted to get the homework finished. But there wasn't much hope of that. Half an hour or so later, the grocery door would swing open once more.

"Eileen, the Major must not have heard you. Could I trouble you to remind him again?"

The same response came from a man clearly enjoying another large whisky as he studied the crossword in the Irish Times. "Tell her I shall be there anon."

Again she would retreat to the car, only to re-enter later, sit on the long stool by the grocery wall and wait for him. Sometimes she took out a small mirror and applied lipstick quickly. It was always a horrible shade of bright red. Mostly she fidgeted with her hair. Took pins from it and put them back in exactly the same place. I thought of my friends again as I tried to concentrate. Wondered were they in Mick's chipper with its new jukebox, listening to the Beatles or Dusty Springfield.

The nearest I got to a jukebox was when a singsong began in the bar. And the songs! Very different to *Please, please me* or *I want to hold your hand*! Some of the customers' favourites were *Que sera, sera, Phil the Fluter's Ball* and *Somewhere over the rainbow*. Tim Jimmy Joy always insisted on singing solo and was useless. Dad's comment was that Tim's voice would improve if he drank more than the two pints he usually nursed all night.

The Major could, occasionally, be heard joining in a singsong, or to be truthful, attempting to join in. He had never grasped the words of the different songs. Ignoring the singing, Mrs. Bridgewater would have more chocolate, read a book or, to my horror, interest herself in my homework, particularly anything literary. Using the small mirror, she fixed her hair again, at the same time telling me stories about her life in Surrey. At times, she seemed to forget I was there. It felt like she was addressing the mirror. Her voice changed completely as she described the big house in the country where she was born. The French maid served meals in the long dining room, on a table full of flowers, silver, glass, flickering candles. Of course, they had dozens of other rooms and she had her own bedroom with a sink in it.

She had a pony named Sammy-Jo and a spaniel named Fletch. She had loved a game called croquet and said it was played on a lawn with balls and hoops and mallets and pegs. "Was it anything like hurling?" I asked. She shook her head and said it would be too sedate for our local GAA lads.

She met the Major at a ball and they fell in love. This I could hardly imagine. But when she brought in an ancient copy of *Town and Country,* I understood more. Their wedding photograph was in it. They stood in front of a stately hall door, looking young, tall and happy. I asked why they had left England. For a moment, I thought she was going to tell me to mind my own business. But eventually she said that the Major was anxious for a change, so they decided to start a new life in Ireland. She stopped talking and stared at me for a second as if she didn't know who I was. Then she said I had good hair and should give it one hundred strokes, morning and evening, like she did. I admired the brown and yellow comb in her own hair and she thanked me with a real smile. Said it was made of tortoise-shell and was one of her favourites.

As she spoke, her eyes kept darting towards the bar door. The left one twitched quickly sometimes and I often wished Mr. Bridgewater would hurry up, for her sake. She never criticised him. But I couldn't help thinking of the dinner getting harder, drier and colder. Finally, he would emerge through the bar door, doing his best not to stumble. "There you are," she would greet him, in a falsely cheerful way. He would shake hands with me and finally leave, often with a half bottle of Jameson protruding from his pocket.

I wished she had a friend she could talk to or go places with. If I was married, I wouldn't spend the day waiting to make a dinner for my husband and then spend the evening waiting for him to eat it. Dad laughed when I told him that. He said she had never settled in Ireland but had made great efforts initially. She started ballet classes shortly after their arrival. I giggled when he told me that, picturing her towering above all her pupils. Dad said she was a great trier but ballet was not high on the list of priorities in our small Kerry town in the sixties. The classes fizzled out.

She joined the Drama Group but criticised their current choice of play - John B. Keane's *Sive*. She said it was rather boring and suggested they do *A Streetcar Named Desire*, of which she had the script. A row ensued as the actors thought the play unsuitable. They said it was her or them so the producer asked her to leave.

A Flower Arranging Club was her next attempt. But the local ladies who joined would invariably arrive at the meetings without the bits and pieces needed. It was difficult to acquire the special glue, the ribbons or even wicker baskets. Each meeting ended with bouquets of flowers but Mrs. Bridgewater stressed that floral arrangements were the aim of the Club. She declared eventually that the whole thing was pointless.

Her days must have seemed very long. The Major worked in town, had sandwiches in our bar at lunch time and returned just after seven in the evening. "Time for a pre-prandial, Eileen," he twinkled. I knew it would be more than one drink.

As Christmas drew nearer, I began to dread her nightly arrival. She was so different, so strange. She didn't wait in the car but ate her chocolate in the grocery. Plucked various books from her handbag but put them back without opening a page. She took off her gloves, turned them inside out, smoothed each one. Turned them again. Moved the pins or combs in her hair. Whispered to herself. I could half hear her repeating the same word "Late! Late!"

On cue, I made my usual excursions to the bar and the Major sent back his message.Eventually, he stumbled out. She stood, belted her coat, pulled on her gloves and assisted him out to the car. Lying in bed at night, I wondered if she missed the pretty villages of Surrey and her life there.

She came in as usual on that last night. It was extremely frosty. I was astounded when I saw her hair - loose, messy, clips dangling. And, amazingly, no handbag or gloves. Her smile was a thin crack in her face. She kept twisting a mother-of-pearl brooch on her coat which was unbuttoned despite the cold.

"Pop to the bar and tell the Major I am here." No "please" that night. No "what are your parents giving you for Christmas?"

She seemed restless, on edge. She paced around the grocery. For the first time, she came behind the counter. Tidied the cigarette shelf. Moved some of the decorations on the tree. Stared at what I was studying. Kept muttering to herself. Just one word "Late. Late."(Or was it "Hate. Hate"?)

My mother took over from me at nine. By then, Mrs. Bridgewater had become calm but seemed remote. She just sat there, gazing at her shoes. Mam said she looked relaxed for once as she left quietly with the Major.

A woman going to early Mass found him next morning in front of his house. He had apparently frozen to death. Mrs. Bridgewater told my parents later that she had sleepless nights thinking of him lying on the ice. She had got out of the car, gone straight upstairs to bed, turned on her radio, and never heard a thing.

Everyone was very sorry for her. Said she was so brave. She went to Mary Lacey's for Christmas dinner. There was a collection for her before she went back to England. My mother bought her a marcasite brooch. .

I didn't tell anyone about her muttered words that last evening. But late at night, in my mind's eye, I picture the scene. Mrs. Bridgewater is standing at the window, brushing her long hair, counting each stroke aloud. Outside the Major is lying on the ice, trying to claw his way up the steps. But slipping back. Slipping, slipping, slipping...

She opens the window, continues brushing. *"Ninety-eight,"* Takes a chocolate from a box. *"Ninety-nine."* Slowly moves it towards her mouth.*"One hundred."*

Calls down *"Don't worry dear, I shall be there anon."*

GREAT UNCLE CHARLIE

By PATRICIA CARTY
Belvedere Park, Belfast

*An affectionate portrait of an old man who was a benevolent
fixture in our childhood home*

Why is it that as houses have got bigger, people have less room for their old folk? I grew up in an old terraced house. Two up, two down with a cold water tap and the toilet in the yard. There was a range in the living room and a tiny scullery with a cooker and a little dresser with a pull down shelf. The house was small but there was room for my mother's uncle Charlie and we wouldn't have been without him.

Uncle Charlie was like the big fire that burnt in the little living room keeping it so warm and friendly. He was an old man when I was a child, a man with a cloth cap and braces and a pipe. He had wise, kind eyes and a shy, mischievous smile. Mummy and daddy were so busy, but Uncle Charlie always had plenty of time for us. He enjoyed his pipe and the horse racing and his bottles of stout, and when we needed to be entertained he had plenty of stories.

On rainy days he would head off to bed for the afternoon and often we would follow him. We would sit on the end of the bed and play snakes and ladders or draw pictures for him to admire. He was full of praise for our efforts and praise is food for children. Often we would beg him for a story. He was a natural. He believed in ghosts. He would tell us tales of meeting a man who had been dead many a long year on a dark country road. He had stories of fairy trees and banshees . He would get into trouble with mummy when we were too frightened after the stories to go out into the yard alone to the toilet.

Then he had plenty of stories of friends he had made of farm animals during his days working as a farm labourer. He had a way with animals. They recognised him as a friend too. He would whistle and the horse would come to meet him in the mornings. He had reared an abandoned pig in the house and he had a friend called Hipply, a hen with a limp.

Charlie's kingdom was our kitchen garden. I never remember him toiling too much. I can picture him yet: still and contented amidst his beautiful vegetables. When I asked him, "What are you doing sitting here on your own?" he would say "Sure I'm watching the vegetables growing."

That used to make me laugh. I was always in too much of a hurry to watch vegetables growing. Uncle Charlie had an abundance of time for his vegetables. Maybe I never noticed the work because he spent so much time there in the summer. He had time to spare, to admire his work and God's creation.

He knew what he was doing. Without books he knew how to tend his soil. He made compost, and always had farmyard manure. He riddled the ashes of the fire every day and used the cinders to keep slugs away from tender plants and threw the ash round the rhubarb. The black fertile soil that he left us was his legacy.

Nothing was forced. He never used chemicals. Before anyone ever mentioned organic gardening he produced an abundance of vegetables for our table every year without sprays or chemicals. He planted in succession so that there was always plenty but never too much. His garden was a beautiful mosaic of lettuce and scallions, peas and beans, cabbages, cauliflower and Brussels sprouts, potatoes, leeks and beetroot. If there was a glut we children would take the old pram packed with produce round the neighbours' houses to sell for money for sweets. It was so exciting to have something to sell. I loved to grow flowers in the little corner he gave me but he would turn up his nose and say "They're lovely Patricia, but I was never fond of seeing them on my plate at dinner time."

Uncle Charlie always remembered to set out food and water for the birds that visited the garden; he was never threatened by them nor them by him. He would sit so still he could enjoy watching them wash and feast beside him and they kept him company in the summer silence.

When he was gone the garden grew up. It was then that we came to appreciate what a clever, artistic and productive man had had his corner in our house and how much comfort he had given us.

I feel so sorry for the people these days that have big houses but never enough room for their old folk.

LOST

By RICHARD LYSAGHT
Walkinstown, Dublin

*Mother feels she has lost touch with her teenage daughter,
despite the nice thing she has done for a stranger*

" Are you going to come in with me and give the letters to Elizabeth?" I said, as soon as I stopped the car in the grounds of St Gabriel's nursing home.

"No," my daughter, Karen, said, staring out the windscreen. "What's the point?"

I mentally counted to three and, keeping my voice as steady and unemotional as I could, said, "Look, Karen, you are the one who found the letters in the first place, you are the one who went to all the trouble to find Elizabeth."

"So?"

I took a deep breath counted to ten. "Well, I just think that it would be nice and fitting it you were the one to hand her the letters, especially this one." I took the sealed envelope out of my bag and held it front of her. She pretended not to see it. "I think Elizabeth would love to hear how you found it, and the other letters, and all the trouble you went to to find her."

"Would you get real, and stop talking as if you know her or that she knows us. She doesn't. Give the letter to someone in the nursing home to give to her because I am not going anywhere near that skanky grey building."

I tried for a count of twenty, made it to fifteen before the effects of a two-hour journey with my fourteen-year-old daughter finally broke through my calm demeanour.

"Fine, stay here then. I'll go." I stepped out of the car, told myself to keep walking but couldn't do so without saying, "Just as well you are not coming, you would probably scare Elizabeth half to death." I ran my eyes over the spiked hair that looked like it belonged to a hedgehog after it stepped on a thousand volt cable, the purple painted lips and fingernails, the black tee shirt, black denim skirt, black stockings and black hiking boots. I slammed the car door and trudged my way along the long gravely path leading up to the steps of St Gabriel's, thankful that I had parked a good distance away from the nursing home as it gave me time to calm down.

At the bottom of the steps, I glanced back in the direction of the car in the forlorn hope that she might have followed me. She hadn't. I sighed. Why had she come with me in the first place? It didn't make sense to me, but then there was very little about my fourteen and half year old daughter that made sense to me now.

I went up the steps, my heart heavy with the memories of a daughter that used to rush in from school with a drawing and always in that drawing there would be a mammy embraced by a halo of red hearts. Where was she? Where was the daughter who a little over a year ago, while rummaging in a derelict old cottage, discovered beneath a pile of rubble a mouldy leather case and within that case a sheaf of open letters and one sealed letter preserved from the elements by a thick wrapping of plastic. Where was the daughter who had tears in her eyes when she read in those letters the words of a girl named Elizabeth imploring Thomas, the man who deeply loved her, for understanding and forgiveness: she would not be coming back to him, could not, because God had called her to stay where she was and continue working as a lay missionary with the Sisters of Charity. Every letter ended with a pleading for him to reply.

Where was the daughter who became convinced that the sealed letter addressed to Elizabeth McCauley c/o the Sisters of Charity, Capetown, South Africa, was his unsent reply, and insisted that Elizabeth had to be given that letter? Where was the girl who despite receiving word back from the missions that they had no record of any lay missionary with the name Elizabeth McCauley, (who in all likelihood was probably dead by now given that so many years had past) came up with the brainwave that maybe Elizabeth might have become a nun. Where was the daughter who had convinced the head nun in her school to investigate that possibility and who, six months later, almost screamed the house down with joy when she got news that Elizabeth was indeed alive and staying in St Gabriel's nursing home on the outskirts of Dublin. Where was she? The answer came to me as I was escorted by a Sister Brigid to the hospital wing of St Gabriel's where Elizabeth was recovering from a chest infection. My daughter was now lost, lost to me forever.

At the entrance to the ward, Sister Brigid said, "please wait here and I'll see if Elizabeth is up to having a visitor." And then, in a conspiratorial whisper, added, "I am afraid that though Elizabeth is much recovered from the chest infection her mood is very poor, has been for many months, though I expect at close to ninety years of age you..." Sister Brigid's voice trailed off as she gazed across at the white haired woman whose emaciated frame was a mere crease in the blankets that enveloped her.

"Don't worry, I can always come back some other time," I whispered, my mind suddenly made up that I should leave. I figured that with Elizabeth not feeling the best what was the point in giving her the letters especially when the one person who should give them to her couldn't be bothered to do so. It really didn't matter now who handed over the letters. I would tell Sister Brigid the story of the letters; leave them with her to give to Elizabeth when Elizabeth was feeling better. That was my plan but when Sister Brigid beckoned me to come to Elizabeth's bedside, it was to Elizabeth told the story of the letters.

"Will you leave them on my locker?" Elizabeth said, in a voice that was both hoarse sounding and gravelly. She took a few slow breaths. "Your daughter has a wonderful kind nature to go to so much bother over some letters, thank her for me."

I nodded and got up to leave. Elizabeth took a thin bony hand out from under the bedclothes and looking at me with rheumy brown eyes pointed to the letters. "Will you open and read the one addressed to me."

It was my turn to take a few breaths, deep ones. What if the letter contained the vitriolic outpourings of a spurned lover? What effect would that have on Elizabeth? I figured this would be a good time to visit the bathroom.

"Please." Elizabeth said.

What could I do?

I took the unopened letter from the pile, sat down, said a silent prayer, took a deep breath and read the letter

"Dear Elizabeth, I cannot tell you how heartbroken I am having read the contents of your letter. 'Tis like you have stuck a pitch fork through my heart.' I paused, glanced anxiously at Elizabeth. Her eyes were hooded, and her whole body seemed to be sinking deeper into the bed. Now I really needed to visit the bathroom. Oh why oh why did I not leave this sorry letter with Sister Brigid?

"Read on, please." Elizabeth's voice cut through my thoughts

I took another deep breath, said another silent prayer and continued.

'When I think of all the time we spent making plans for the cottage, you saying that we would have to convert the barn to accommodate the size of the family we were going to have. 'Tis like a bad dream to me now; a dream that knows no day.

'I am moidered by the memory of your brown eyes, with the shine off them like chestnuts after they've been squeezed from green cases. I can no longer listen to a bit of music without seeing you up on the floor smiling and jigging around. 'Tis as if my mind is full of the vision of you all of the time, which I suppose it is. Just as well because it is as clear as daylight from your letters that I won't be setting eyes on you again. To be truthful with you, I knew it'd be so when you first got the notion to go away foreign for a year to help out those nuns. I felt it in the flesh on my bones that once you'd go you'd ne'er come back. And now that I am after reading that you feel called by God to be doing what you are doing, I know that you would never be able to sit easy with me no matter what I'd do.

'But I'd be lying through my back teeth if I didn't tell you that I would burst every blood vessel in this body trying to make you happy. God's truth.

'Elizabeth, your decision is bitter medicine for me to take, so before the pain of missing you builds up a head of steam in me again, I'll tell you that you have nothing in the wide world to ask my forgiveness about. I respect and honour your decision and if it does the trick in making you happy, so be it. As God is my witness, you have my backing on that one, till the last breath leaves my body.

'Elizabeth, I'll say no more. I want to catch the postman. Love, Thomas.'

I looked at Elizabeth, at the tears spilling from her eyes, spilling on to a face that was a wreath of smiles.

"I am so happy and I cannot tell you what joy and relief you have brought to my heart." Elizabeth said, in a choking voice. "I cannot thank your daughter enough. This means so much to me." Elizabeth became silent and for a long time laid there, the light of treasured memories resurrecting a bygone luminance to those chestnut eyes.

I stood up to leave.

She looked at me, the light dimming in her eyes. "I wonder why he never sent me that letter?"

I reached for her hand and caressed it.

"I think Elizabeth that some part of him always hoped that you might come back, sending you that letter would have meant giving up that hope."

Elizabeth smiled a sad wistful smile and then she said, "Please make sure to tell your daughter how grateful I am to her."

"I will." I bent down and kissed Elizabeth on the cheek.

As I drove out of the grounds of St Gabriel's, I related everything that had happened to Karen emphasising how grateful Elizabeth was for what Karen had done. My daughter said nothing, just sat looking out the side window.

I shook my head and then as I was turning out of the main road and looking to my right, I noticed what appeared to be a tear in my daughters left eye. I shook my head again; it had to be a trick of the light. Then I heard mumblings about flowers.

"What's this about flowers?"

"You should have brought some to Elizabeth."

"Well, we can always stop and at that florist over there and bring her back some, if you like." I said.

No answer.

I glanced at my daughter convinced now that I had to be hearing things. She was nodding her head and there were tears running down her cheeks. I couldn't help smiling. My real daughter wasn't lost after all, only hiding. I stopped the car.

Beginners Runner-up

AT THE FAIR

By GARRY LOMBARD

Gorey, Co. Wexford

Young Timmy is going to the fair with his Granddad for the first time, an experience eagerly anticipated

When the cock crowed first it didn't really register in Timmy's sleepy head, but the second time he awoke, and blinked. There was only a little light coming through the window as the day dawned. He lay there for a moment and then he remembered. Today was the day, yes, it had come at last, and Granddad was taking him to the fair at Glynn. Oh! It had been so long in coming, but now it was here. He felt the excitement like a tickle in his throat as he slipped quietly out of bed, careful not to wake his brothers. He dressed quickly pulling on his shirt and trousers, his coloured gansy, socks and boots.

Granddad's room (not really a room, more of an attic) was still quite dark as there was only one small window. He could hear the old man snoring heavily. He shook him by the shoulder, "Granddad, wake up Granddad, its morning Granddad, wake up." The old man stirred, grunted, peered at Timmy in the gloom, "What?" "Its morning Granddad, we're going to the fair." Granddad leaned over and took from his waistcoat pocket a large turnip watch. He peered at its face, ten past five.

The old man blinked several times gathering his thoughts. "Alright Timmy, you go down to the kitchen, stir up the ashes in the fire and put on some turf. Can you then go out to the shed and feed the donkey." "Yes Granddad, I know what to do." In the kitchen he took the heavy poker and stirred up the ashes until he exposed the red embers underneath. He took three sods of turf and placed them on the embers.

When he entered the stable Neddy seemed surprised to see him. He poured out the oats in a basin and gave the animal a bucket of water. He then climbed the ladder up into the loft where he knew there was a sack of carrots. He took two carrots and gave them to Neddy, "We're going to the fair Neddy, you and me and granddad. We're going to the fair in Glynn to sell the goats."

After breakfast granddad tackled Neddy with two turf creels one on either side, into one creel he placed the nanny goat and in the other her two kids. The sun had risen and was shining brightly as they set out to walk the three miles to Glynn.

As they walked steadily down the long hill towards the tarred road, the countryside spread out in front of them like a map. Everything seemed fresh and newly washed, and each field contained a pool of mist that gradually shrank and shrank until it disappeared in the rising warmth. Soon they were on the tarred road and passing the school that Timmy had attended for the past three years. He longed to hold granddad's hand, but didn't want to appear too babyish; at last he could resist no longer and raising his hand touched granddad's fingers. The old man enveloped his hand in a huge grasp and looked down and smiled reassuringly. A tide of love swelled up in Timmy's throat so that he almost choked, "I love you granddad" he thought, "I love you more than anyone in all the world."

It was good to say that, even if only in his head. Yet it was true, he did love granddad more than anybody, even more than his mammy and daddy. He thought about this, was it wrong? He tried to remember what Mother Theresa had told them about love. You must love God and you must love your mammy and daddy, yes, but nothing about loving granddad. If it were a sin he would have to tell it at his first confession next month. Mother Theresa had spent a long time teaching them about first confession and Examination of Conscience. That meant making a list of sins to tell the priest. Mother Theresa had told them that this was a very important thing and he had given it a great deal of thought. He had his list of sins ready, three sins; he thought that was enough.

He had pulled his sister Nora's hair when they were fighting over the spinning top. He had stolen a handful of raisins out of the jar his mammy kept for making curney bread (stealing carrots for Neddy didn't count). He had said that very bold word beginning with "F" the day the gander had tried to peck at him. This last sin caused him a problem. How could he tell the priest this sin without saying the word again – and maybe committing another sin? Saying that word in the confession box might even be a mortal sin and they were the worst of all. Now he wondered had he a fourth sin to tell, loving his granddad more than mammy and daddy. His thoughts grew troubled and he put them firmly out of his head deciding to think about them another day, today he was just going to enjoy.

They walked on and on for what seemed ages and he grew weary, he thought his knees would buckle and there was a blister on his left heel that hurt with every step. At each bend in the road he hoped to see the town, but no, the road ran on, and on. How much further could it be? He noticed granddad glancing down at him, he lifted his head and quickened his step to show that he was fine but granddad bent down and swept him up onto Neddy's back. "It's less than a mile now, Neddy will be able to carry you for the last bit." The tiredness left him at once, and all of the anticipation and excitement came flooding back. Granddad had let him sit on Neddy's back a few times before, but here he was now, riding Neddy, riding Neddy on the road, on the road to the fair with granddad.

At last they crested a hill and there below them was the town. Each street was crammed with people and animals. There were hundreds of cattle herded into groups by men with big knobbly sticks, makeshift pens full of sheep and lambs, carts and creels loaded with pigs, goats and chickens. Timmy had never seen so many people in one place, not even at mass on Sunday, or at the football match to which granddad had brought him. The crowd was so thick now that granddad had almost to push his way through until he found the street in which goats were being sold. He lifted the nanny goat from the creel and tethered her with a piece of rope, he then lifted out the two kids who rushed instantly to their mother and suckled greedily.

During the morning a few men stopped briefly and looked at the goats but made no offer. About midday, a heavyset man, whose enormous stomach hung out over the top of his breeches, approached them. The breeches were supported by a pair of braces that appeared under such a strain that they would snap at any moment. His face and jaws were so fat that his chin had disappeared, and his mouth was full of bad teeth. He scowled rather than looked at the goats and without looking at granddad he grunted "How much?" Granddad told him the price and he grunted and walked away. Ten minutes later the fat man returned, for some minutes he and granddad bargained over the price. Eventually a price was agreed and the fat man handed over the money to granddad with a begrudging air.

He turned and was about to go when his eye fell upon Neddy. "How much for the ass?" "He's not for sale" Granddad told him. As if he hadn't heard, the fat man put his arm tightly around Neddy's neck and roughly forced his lips apart exposing his teeth. Although granddad continually told him that he was not selling, the man kept increasing his offer. "Throw in the two creels and I'll give you two pounds ten shillings." Eventually the man said: "Two pounds eighteen shillings and that's my last offer." Granddad seemed to hesitate. There was a long silence and then granddad said "Make it three pounds." "Alright then" the man said angrily. He spat on his palm and held his hand aloft, "Hold out your hand."

An involuntary sound escaped Timmy's mouth, not so much a gasp more of a whimper. His Granddad looked at him, Timmy's eyes were wide with panic, his little mouth open, his jaw slack. He looked into his granddad's eyes with disbelief, desperation, despair. Granddad held his gaze for what seemed a very long time and then he tuned to the fat man "I've changed my mind, I'm not selling."

On the way home as he sat astride Neddy a look was exchanged between him and his granddad, between child, and adult, and though nothing was said, Timmy knew that there was something new between them, a new rapport, a new understanding, a new relationship. Timmy knew now more clearly than ever that he loved his Granddad more than anything in all the world. He didn't care if it was a sin.

YANKS AND DOLLS

By MAURA FLYNN
Westport, Co. Mayo

The visiting Yanks cause weeks of frantic preparation and much anticipation of what they might bring

They came every year in search of their roots, once removed from their Irish cousins, sons and daughters of Mike, Pat and Nora who left Ireland when water came from the well not a tap. Cars hired at Shannon made their way down country lanes and dogs barked at the strange noise the engines made.

For weeks beforehand our house would be in turmoil, every room turned inside out, the smell of paint and new lino filled the whole house. Bottles of Guinness and whiskey were bought and some of my mother's chickens died for the American cause. Currant cake, treacle cake and soda bread were baked the day before, fresh lettuce and scallions were picked from the garden and laid on the cold shelf in the pantry where they fought for space beside the rhubarb and apple tarts made by my mother. They were alongside a large bowl of trifle that wobbled and shook every time the door was banged, which was very often, as we went in to see all the goodies lined up, our mouths watering in anticipation of the feast to come when the yanks finally arrived.

At last the great day arrived and the final preparations were mad, children were scrubbed, boy's hair brylcreamed and girl's hair released from the rags that were put in the night before. Beds were changed and the Yanks were given the good room which meant us children had to bunk in together, not that we minded as the excitement was well worth any discomfort.

We had never seen Yanks before and could only conjure up pictures in our minds of what they might look like. Those cousins of my fathers were faceless people to us, the cousins who sent the dollars and parcels at Christmas and memorial cards of dead relatives we did not recognise and would never see now.

We sat on the wall by the roadside listening for the sound of an engine in the distance.

Cars were few and far between in those days; the odd bus made its way between Ballina and Galway. Once a week the Benson Box lorry passed by on its way to the factories in Westport and Castlebar. Moran's and Lavelle's bread vans made their way to Ballinrobe with fresh bread a couple of times a week. Our local insurance man known locally as Tommy Windmill had a Baby Ford that did not always stay on the road and more than once ended up in the ditch outside our house.

We would sometimes have to sit on that wall for hours as flights could be delayed and there was no telephone to let us know what was happening. Hands and knees became grubby and we were hauled into the house for a quick repair job and warned that we would be put to bed before the Yanks came if we did not behave ourselves.

And then they were here in a black shiny car, my great Aunt Ellie and her daughter Patsy who, to our amazement, looked like us; two arms, legs and ears and, the biggest wonder of all, only one head. My mother and father rushed out to meet them as they climbed out of the car. There were hugs and kisses and a few tears from Aunt Ellie at her first trip home in forty years. Our cuteness was commented on. Suitcases were taken upstairs to the good room, but to our dismay not to be opened until after dinner, leaving us in limbo as to what they contained, presents for us we hoped as my mother had hinted.

Finally the time came to open the cases and the presents were handed out. My mother got perfume that filled the air with the most beautiful scent. May father's carton of Camel cigarettes soon filled the room with a different aroma. My brothers received two beautiful wooden hand painted boats complete with sails, for years they sat on my mother's sideboard as they were much too good to play with. My sister's gift was a fancy muslin dress embroidered with flowers. Then it was my turn, the most fabulous doll I had ever seen was produced from the bottom of the suitcase. She had arms and legs that moved, her head was covered by lovely golden curls and my rag doll paled into insignificance compared to Rosebud.

During their stay they brought us to Knock and we had our first visit to the seaside where we played on the sand in our knickers and vests. There was always a party when the Yanks came and all the neighbours and relations gathered to meet our American cousins. It went on well into the morning and people sang and danced the night away. Fiddles and accordions threw their sound out into the night and hobnail boots beat time on the stone floor. We children were sent to bed before midnight but we sneaked out and sat halfway down the stairs. The aroma of cigarettes and pipe smoke curled its way up between the banisters and the aroma of strong black porter and hot toddies gave the whole house an exotic smell that was strange to our nostrils. Most people had a party piece and as the night wore on our eyes closed and we drifted off to sleep, lulled by the music from downstairs and we dreamt of dolls and Yanks and trips to the seaside....

While Lucifer Watched

By Paul McLaughlin
Marmount Gardens, Belfast

As the angelic baby and perfect child approaches his teens, his doting parents are in for a shock ...

Deckie Rooney had been an angelic looking child. Praised in his White Cross pram by strangers at the shops on Belfast's Lisburn Road, spoiled rotten at home by parents who doted on him, little Deckie had won hearts wherever he had toddled and often had the dimpled cuddle marks to prove it.

In turn, he was a bonny baby, an inspiring infant and a child with a face to die for. Yet, despite or maybe because of all these bounties, Deckie was blessed with a charm and pleasance of personality that could be measured in bucketfuls. Everybody said so. Even the spinster woman from the Methodist church down the road had lavished her "Sunday going to meeting" smile on her "wee dote" as she called him. And she hardly spoke to a soul without a definite sourness curdling her lips, especially not the "other sort".

All in all, Deckie had been the perfect son for Mary and Manuel Rooney of the leafy suburb where 31 Berryvolga Avenue shone out, as if from an estate agent's brochure, as the happiest of homes. A child born fourteen long years after a Rome wedding, Deckie had been a gift from God himself that came after a thousand Novenas and a mother's dip in the holy waters of Lourdes.

His devotion to his prayers and his love of the chapel, no fidgeting at all even when Father Gillespie droned on and on, had his mother talking of the joys of a vocation within days of his not unexpected 11 plus success.

"God gave him to us, Daddy," said Mary, reverently, to her husband one night after the family Rosary, "And I think the boy's heart lies deep within the church".

Mary and Manny had forsaken their own Christian names on the day the baby had been born to prepare themselves for the family cocoon they would spin to envelope Declan Majella Rooney. Declan after Mary's late father, Majella after the patron saint of expectant mothers.

A dream birth in the private ward of Belfast City Hospital had signposted the way for a new baby that would be a stranger to pitfalls. The Rooneys had had the A to Z of parenthood planned carefully ahead. They were both in their mid-thirties, mature and sensible, just as their mothers and fathers had been before them, and with their four pubs thriving, albeit in the less salubrious areas of the city, money would never be a problem.

But the Devil, who learned his trade at the feet of the master, works in his own mysterious ways and, as Deckie approached his thirteenth birthday, hormones, straight from Hell, were already sharpening the rounded face and black-heading the turned up nose of the cherub into something that would prove unrecognisable to Mister and Missus Rooney. Deckie Rooney, in the March of 1964, was about to become a teenager.

Mammy had thought Deckie unusually quiet before his birthday Mass and not at all his jokey self, but she had put it down to nerves on his big day. Maybe even a little embarrassment at being the centre of attention yet again. For Deckie had always been the most modest of boys.

Deckie wore his new pair of grey, terylene trousers, his first pair of longs as everyone called them, and had looked so grown up as he had paraded to church. But those new shoes from McAfee's shop must be just a little too tight, she thought, or why else would he drag his feet so. He had hardly been able to keep up with them and it was only a short walk.

Daddy left for work at 11am with promises to return before 3pm, but Deckie did not wave from the sitting room as usual and Daddy thought him preoccupied with the day that was in it. "He's such a great fella," thought Manny as he drove down the Malone Road, " and the double of his Granda Rooney. He'll break a few hearts if the clergy don't get him first." Manny Rooney smiled contentedly as he motored past the Queen's University of Deckie's future. There could be no doubt about it.

By three o'clock that afternoon, both sitting rooms of the double-bay windowed house were packed with other Mammies, sporting freshly set hair do's and remarkably-behaved offspring who queued up to present gifts to the birthday boy. Mary thought it all a little too much for her son. His ever-present smile, sure it was the gift of the angels, had disappeared and he looked drawn and somewhat distant during the entire proceedings.

Eventually, all the visiting children were hustled into the breakfast-room where the party had been deposited earlier and Malcolm the Magician, who had enjoyed a season at the Empire Theatre back in the 1940's, Daddy said, was practically tied up in silk hankies when Daddy wheeled in the "Raleigh Rapier" bicycle. A chorus of oohs and aahs bubbled breathlessly from the two dozen assembled boys and two girls.

Mammy had written out the guest list herself and only two girls, Father O'Dwyer's nieces, Attracta and Concepta, had received invites. They were such sweet girls and so natural. Mammy had heard stories about some of the families that were moving into the avenue, tales of kitchen houses, sauce bottles on the table and ill-mannered girls. One couldn't be too careful. But, Mammy had been.

Preparations for the big day on the seventeenth had been underway for weeks.

Mammy had even overseen the catering arrangements with the help of her "daily", Missus Mac. Father O'Dwyer had promised to say grace and stay on for a wee half'un. The ladies of the Sodality, Mammy's Tuesday evening group since she was a wee girl, would sing for their supper, "Blow the wind Southerly", of course, and everything would be just right for the big occasion. Mammy had been saying so for weeks to anyone who would listen and open house at the Rooney's would be the parish's party of the year.

Invitations, printed on little gold-framed cards had been sent out in the third week of February, with RSVP's, of course.

"Declan Rooney cordially invites you to share in his birthday on 17th March", they read in a fine italic type that Mammy had thought tasteful but not over the top. Nearly thirty replies had been received and filed away alphabetically in Auntie Agnes' bureau in the back parlour. Nothing had been left to chance. The baker had been instructed, with a wagging finger, to provide only the very best pastries and fancies and Missus Mac, who normally worked from 9am until 3pm, had agreed to stay on as a guest and, of course, a waitress, until teatime. Her wages would be paid until 3pm only. That went without saying. Even the school closed down for St Patrick's Day and Deckie's birthday, thought Mammy.

Monday the 17th had seen the family breakfasting late. They had gone to St Brigid's for 9 o'clock Mass and Communion and had the hearty appetites that they, inevitably, created. Missus Mac had had the Ulster fry ready, "cooked breakfast please, not a common fry, Missus Mac" said Mammy; and the birthday cards, with their envelopes ripped and tossed away, flew over the great mantelpiece of the "little" parlour like the flags of all nations.

Deckie's reaction to the "two-wheeled wonder" Raleigh Rapier as the advertising blurb had described it, came as a shock to everyone. "Cud you not git it in red? That silver colour's for wee girls."

His words cut through the crowd like a knife through birthday cake and Mammy rushed to switch on the record player in an effort to drown everyone's embarrassment.

Freddie and Dreamers' "Who wears short shorts" blasted out from the little Dansette player and, with cakes, ice-cream and minerals for camouflage, the bitter pill of Deckie's obvious disappointment was swallowed in the sound and fury of the afternoon.

Mammy and Daddy guided the other mothers and a couple of fathers into the conservatory, with little nudges and shoves disguised as the friendliest of touches, along with Father O'Dwyer and a clutch of the church choir. The good ladies' rendition of "Hail Glorious Saint Patrick" had been received with silence and they looked glad to make an early exit. But Daddy had excelled himself.

Drinks of all colours were on display on the long trestle table that ran the considerable length of the room. Johnny Madden, the charge-hand of Daddy's public house on Donegall Pass, dressed in a new white bar jacket, hired especially for the occasion, did the honours, speaking only when spoken to as instructed, while canapés and savouries, that tasted as good as they looked, were handed round by Missus Mac, dressed in a black and white outfit that had seen more cocktail parties than King Farouk.

Mammy relaxed at last and enjoyed the refreshments and eager chatter of her neighbours as they praised her to the high heavens. Even Father O'Dwyer, no stranger to the higher social scene, said something complimentary in Latin. Very impressive. And the time flew past as it does only at the best parties.

No wonder then that Johnny Madden's drunken outburst, as the Westminster chimes of the conservatory clock signalled 6 o'clock, threw everyone into shock.

"And you Manny "hi-falutin" Rooney can shove your tuppenny, ha'penny pub where the sun don't shine", he screamed. Johnny's words, no little slurred, but perfectly audible to all, were his first and last of the afternoon. He collapsed on the trestle and came to rest on top of Miss Imelda Fitzsimmons, of the Fortwilliam Fitzsimmons', felled by the guts of a bottle of John Power's Gold Label.

Her bright, pink bloomers were as vivid as her face as she lay gazing up into the glazed eyes of Madden's imposing thirteen stone. For a moment, chaos reigned. Gasps and squeals were uttered on cue, Miss Fitzsimmons fought to restrain Johnny Madden's hairy, Co Armagh hands with kicks and screams, not all that loud said Missus Gogarty afterwards. Only Manny Rooney, publican to the end, had the presence of mind to lever her to safety while removing his employee to the relative security of the downstairs' washroom, courtesy of a half-Nelson.

Mammy apologized and apologized louder again, firing salvo after salvo of "Sorrys" at her distracted targets. She soothed tempers and bruised sensibilities and even smoothed down Imelda's party frock that had seen action for the first time in its uneventful life. But the damage had been done and Mammy knew it. She rushed to the breakfast room to find solace in the embrace of her beloved Deckie. He would understand and make the bad things go away. Her only son, the joy of her life, would comfort his Mammy with eager arms.

She stopped dead in the doorway, beneath her blessed St Brigid's Cross, as if she had been hit by a sniper, but her disbelieving eyes continued to see. She focused on the "Raleigh Rapier" lying overturned on the heavy Wilton carpet, like a wounded animal, splatters of red paint running from handlebar to tail light.

"Where is Deckie, where is my baby?" she cried, the sickness in her stomach rising with her voice. "What in heaven's name have you done with him?"

The dozen or so guests looked bleary-eyed and vaguely unaware of her cries of anguish as Deckie appeared, crawling from behind Grandmother's best settee, red-faced and crumpled, with a bottle of stout in his fist and Father O'Dwyer's niece Concepta on his back.

"I'm here Ma. Are ye lukin a spin on my bike?"

THE MEAL

By GERARD O'CALLAGHAN
Tockwith, York, North Yorkshire

*It's a special occasion for Julia and Miriam as they have their
friends and neighbours in for a meal to thank them for their
support, but where is John with the meat?*

Watching Julia stand on tip toe at the kitchen window
reminded Miriam of the rabbits she saw in the lane
on her morning walks. She watched as her older sister
drummed her long fingers on the windowsill, her grey narrowed
eyes peering over the net curtains and down the gravelled drive.
Miriam, amid the growing tension, stopped folding napkins
and began to polish the cutlery instead. Both women looked up
at the large clock on the wall, the pendulum now appearing to
swing faster than normal.

The light in the kitchen suddenly faded as the last remnants
of the winter sun began to sink from the sky. "Put the light on
Miriam before we both go blind" Julia snapped, her eyes remain-
ing fixed on the drive. Miriam did as she was asked and then
wished she hadn't.

Under the harsh glare of the kitchen light Miriam scanned
the room and all that had yet to be done. On the table by the far
wall, two pies waited to be finished. A rolled blot of pastry lay
stretched between a bowl of beaten egg and a mound of apple
peelings. On the draining board were unwashed and unpeeled
carrots, potatoes and turnips. John left them there earlier before
rushing off to the next job on Julia's list. She smiled remembering
the way he rolled his eyes and winked at her before heading off
down the drive with his wheelbarrow.

Julia's voice boomed across the kitchen. "If John Sheehan isn't
standing in front of me with a joint of beef in his hands within
the next ten minutes, all hell will be let loose, I promise ye". She
threw the tea towel she had been holding on top of the dresser,

tipping over a picture frame and stormed out through the kitchen door. Miriam listened for the footsteps on the stairs before skipping to the window. Outside, a light wind was rolling leaves across the lawn and down the drive. Down at the gate, sentinel crows called to each other in the trees. Long blue shadows reached up the drive from the gates to the front steps of the house. There was no sign of John. Earlier, between fetching coal for the fires and carrying chairs down from upstairs, Julia had instructed him to take the bike and to go pick up a joint of beef from Quinn's in the town. That was over an hour ago. She glanced at the clock. Four thirty. The guests were due at seven.

Sighing, Miriam busied herself with finishing the pies. She covered the fruit with sugar, sprinkled a little cinnamon and put the pastry lids on. She sealed both pies with some beaten egg and carried them to the oven. After wiping down the floury surfaces she moved to the draining board and began preparing the vegetables. Julia would see to the soup. Upstairs she could hear her stomping between rooms. If she finished the vegetables quickly, together they could set the table. John would be back with the meat soon, which Julia would insist on cooking herself, not trusting Miriam or John to jeopardise the day any further. In the meantime, Miriam and John could see to the fires and wine glasses. For the first time that day, Miriam started to believe that this meal might just be a success after all.

The meal had been Julia's idea. Since their father's death the previous winter, people had been so kind that Julia decided to repay the kindness by hosting a small dinner party. Nothing too grand, just a small gathering for a few close friends and neighbours. Doctor Collins and his wife were invited. The Barry's from across the field, who had been such strength to the sisters in helping to organise the funeral, were also expected. Bob Sullivan the solicitor from town and his wife also agreed to come.

A bedroom door slammed upstairs startling Miriam. She gathered up the chopped vegetables and dropped them into a pot of cold water before running to the window to search for John.

It was now dark outside. The pillars of the gate were barely visible. Orange and yellow lights glowed in the blackness from surrounding houses. It was nearly five o clock. "Please John" she whispered. There was no sound from upstairs but Miriam knew that Julia was keeping watch from the landing window. If John was to turn up the drive this very minute he would see two pale and anxious faces staring back at him. Miriam turned away from the window and considered ringing Quinn's. Instead she picked up a tin of furniture polish and tip toed down the hall towards the dining room.

Upstairs, Julia watched from another window. John could be absent minded at times especially when Miriam was about but this time he had taken the proverbial biscuit. She had planned this dinner party for months and now she was about to be mortified in front of friends and neighbours. She could hear Miriam downstairs and knew she would be worrying about John. What if he had come off the bike on the dark road? He could be lying in a ditch hurt or even dead!

Julia couldn't imagine the house now without John in it. He had come to help in the garden after their father had had his first stroke. That was nearly five years ago. Now he did all sorts of odd jobs around the place. Julia had interviewed him for the job and although there were things about him that she found fault with, his eating habits for one, not to mention his wild and unkempt hair, she had to admit that he was a hard and honest worker. She also remembered his face that day when Miriam came into the kitchen and the shy way he rose to shake her hand.

Suddenly outside, she heard the crunch of footsteps on gravel. She quickly moved away from the window and headed for the stairs.

Miriam had also heard the crunch of gravel and she ran down the hall towards the kitchen door. She heard Julia, her footsteps sounding like furious thunder on the stairs.

John entered the kitchen quietly with the wrapped parcel of meat under his arm. "Thank God you're back John," Miriam cried, "I thought something terrible had happened to you"

"Ah no, I'm fine" he said "a bit delayed is all. I hope I haven't upset the arrangements."

At that moment Julia marched into kitchen, her arms folded tightly across her chest.

"And what time do you call this John Sheehan" she shouted. "Now Julia" Miriam pleaded, "John's here with the meat and everything's grand so don't go getting upset. We have a lot to do".

"Don't remind me what we have to do Miriam Buckley, thank you very much" snapped Julia. "I'm well aware of what we have to do, although at this late stage however we might as well cancel the whole thing". Her face was beetroot red from a combination of shouting and the heat in the kitchen.

Miriam gently took the meat from John and put it on the table. The three of them stood in silence. Finally, Julia sighed loudly and moved towards the table. "Well" she said, "we'd better get a move on then if we don't want to look complete fools in front of all our friends and neighbours".

"I'm sorry Julia" said John moving towards her, "it couldn't be helped, I swear".

"What couldn't be helped exactly" she snapped. "Such a simple errand and now look at us all in a right state, what in God's name are we going to do?"

John stepped towards Miriam and shook his head. "Look" he shouted startling the sisters. "I didn't expect to be late. I picked up the meat as planned and then I had to go to Kelly the jeweller to pick something up." He put the cap he held in his hand on the table and reached into his inside pocket. He turned to Miriam and placed a blue velvet box in her hand.

"I brought you this" he whispered "because I was hoping to ask you to marry me. I planned do it on Sunday but now that the cat's out of the bag", his voice trailed off. "I waited to have our initials engraved on it, that's why I'm late. I know how important tonight is for you Julia, I didn't mean to upset you and I'm sorry". He sighed and shook his head again. The kitchen fell silent. Miriam stared at the box in her hand. She turned to Julia who was wringing her apron in both hands and struggling to keep the tears that were brimming in her eyes from falling.

She opened the hinged lid and looked at the diamond ring inside. "Oh John" she said and reached for his hand. "I've never seen anything so beautiful". His eyes were dark and serious. "Is that a yes then?" he said. She looked at Julia. Tears were now streaming down her sister's face. "Of course I will" she cried out and threw her arms around his neck. He lifted her up and kissed her gently.

Julia wiped her eyes with her apron and sniffed loudly. She moved towards the parcel. "You don't half pick your moments John Sheehan" she said. "A dinner party to organise and you start proposing marriage. I never heard the like of it in all my born days". Her voice was soft and fragile. John and Miriam remained in tight embrace and appeared not to have heard her. She smiled, watching them standing together in the warm kitchen.

"Maybe, just maybe, we could save this day from being a complete disaster if we put our backs into it" she said. "Right you are, I'll get the fires started" John said stepping away from Miriam. As he was leaving the room he paused and turned to Julia. "I'd say the whole parish will be talking about that piece of beef tomorrow after you've worked your magic on it Julia". With that he beamed a bright smile and left the room. The two sisters watched him walk down the hall, shaking his coat off as he went.

Julia was still crying. Miriam moved towards her and held her tightly. "You are happy about this Julia?" she whispered. Julia's back shook and she nodded her head. "Oh Miriam" was all she could manage to whisper. The two women stood holding each other. "We'd better get a move on" Miriam finally said "or the people will starve!"

Julia straightened herself and began fussing with her apron. She let out a long sigh and gripped her sister's hand firmly. "Haven't we the long night ahead of us Miriam to be eating and drinking". She turned and looked at the kitchen. "Right so" she said heading towards the cooker. "I hope you've not made a mess of those pies, you know you can't be trusted. I should have done it myself". Miriam smiled, watching her sister clattering about in a cupboard searching for a roasting pan. As she turned to go in search for extra wine glasses she could smell the cinnamon from the apple pies.

From the sitting room she could hear dry logs spitting and sparking in the fire. Pausing at the doorway she saw John kneeling before the flames, his eyes lost in thought. She made her way upstairs, her footsteps soft on the worn carpet. At the landing window she stopped and looked out at the blinding darkness, her hand clutching the blue velvet box.

John listened to the footsteps on the stairs and locked forever in his heart the look in her eyes when she opened the box.

In the kitchen Julia seasoned the meat quickly before shoving it into the hot oven. Dabbing at her forehead with her apron she glanced about at the prepared vegetables and the cooling pies before loudly exclaiming "thanks be to God".

CATCHING RABBITS

A Memory from JIM FOGARTY
Two-Mile Borris, Co. Tipperary

Rabbit-hunting was an important source of income, and food, for many country people just after World War 2

A large amount of my childhood and teenage memories are of days catching rabbits. Our main hunting dog was a mongrel of sheepdog extraction but with some greyhound blood in its breeding. In this far- off age our adventures covered large tracts of land and bog. By evening we were usually very tired but if we had a good catch it was considered worthwhile. It was certainly a great method of keeping fit before the gym age.

Our household had a mongrel called "Sport" and a couple of terriers "Darkie" and "Spot". The mongrel seldom failed to catch his quarry, once the terriers raised a rabbit. "Sport" followed with great enthusiasm and the speed of a greyhound and was able to catch his prey without doing much damage to it. After World War Two there was a great demand for rabbits in Irish cities and a great overseas trade in England. Ship loads were dispatched twice weekly to the U.K. Rabbits boiled and fried with fresh vegetables and potatoes made a magnificent meal and could be said to be the "gourmet food of the poor" then.

Rabbits sold at two to four shillings depending on size and quality. My old pal Paddy Connolly was my companion on our Saturday outings. The following day our dogs would be required by my father and his adult colleagues. Sunday for two young boys was reserved for hurling and football.

Our catch one Saturday amounted to over forty animals. We spent the night sorting out the rabbits according to size and any that were slightly damaged had to be sewn up with thread to disguise the open skin. Of course that was slightly illegal but two young boys on the verge of some good money never worried about the regulations. Up to ten pounds could be made, a lot of money in the 1950's.

After grading the catch and dividing them into two lots and securing in two half beet pulp bags, the catch was ready for delivery. It was my task to take the two bags into Thurles on Monday morning on my bicycle on my way to school. It meant an early start, around eight o'clock, to be outside the purchasers, Lawlors of Friar Street, when they opened. One had to first in the queue as the excuse that you had to make a rabbit delivery would hardly be a valid one in the Christian Brothers School if you were late. Whatever the school day brought I felt in a good mood with around ten pounds in my pocket. Of course, I had to give Paddy his share which would be about a third for I had to deduct the carriage and a charge for use of the dogs!

We also had to be very careful that crop owners were not around in the summer time for ""Sport" had a habit of chasing rabbits in corn fields and left a trail. We always checked that our selected fields were vacant of the owners.

The poor rabbit was disliked by farmers. Rabbits liked young corn and root crops leaves. In the 1950's a disease was introduced by the Government, called myxomatosis, to cut down on the numbers of rabbits as the farmers were complaining about all the damage caused. Myxomatosis brought on blindness and multiple tumours causing the rabbit to die a fortnight later. As a result of introducing this disease deliberately, thousands of rabbits died. It was a sad scene then to see rabbits dying out the fields with swollen heads and eyes and often crows, jackdaws and magpies plucking at them for food. It stopped their value as domestic food. One wonders did the spread of the disease really benefit farmers for bad weather in subsequent years also militated against crops and grass management. Maybe a weeding out process was needed to keep down rabbit numbers, but two schoolboy hunters of fifty years ago considered our method more humane!

Today rabbit numbers are beginning to grow again, very slowly according to a survey despite the advent of motorways, and the removal of ditches to make larger fields out of several smaller ones, all in the name of modernisation. The rabbit has lost a lot of its normal habitat.

Writing this article brings back wonderful memories of a childhood era and an old pal, Paddy Connolly, who later emigrated to Australia and died there some years ago. And, of course, memories of three very loyal dogs.

LETTER TO MY DAUGHTER

By EILEEN CASEY

Old Bawn, Tallaght, Dublin

*A mother remembers her 'first love' as she watches her daughter
constantly texting her boyfriend; though the technology might
change, the agony and the ecstasy remain the same*

There, it's gone off again, making a buzzing sound, like an
alarm clock. I know by the brightness flashing from your
eyes, the pink glow on your cheeks there is a message on
your mobile from that 'special' someone. A message that makes
you oblivious to my presence here at the kitchen table writing
what you probably imagine is a dull shopping list.

No doubt you are thinking that such a middle-aged, grey-
haired matron as I am would not appreciate the urgency of these
text messages or the need to reply so immediately. Or the beauty
of technology! I can't blame you on that score, it took me ages
to resist using the mobile. I'm so glad that you insisted I learn,
sure it was a piece of cake once I picked up on it. And .....to be
able to text you when you're out eases a lot of the worry of these
teenage years.

Your fingers fly along, deft as the finest concert pianist, making your own peculiar notes, abbreviations no doubt for the language of love.I know. And you have told me so often, I mustn't
be so old fashioned.Lv., though a consonant and a vowel short,
still stands for the word love. And I am so much older than you,
my darling, my first born daughter coming to me after such a
long gap after the birth of your two brothers, who are now full-
grown men and married themselves.

Yet, I was sixteen once upon a time and beautiful too, as you
are now. My hair was long and glossy just like yours and I was
always listening to music on the radio. We didn't have IPods or
earphones or anything like that. Instead, my fingers flew across
pages and pages like winged messengers trying to keep up with

my thoughts. My thoughts were speedy and swift and I was lifted airborne by the magical world of love. How could I ever forget that heady time?

You see, I too had my first real boyfriend at sixteen. We had no telephones or texting machines then. Our thoughts were hourly filled with each other but there was no quick way of communicating these thoughts. No abbreviations, no shorthand. And just as well because the memories of getting those letters, are still very vivid. You see, he lived on a farm outside the town. As a result he was very close to nature and was very appreciative of the seasons and their meanings. From him I too learnt to savour the changing colours of the year and I looked for the coming and the going of the swallow, that tiny little bird that so bravely makes such a long and hard journey every year to our shores.

Although the object of my heart's desire travelled in from outside the town and I saw him at lunch times and briefly after school, most week-ends were endless without sight of him. Yet, love finds a way! His cousin worked in one of the larger bakery shops in the town and most Saturdays this cousin would bring in a package for me from my sweetheart which I, or your grandmother, would collect. Mostly your grandmother did because she was up so early and out getting the shopping while I was still dreaming sweet dreams. Like you, dear daughter, I always needed that extra hour.

But just imagine! There, under a counter bursting with fresh made bread and delicious cakes, that parcel waited to be collected.When she'd return from the town your grandmother would wake me up and my first sight of the day was that brown paper parcel secured with string or strong Sellotape. Barely awake, I'd tear open the prize to find a book recently finished and much enjoyed, and passed on for me to share. There was an indefinable sense of that package being wrapped at a table late at night, sprinkled with moon dust or folded together in the early morning when the day was only beginning.

But the biggest prize of all would be the letter that tumbled out of the centre of the book. That letter would be read and reread and the whole world was made fresh again as I savoured each line, each word, going over it and over it. Those words wound around my heart like a soft silky breeze. All those envelopes, full of letters written in quiet moments at windows filled with canopies of sky or leaf and birdsong, all those pages covered with such strong handwriting, were kept in a drawer beside my bed. What other treasures need I have wished for?

First love is so special. But first love isn't always the one that lasts. I still think of that kind gentle boy with much fondness but as the months passed, like the seasons our romance changed. One day I opened your grandmother's range and burnt those letters and I knew that it was right that ashes were all that remained of a romance grown cold. I still had a good friend at the end of it all, however, and fine preparation for when I eventually met your father some years later. Your dear father, my truest love.

I had come to Dublin to work in Heuston Station as a typist. Your father was very young also but our homesickness and loneliness was less sharp when we caught sight of each other one evening, both of us walking home to our bedsits along the canal that, as luck would have it, were literally around the corner from each other. The hours didn't seem quite so long in the typing pool after those glimpses though it was ages and ages before I plucked up the courage to say hello one summer evening when my heart was filled to overflowing with such longing.

Your father had the most beautiful raven black hair, black as black could be. He had been born and reared under the nestling presence of Torc Mountain in Muckross, Killarney, a place full of the passion and wildness of nature. That evening when I said hello, I was rewarded by a wonderful smile that swept away all thoughts of loneliness for my own home, a small town in the Midlands. We were drawn, two lonely young people not long left home, a loneliness that we eventually put down into words when the letters between us began to be written on various occasions over the years. Letters that often returned to those times when we first met. How else could we have expressed those early days of love and longing? Of trying to find ourselves in the strangeness of a city landscapes?

Sometimes, there is only the white space on a page that is like a silence which when broken, can only say exactly what you want to say. A line of words rippling into another, as the fishing line is reeled out onto the water, finding the deepest part of the lake, bringing the 'catch' to shore, glinting in the light. On those pages I still can see the sheen of your father's dark hair, as it was then, and the blueness of his eyes, as they still are! and the stretch upwards of his tall, lean, frame.

On those pages the dancing music of your father's Kerry lilt perfectly compliments your mother's Midland brogue . In the same way as mountains compliment flat landscape. Your father, coming from a place abundant with mountains and lakes, was the perfect companion for a young woman reared so near the bog. He used to joke that my brown eyes had shades of turf in them! On those white pages, between those lines, laid like a track, were journeys I never dreamed of, journeys I savour each time they are read and re-read. I learn again of your father's big, wide generous heart, of his own loneliness fading like the night sky once we became sweethearts, a love that has lasted over thirty years. I still hear the beat of his heart flutter into my own because we were both brave enough to say things on those pages that shyness might have prevented us from saying. He was, and still is, my angel.

Daughter, I have kept those precious letters. They will be a legacy to you. Someday you might read them and our story will give you comfort. You'll read about the young woman who wore a red raincoat her sister (your Aunt Rosy) sent her all the way from London. I could hardly wait to write to your father and tell him about that wonderful gift. Through reading those letters, you also will open that crinkly parcel, delivered by your own grandfather who was postman in that Midland town for most of his life. You will hear the sounds and scents of the bustling city Rosy emigrated to so she could train and become the fine nurse she did. All that excitement tumbling out onto the table as the vibrant colour of that coat lighting up the kitchen.

Your grandmother's worried creases smoothed away as she read the letter enclosed for her. All well, a Christmas visit home planned and immediately looked forward to and prepared for. Your grandmother carried it around in her apron pocket all day and that night as she did her rounds, checking the sockets, turning off the lights and then sprinkling holy water on me, her youngest daughter, we both prayed for the safe keeping of Rosy.

Daughter, you might actually be able to see the girl, now your middle-aged, grey haired mother, who wore that coat, crossing the bridges of the town she grew up in, loving every nook and cranny of it, from the outline of the steeple of St. Brendan's Church to the winding journey of the Camcor. How often I'd walked by those drifting waters, under the sheltering branches of oak and willow. How I loved the drapery shops in the town also, smelling of oilcloth and linen. Those journeys were often replayed in my mind as I woke up in Dublin to hear the sounds of buses screeching by the door of the house full of bedsits, where I was so lonely for one whole year before I met your father and the light and happiness of enduring love came into my life.

Ah! my darling, I see that your special someone has not text-ed back now for oh, ten minutes! Ten whole minutes! Daughter, it is my dearest hope that the time will come when you real-ise that only a letter will do to bridge whatever gap separates you from the one you love. That the message sent out in haste and without much thought, is like the message scrawled on the sands, washed away with the incoming tide. I want much more for you than that, a legacy of tangible treasures that can be read and savoured on those rainy days when the heart and soul need nourishment. When you might open the envelope as it were a portal to a very magical place and say 'Ah, I remember now, that day, that place, that very special someone'.

THE CONFIRMATION HAT

By MARY D'ARCY

MALONE ROAD, BELFAST

She wanted the expensive hat to complete her Confirmation outfit but her father was struggling to bring his family up on his own and just couldn't afford it

I wheeled my father from the home. Out. Out. Into the stinging freshness of a cold December day, and home to our new remodelled house where he would stay - for Christmas, for New Year, for Easter. Forever.

And as I drove the seven miles to the midland town of Ballinore, father turned to me, a question in his troubled eye. I leaned across and touched his hand, the one contracted into a cone. "You're coming home and staying home. The kids and Ed can hardly wait. And Da," I added, as I turned the windscreen wipers on, for the first frail snowflakes were sifting through the air. "You don't need to wonder why".

For a moment he watched the passing scene – hedgerows, fields, and leafless trees - then fixed his gaze on me again.

"It's not that we're tired of London –" I answered the question I saw in his eyes. "Or want the good life for the kids. Or prefer this different kind of work." I paused. "What we want is yourself".

His slow, half-hidden smile was father's answer to that, for speech was a struggle ever since he'd had the stroke. And as I boggled along the country road, the snowflakes brought back with a piercing clarity, ringing across the years, childhood memories, a warm nostalgic tide which welled up inside me.

"Da?" I forced a smile. "Do you remember the hat – the Confirmation hat? I seem to think of it when it snows".

It was a small white hat that called to me from the window of Cassidy's, a drapery store in Ballinore. More than anything in the world I'd coveted that hat, an arrangement in white - velvet,

74

elastic, streamers and bows, and designed to go with nothing so much as Confirmation clothes.

It was March when I'd pointed it out to father, who was bandy-legged under the weight of a sack of potatoes. "Thirty-five bob? For a snowball like that?"

Pale with outrage, father set down his burden the better to remind me that he was by himself with seven mouths to feed, and after shelling out for costume and shoes it had to be No. Sorry. He couldn't afford that extra fal-lal.

But that extra fal-lal was all I had wanted.

"Price of a leg a lamb," bawled father, hoiking up his bag again. "Sack a spuds, and a stone of flour."

I turned on him in a kind of blaze. "Maura Rattigan has one. And Aine Coyle -"

"And what," cut in father, "is wrong with the cap your granny knit you?"

"It's a hat I want, like Maura Rattigan has!"

Maura was a friend who invited me to her home every Friday after school. She lived with her parents above their pawn shop on the prosperous side of Ballinore.

On days when he wasn't busy, Mr Rattigan would permit his daughter and myself to rummage round among his goods. "And while ye're at it -" He would open a drawer and throw me a chamois. "You might as well earn yer keep."

With all my anguished soul I envied Maura for, although her father was known to be miserly, she got everything she asked for, and was never without a sixpence in her pocket. But then, neither was I, until mother left us. She had died the August before `after a brief illness borne with fortitude`.

We'd never heard of pancreatic cancer, but it swept her away in the space of a month. This forced Hughie to leave his job, for nobody else – not even our grandma - was prepared to take the Sullivans on.

That first terrible Christmas, Grandma Sullivan came all the way up from Kerry to show "pore Hughie" how to pluck and cook the Christmas goose. Although a joiner, in whose great big work-man's hands wood turned into miracles of elegant tables, claw foot sideboards and graceful chairs - when it came to work in the kitchen, father was nothing but fumbling thumbs.

On Christmas Eve, unable to sleep, I stole down the stairs in the dead of night to find father standing before the fire, eyes fixed on a picture that hung above the mantle clock. It was a black and white photo of mother, enlivened by the beauty of its frame. Tortoiseshell in a fern-and-floral decor, it was a treasure that mother brought back from the States, bestowed on her by an employer for eight year's service as a cook in her house.

And here Hughie was, his first Christmas without his wife, transfixed before her image, his lips drawn back in an agonised spasm. I backed from the kitchen tightly clenching my teeth to keep the tears from falling down.

Christmas came and went and I found in the face of other preoccupations I was slowly getting over mother. Then came the month of May and I suddenly yearned to see her again. "Where are you?" I accusingly addressed the tortoiseshell frame. "Can you hear me? I'm making my Confirmation and I want a hat."

I ought to pray, I knew. But the trouble with praying was that it was one-sided, and with only a week to go before the event, I needed to be sure I was being attended.

I had a suspicion neither God nor Mother existed, because ever since I saw that hat, I'd done everything a mortal girl could do to raise enough to buy it – messages for neighbours, returning bottles to various shops, searching through father's pockets, nicking a shilling from Rattigan's till.

And still I didn't have enough.

In desperation I applied to father once again. An untimely approach, for it was a wet Saturday morning and Hughie was using a ruler to separate Jimmy and Aidan who were locked together in mortal combat, kicking at each other's shins. Nevertheless, I couldn't wait. "D'you hear me? I want that hat."

"For the last time," father turned from the squabblers. "I haven't any money."

I was ready for him, for Rattigan had put the words in my mouth.

"`What about Children's Allowance?"

The straw to break the camel's back. "How do you imagine," said father, in a menacingly low voice, "I get food on the table, turf in the fire, books in yer schoolbags?"

I grabbed my coat and made for the door. Father followed me into the hall, and stood with his back to the door. It was drizzling outside, and high in the tower of the Franciscan Friary, the bells of the morning Angelus rang splendidly over the town.

"Where are you going?"

"To the church."

"To Confession or what?"

"No."

"Well, what then?"

"To pray," I said, "for a miracle."

At those last three words, uttered on a sob, father kept his eyes on beam with mine, and his lips dropped open in an expression I was to remember for the rest of my life. He narrowed his eyes, and turning round, silently opened the door.

For an hour I sat in the Friary, bargaining with God. "A hat. That's all I want, or the money to buy it." I rounded off on a husk: "Amen", just as something came down on my shoulder.

I twisted round, to find our neighbour from down the street smiling with all her dentures.

"I hope you said one for me?" I returned Mrs Mulligan's smile, and was forthwith rewarded – to think I'd doubted the existence of God – by the shiny florin she pressed in my palm. I stared at this windfall, then at my neighbour, and managed somehow to choke out the words. "Thank Mrs Mulligan. Thanks very much."

Charged with purpose, I left the church and flew to the other end of town to look again in Cassidy's window. Possibly they might accept a deposit, for what with the florin, Rattigan's shilling and the other bits and pieces, I had altogether nine and six.

Breathless, I crossed Mardyke Street, and beelined towards the draper's, to find that the hat was gone from the window.It was as though a bucket of water were thrown in my face.

Where was it?

With a rush of panic, I turned into the shop. "No more hats," The assistant was gleeful. "How about a crochet cap?"

With hate in my heart, I returned to the house and up to my room, ignoring the aroma wafting from the kitchen. I resolved, there and then, I would not be making my Confirmation. I was going to be sick on the day, green, from all the sweets that nine and six would buy me.

"Don't want it," I squawked, when Hughie called me down for dinner.

"Sausages," he said, in a cajoling voice but I stayed in my room, heroically brooding. In the end, a growling stomach forced me downstairs. Although my brothers were gathered round the table, a pall had descended on the house, as though everyone were holding his breath in fearful curiosity for what would happen next.

What happened next was rather dramatic: Father emerging from the scullery, and with a hand behind his back, escorting me to the table in the manner of a waiter, and grandly pulling out my chair.

"Yer majesty," said Aidan, which occasioned laughter from the others. Imposing silence with a finger to his lips, father swung his hand around, and set a plate before me. On it was not a dinner, but a box tied up with string, drum-like, white. I stared at it, then at my brothers.

"Go on," said father. "Open it up."

With a queer acceleration of my pulse, I undid the string, while father watched with an expression of affectionate expectancy. Slowly, I lifted the lid. And I found within, encased in tissues, the hat I'd so passionately prayed for - a queer feeling came over me. It was a moment that could never be repeated, this lifting of my insufferable disappointment.

I raised the hat from its rustling nest, and held it away from the table, but I couldn't really see it. My vision had blurred. And when I turned to look at father, I found I couldn't speak, for something had risen and knotted in my throat.

The day after my Confirmation, I found that I was rich.

A pound from Granny Sullivan was teamed with another from Mrs Mulligan and a dollar from an aunt who lived in the States. I was joyfully counting my savings, setting aside the shilling owing to Rattigan, when I raised my head and looked around: something in the house wasn't right.

I tried to think what it was. My eyes did a quick flight about the kitchen, but nothing appeared out of place. And yet I was sure that something had changed. Puzzled, I pocketed my savings, found my raincoat, and made my way across the town.

"Homework," said Rattigan, when I asked after Maura. "See yeh Friday."

Stung by this chilly dismissal, and my thwarted desire to return his coin, I waded my way through an obstacle course of knick-knacks. Half way to the door, I halted slightly, continued three steps, then, frowning, turned back. On a shelf, wedged between a po and an ornamental clock, was something that had no business being there, a tortoiseshell frame with a fern-and-floral decoration.

For how long I stared at it I will never know, but seeing it there, I knew a terrible grief.

Father. Poor father. Lifting my eyes, I gazed at Rattigan, and enquired the price of mother's frame.

"Thirty-nine bob," came the flat, uninterested voice. I quickly computed: four shillings profit for the cold-blooded miser. Well, he would never get his shilling back! With gritted teeth, I dug in my pocket and threw out the money.

If Rattigan sensed my contempt, he showed no sign of it. And as he parcelled the tortoiseshell frame, his smile warmed up a fraction. "Let you come back after tea."

My chin went up a defiant notch as I grabbed the change he was holding out. "I won't –"

"Oh. And why not?"

I ordered myself not to say it. I said it. "Because you're a rat, Mr Rattigan."

And with that as an exit line, I took to my heels.

I never did go back to the shop, until the day my husband bought it. It is now our guesthouse with airy rooms, open fires, gleaming windows, hanging baskets. Oh!

And a ramp to the front to make it easy for father.

THE MILK RUN

A Memory from SEAN MCCANN

Newry, Co. Down

*Son does the daily round of the local farms with his father,
especially during the Summer holidays*

My unique relationship with my father was firmly bonded on the road, on the byways and highways, such as they were in the late fifties and early sixties in a delightful little corner of South Armagh. He drove a milk lorry and collected the daily produce in ten gallon steel cans from the local farmers for the Milk Marketing Board.

During my summer holidays I was his constant companion on the lorry and I vividly recall those halcyon days when the sun used to shine continuously day after day and the sparse tar on the roads used to bubble and burst under the constant heat.

I was about eight years old when this magical experience began out of sheer necessity as there wasn't anybody at home to mind an energetic, fun loving boy whose endless curiosity knew no bounds.

The daily 'milk run' created the odd problem for my father but my participation doubtlessly satisfied his main source of concern. He knew I was safe with him. We chatted and laughed, he would show me where different people lived and he always had a sweet in his pocket, a Fox's glacier mint or a barley sugar!

The wee Commer lorry, later replaced by a bigger Bedford, would rumble down the winding narrow roads and lanes at a snail's pace and the clatter of the chains against the steel cans, later to become aluminium, would echo sharply across the valley as my father skilfully negotiated an often difficult passage to the farmyards for the pick-up. I marvelled at the superb knack he had for lifting those heavy cans, each easily identified by a red number painted on the lid, from the dusty ground onto the wooden body of the lorry. It involved a sweeping action using both his arms and knee.

It never seemed to bother him then but in later life arthritis would invade his knee joints as a direct consequence of this work in wintertime. Oilskins were a mere futuristic idea at that time!

Deep potholes would cause the cans to rattle like thunder and thick briars, as well as overhanging branches, would sweep over the windscreen as blind corners and steep inclines were negotiated gingerly. Cows, sheep and goats would gaze curiously at this noisy intrusion and the odd barking dog would playfully run at the revolving wheels.

Breakfast, believe it or not, was served each morning in the same farmhouse in Umericam about half past ten and the kindly farmer's wife, Molly was her name, would provide us with soft boiled eggs and homemade wheaten bread; a tasty feast enjoyed with a piping hot cup of tea.

My lofty perch in the cab provided me with the perfect vantage point to behold the rough countryside erratically divided into small fields by walls of loose stones, the work of craftsmen in times gone by. The rich musical names of Annaghclochmullion, Carricknagavna, Aughanduff, Cashel, Dorsey, Umericam and Tullymacrieve became firmly embedded in my mind as we trundled along together on the first part of the 'run', when only the odd rusty tractor would cross our path.

The second part through Mullaghbawn, Adanove, Carrickaldreen, Tievecrum, Dromintee and Killeavy was much busier with traffic, in complete contrast with the more outlying area. Here the rusted tractor was transformed with a shiny coat of paint.

My father never rushed and a brief chat with some farmers was an integral part of each day when local happenings were discussed and digested while leaning against the lorry or sitting on the ditch smoking a cigarette. The engine was rarely switched off for fear that it mightn't start again and the smell of diesel was palpable as the fumes wafted through the cab and exited by the open windows. I would usually read my comic, a story from the 'Dandy' or the 'Beano', during this lull.

The milk cans were unloaded in the creamery based in Newry. The cans were placed by my father on a carousel for emptying amid a cacophony of noise and samples extracted from random numbers in order to test for freshness.

Cans emptied and reloaded in a certain order for the following day, we headed for home to make the dinner. Sometimes on a Sunday my father would buy me a Mars bar or a quarter of wine gums; this really was the icing on the 'Milk Run.'

I grew very fond of my daily safari on the lorry; it was an adventure, a knowledge accumulating journey but above all, quality time spent with my lone parent. It was a time never to be forgotten and quietly treasured; a bonding that was never broken.

The End in the Beginning

By Fiona Ferguson
Kilbeggan, Co. Westmeath

An older farmer is struggling to keep up with the work but he finds it difficult to contemplate retirement and handing over the reins

Father and son stood regarding the dented farmyard gate as if it had just dropped from the sky. "I never saw it," Seamus remarked, scratching his head.

"Sure it has always been there, Da," Kevin replied.

"I know that - didn't I put it there myself donkey's years ago," Seamus snapped.

"Like everything else around here," his son muttered under his breath.

Seamus turned and climbed back into the cab of the tractor. A new fangled yoke, full of dials and switches that his son had persuaded him to buy. Sure, was it any wonder he had reversed the trailer into the gate, distracted by all this technology.

He shook his head as he watched his son manhandle the gate off its hinges to be repaired. This was the last thing they needed at this busy time of year, between drawing in and wrapping the silage and now cutting the corn, he had been running at full tilt for several days now.

Seamus knew his concentration waned when he was tired and recently he had felt tired all the time. This incident was the latest in a list of near calamities over the last year that his son never tired of rehashing, especially the incident involving the dung-spreader and chicken coop. The surviving hens still weren't right. Then there was the close encounter between Kevin's new car and the load of gravel; a simple miscalculation in distance. Kevin's day job as a panel beater had come in useful.

Seamus turned the ignition key and the Massey Ferguson chugged back into life. He reversed the tractor across the yard and drove gingerly through the now gateless farmyard entrance.

He headed back down across the fields towards where their corn was being harvested with the help of their neighbours, the Healys, who ran a farm contracting company.

As he drove Seamus surveyed the fields he had known and nurtured all his life. Each square foot of this land held memories for him. From his first recollections of listening to his father's stories of the generations who had farmed the land before them, through to his own son and daughter walking the fields with him and helping bring in the cows for milking.

Now the next generation, his beloved grandchildren Sam and Ella, came to visit occasionally from the city with his daughter and were entranced by the animals and the freedom of the countryside.

Kevin had worked his whole life on the farm, as he had himself. Seamus regretted that his son had to take on a day job to support himself and his fiancé but there was simply not enough income to support two families.

In his day a man waited until he was ready to take over the farm before he thought of marriage but these were different times. Kevin helped on the farm at weekends and evenings. He had been bitten by the farming bug early and worked eagerly in his free time.

His wife Alice had taken to retirement from her job as a nurse several years ago like a duck to water. She had become involved with numerous voluntary groups and set up a sewing, or gossiping, club in town. Alice constantly encouraged him to consider retirement and take up his generous pension.

Seamus could not bring himself to relinquish his control over the farm, especially at such a busy time. He knew his son's long suffering fiancé nagged Kevin to encourage him to retire so they could afford to marry and start a family, but there was still so much Kevin had to learn.

He pictured retirement in his mind with dull dread. Mornings, afternoons and evenings by the fire, watching television, fading away. He was a respected member of the local farming community, head of his family, the man everyone came to when they needed something fixed. Who would need him if he weren't working? What value would the opinion of an armchair farmer have?

Seamus arrived at the field where the Healys were working away in their combine harvester, cutting the corn in ever decreasing circuits of the golden meadow. He greeted Ger Healy, son of his good friend Andy.

"Afternoon Ger, where's your father today?"

"Hmm... sun splitting the rocks .... work to be done ... I think you will probably find him out on the golf course."

"Golf, is it?"

"He has taken to it like a demon. We bought a set of a golf clubs last Christmas to see if he would give it a try. Now if the sun shines we don't see him for dust."

"So you are doing all the harvesting then this year?"

"That's right, myself and two lads I have taken on; took both of them to replace the old man."

Seamus ruminated on this turn of events as he trundled alongside the combine harvester to allow it unload the corn into his trailer. He had lost touch with his friends, he didn't even know Andy had retired. It was so hard to keep up with the intensive business that the farm had become. He was constantly running to stand still, to do the bare minimum that needed to be done and then falling into bed in the evenings and sleeping all day Sunday.

He noticed his daughter, Joanne's, car down at the farmhouse as he drew the load back to the shed in the farmyard. He brightened, thinking maybe the children were with her. His wife was no doubt filling them full of biscuits as they regaled her with news of school projects and their friend's antics.

He parked in the farmyard and told his son he was heading down to the house for a while. In the garden behind the house Sam and Ella were playing ball with Prince, the farm dog, who was delighted with the unexpected frivolity.

The children ran over to greet him with overjoyed cries of "granddad". They hugged his legs and squealed as kept walking, pretending he could not see them. He relented and picked up a grandchild under each arm and gave them a squeeze.

In the kitchen, Joanne greeted him with a kiss and he nodded a greeting to Philip, his son-in-law. He noticed Alice was
uncharacteristically lost for words and he gave her a quizzical
look. "Wonderful news," she mouthed, choking back tears.

Joanne smiled: "We bought a house down the road Dad, so
we can stay here during holidays and come out for weekends
now and again. The children love it here so when we saw the
chance we took it. We kept it a secret because we didn't want to
get everyone's hopes up in case it fell through."

Seamus grinned with delight: "That's great news, sweetheart,
great news."

The small group decided to take a walk down across the road
to take a look at the soon-to-be holiday home. The children ran
amok in the overgrown garden as the adults took stock of the
rundown house.

"The widow Brennan's old cottage" said Seamus, "I always
liked this place."

"She was just living in two rooms towards the end apparently," said Joanne, "the rest of the house is pretty neglected.
The garden needs doing up as well."

"Don't go spending money now," Seamus cautioned, "we
could do a job on this ourselves. It only needs bit of cleaning
and repair work."

"Sure you don't have the time Dad," Joanne countered, "we
were hoping to get set up as quickly as possible to take advantage of the rest of the summer."

Seamus dismissed her concerns with a wave of his hand.

"Kevin has some holidays coming up, he can keep the farm
ticking over while I help you out."

Over the next few weeks Seamus saw little of the farm. He
spoke with Kevin at breakfast and gave advice to his son on
the running of the farm. Kevin even took over the filing of the
annual tax returns that had left Seamus increasingly befuddled
over the last few years.

He became absorbed in the work at his daughter's new house.
He stripped away all the old wood and debris around the house
and began sanding and plastering. Joanne and the children came

down to check on progress and stayed around to help him with the painting.

Alice picked out pieces of old furniture from the cottage that could be restored and made regular trips to the garden centre to pick out plants and decking for the garden that Philip had made a start at revamping at the weekends.

Soon it was time for the family pick out a kitchen and bath-room and to furnish the bedrooms. Before he knew it, Kevin's holidays were over and Seamus had to go back to work. He was satisfied that the house would soon be ready for his daughter and her family to stay in.

Seamus rose early to do the milking for the first time in a couple of weeks. As he approached the farm yard he noticed the piles of flotsam and jetsam that had built up round the yard were gone. The shed door that had been hanging off its hinges and the corrugated roof that clanged in the wind were fixed.

Inside the milking parlour the machines and walkways were spotless and the cows seemed more contented coming into a clean environment instead of the slippery, dung encrusted shack he had allowed the parlour to become through benign neglect.

He wasn't the only one who had been working hard for the last few weeks. All the things he had never got around to doing had been done by an enthusiastic young man with the energy to match.

The farm looked modern and functional instead of patched and ramshackle. Seamus remembered his father telling him: "You never own a farm, you look after it for the next genera-tion." His son had shown he had the capability and commitment to continue the family tradition.

Seamus returned to the farm house after milking with a heavy heart. He knew he would be financially secure with his pension but money seemed to have little importance to him at the mo-ment. He felt there was little for him to do but fade away and stop being a nuisance.

Alice beamed at him from the kitchen table as he took off his boots in the porch.

"Joanne, Philip and the children are coming down next week," she said excitedly.

"Yes, they wanted to have another look at their holiday home," Seamus replied.

"It's not a holiday home anymore," Alice gushed, "they have decided to move down permanently. The children are so happy down here that Joanne decided to apply for job at a bank in town and Philip will commute to the city on the motorway."

Seamus smiled, happy at the news

"There is one problem," Alice said, turning serious. "They are struggling financially, that's why they are leaving the city and Joanne is looking for work."

"Well, we will help them any way we can."

"That's what I hoped you would say." Alice hesitated, before continuing effusively. "I know it's a lot to ask as you are so busy on the farm but I told Joanne we would look after the children to save them money. The problem is I will be busy with Meals on Wheels during the week so a lot of the work will fall to you."

Alice stopped and looked at him expectantly: "What do you think?"

Seamus paused, wondering if he could reinvent himself at his age. He pictured an alternative retirement of discussing the farm over breakfast with his son, followed by afternoons chatting at the school gates, supervising homework and teaching the children about nature.

He tried to force his facial features, which were threatening to break into a grin, into a thoughtful expression. "I suppose we could give it a try. Back to the beginning for us, Alice!"

JENNY'S SONG

By SHANE FAGAN
DROGHEDA, CO. LOUTH.

Shay's feelijng a bit down and missing his wife. He has jaundiced
views on modern young people, but events change his mind ...

" " I can't do this," the elderly man muttered to himself shak-
ily ... "not yet... I'm not ready!" Shay Grady had been
making his first visit to the lavish new shopping centre
in town when he was beset by a sudden, clammy anxiety. He
needed to be back in the sanctuary of his home. He needed
to be away from all the hustle and bustle of the place. Shay
was just about to turn and head hurriedly for the exit when the
music system of the shopping centre, which had been providing
barely audible background sounds, slowly began to swell in volume. He stood transfixed. It was that song again, the song that
had emerged from the musical wilderness to become the theme
music of a smash hit movie. He listened, almost mesmerised,
to the haunting melody. How often, over the decades, that fifties chart-topper had flitted into his life. And always, it seemed,
during times of profound emotion. And here it was, once more,
weaving its nostalgic web at this desolate time.

Shay continued to listen to the enchanting strains and, as he
did so, soothing, comforting images of a memorable night of
long ago began to supplant the painful ones and his fretfulness
started to recede.

Taking a deep breath, Shay decided that he would, after all,
take a look around the impressive complex.

The spacious, new stores and the colourful window diplays
did have a certain novel appeal. Besides, it was almost six
months since he'd last come into town. Mustering up the remnants of his fortitude and energy, he decided to soldier on.

The evocative melody was coming to a close when Shay found
himself drawn to the attractive little boutique that called itself

"Elegant Lady." In it's artistically laid out window, three mannequins were draped in sumptuous evening gowns. His eyes started to sting again and an alarming tightness came to his chest. He could almost hear the voice of his beloved Jenny and what she might say when they were out shopping.

"Off you go, Shay," she would suggest, while flashing her beautiful, winsome smile, "ramble off and get yourself a nice cup of coffee in 'Romano's' while I have a quick mosey around all the style ... I'll join you there shortly."

Shay blinked hard and straightened up his shoulders. Jenny's suggestion was still a good one. A hot cappuccino might just put a bit of new life into him.

He ventured deeper into the shopping fantasyland and, turning a corner, the deliciously appetising aroma of coffee and freshly baked confectionary wafted invitingly past his nostrils.

A few minutes later, Shay managed to grab the last available table by the window; and was seated comfortably in the "Coffee dock."

The air seemed less oppressive in the café and after a few sips of cappuccino, his breathing was getting easier and the aches were beginning to leave his bones.

Shay gazed at the empty chair opposite him and tried vainly to make sense of it all. "Dear God," he whispered, "how could fate have been so cruel? How could events have unfolded with such unexpected and tragic consequences?"

It was Jenny who had showered him with devotion and attention during those long painful months after his heart surgery. It was she who had given him the will to take up the threads of his life again. They had even been planning to take a short holiday to celebrate his recovery when, like the fearsome "thief in the night," the stroke came. For twenty-four hours, Shay had sat by Jenny's hospital bed and had watched helplessly as slowly but inexorably her precious life ebbed away.

From his vantage point at the café window, Shay tried to divert his thoughts to what was going on outside.

He soon realised that Saturday afternoon was, of course, the favourite time for the younger generation to converge upon the shopping centre.

He watched with rising interest as teenage boys and girls, their hands clamped to their ears as they shouted into their mobiles, frolicked their way eagerly among the bustling bargain hunters.

What, he wondered, would his old, departed friends make of this hubbub if only they could return - even for a short visit? A hint of a smile played around his lips as he himself supplied the answer. They would probably surmise that the ear-clutching young folk had succumbed to a nasty, virulent ear bug that was rampaging through the populace.

Shay was still pondering on the changing times when a laughing, young voice rang out and sent the friendly ghosts scampering from his mind.

"Hi, Grandad, we spotted you as we passed by the window … you seemed to be on another planet."

Shay smiled delightedly as his favourite grand-daughter, Fiona, and three of her exuberant fifth-year school friends crowded around his table.

In a matter of moments, the hitherto tidy table had become strewn with crisp bags and latte mugs and the bubbly Fiona launched into a series of breathless introductions.

"Grandad, this is Clodagh … and this is Julie, and, the one with the funny, frothy moustache, that's Millie. Girls, this is my Mam's Dad --- Grandad Grady."

Shay never failed to marvel at how uncannily Fiona reminded him of Jenny, and of how whimsical were the vagaries of family resemblances. His only daughter, Katie, had followed him. Her dark complexion and raven black hair attested to that.

Fiona, on the other hand, with her willowy form, pale-skinned beauty and, above all, a crowning glory of flowing amber, was the living image of Jenny.

How confident and self-assured these young people seemed to be, Shay observed. How effortless it was for them to cast off all those confining restrictions of childhood and launch into their adolescent years with such unfettered abandon.

All this sophistication was a far cry indeed, Shay concluded, from those much simpler times when he, and his boyhood friends, had searched so valiantly to find their niche in life.

91

Sitting among these effervescent young people, Shay's downcast spirits started to rise. It was such an uplifting experience to be in the midst of all this giddy, youthful exuberance. But then, almost as quickly, a niggling new worry crept into his thoughts.

After the initial burst of conversation had abated, Shay feared that most unsettling of social syndromes – the dreaded generation gap - would stage an unwelcome appearance.

He would find himself unable to engage, in any real sense, with these young sophisticated people and, after a few awkward silences, the girls would politely take their leave.

It was at that precise moment, when Fiona, unwittingly, put that particular concern to rest. In a voice that exuded a fair degree of pride, she spoke above the girlish chatter.

"Grandad used to play in a show band. You know, girls, he's a really, really brilliant trumpet player … aren't you, Grandad?"

At that point, Millie, the one with the Latte moustache, piped up. " Oh please tell us, Mr. Grady, what was the scene like during those showband times … it must have been so cool."

"Tell us about those beehive hairdos that we sometimes see in old movies, Mr. Grady." Clodagh joined in perkily … " were they really that high?"

Shay smiled, somewhat sheepishly, at Fiona's rather biased assessment of his musical prowess.

It had been nigh on three decades since he, and his fellow troubadours had, outdated but unbowed, huckle bucked their way into folklore. Still, it was nice to get such a lofty introduction - one that might well banish all generation gap problems from this table.

These girls, Shay was starting to suspect, might not be quite as sophisticated as he first thought.

Whether they were or not, they did seem anxious to embark upon a retrospective journey.

They were eager to hear all about their intrepid forerunners of the swinging sixties and the part the showbands played during that decade of cultural revolution.

Shay surveyed the young expectant faces round the table and for the first time in a long while a once familiar spark of mischief entered his thoughts and he gave way to a rare moment of levity.

"I was the very first chap," he disclosed with mock pride, "to strut down our road sporting a pair of drainpipes and a duck's-ass haircut."

Well, this personal contribution to the "rebellion" certainly set off peals of laughter round the table. And, with credentials of that magnitude, Shay's standing was quickly assuming an extra measure of weight.

His avid audience was now expecting revelations even more startling in nature.

But, true to form, Millie was nothing if not persistent. "Tell us about the showbands, Mr. Grady," she urged again. "Tell us all about those famous 'ballrooms of romance'... the ones I've heard my Granny go on so much about."

Shay had, long since, realised that for those who hadn't lived through that wondrous era, the very term "Ballrooms of Romance" had become something of a cliché. He grasped the opportunity to put that to rights.

"I do happen to know one true story," Shay said to the girls with a touch of earnestness. "It's about two young people who met in such a ballroom, and how the magic of a special song led to a meeting that was love at first sight."

These words seemed to capture the girls' attention - especially the love at first sight bit, and the noisy, crisp crunching and the frivolous chatter quickly dissolved into temporary suspension.

"Well," Shay began, "I was playing in a beautiful ballroom right on the very edge of the Atlantic coast, when four young ladies, very much like yourselves, approached the bandstand at around midnight.

They had a 'very important' request. It was to play a certain song for someone. It was for a girl who was 'feeling a bit down,' they said."

An expectant hush falls round the table, but just as Shay is set to continue, Julie's mobile goes off. After a brief, garbled exchange, she tells the others of an interesting new development.

"That was Gavin," she informs them. " He, Jason and the others are down in Romano's, and there're wondering if we'd like to hook up with them."

Fiona looks anxiously at Shay. "Carry on with your story, Grandad. We don't have to rush off straight away."

But the spell is broken. Shay reaches out and, briefly, covers her small hand with his. "Away with you and join up with your friends, young lady," he says, "sure, the story will keep for another time."

A few minutes later, Shay watches from the cafe window until Fiona and his new young friends melt into the crowd and disappear from view.

Shay looks at his watch - ten past four, that's not bad! By the time he visits the cemetery, and fixes Jenny's flowers, it will be six. Then, if he takes it easy going home, it will be time for a bit of supper. The nice piece of quiche that Katie dropped in should be grand.

After that, he will repair to the small conservatory to the rear of the house - his favourite place of all. And, there, in the fading August twilight, his thoughts will follow the sunset to an unforgettable night of long ago. And to the ghostly rhythm of the distant Atlantic breakers, he will raise his trumpet to his lips and he will respond, once more, to that "very important request". As sweetly as he knows how, he will play "Unchained melody" - that was Jenny's song.

CHRISTMAS BOVVER

A Memory from JOE KEARNEY

Enniskerry, Co. Wicklow

A group of Irish emigrants spend an early 1970's Christmas in a London flat

Frank resembled a skinhead, but he was far too gentle to be one. The reason he wore his ox-blood, 14-hole Doc Martin's was he loved those boots. He adopted the fashion of rolling up his jeans to display his lovingly polished footwear. The joke in the flat was that he wore them in the bath and maybe even to bed. On the night of 21ˢᵗ December, 1971, their rubber soles saved his life.

Our flat on Willesden High Road in London was what my grandmother would have described as a 'rambling house.' There were more comings and goings than at Piccadilly Station, myself being one of its more recent transients. Sleeping bags sprouted overnight like magic mushrooms and the teapot seldom got a chance to cool.

On the night in question, there was a handful of us slumped in front of The News at Ten. We were bemoaning the lack of upcoming festive entertainment. We had no plans to go home, and our Christmas Day options were The Generation Game or Mike and Bernie Winters' All Star Comedy Carnival. But our torpor dissolved when Frank leaped from his beanbag and drove his boot through the 19-inch screen of our black and white Telefunken. We had been watching a news item about a man who had been shot dead outside a social club in the Ardoyne area of Belfast. He was Frank's brother.

As soon as they were married, Frank and his wife, Cathy, had fled from the troubles back home. London was a place where they could make a new life. They had much to live for. She was pregnant with their first child on that night when Frank broke the television. We scraped up a collection, and Frank flew home the next day. Nobody cared too much for Christmas that year. I have no recollection of shopping or decorations, and there was certainly no turkey.

Frank phoned to say he'd landed safely but, even so, Cathy worried. Would he get caught up in the old world of hatred? Surely, she reassured herself, the baby would bring him safely back to her and to the flat on Willesden High Road.

She fell ill on Christmas Eve; the baby might be on its way. We called an ambulance. As we waved her off, we joked that she would have to call the child Christy or Nollaig. There was even a suggestion of Rudolph!

Christmas morning dawned cold and bright. The air smelled of metallic frost and there were ice flowers on the windows of the unheated flat. A Pakistani greengrocer rented the ground floor premises and he was open for trade. His floral displays were past their best, but we got him to dress up a bouquet with tinsel, anyway.

At Willesden General we were shown into Cathy's ward. She was propped against the pillows, lost to her visitors, lost to her surroundings. When we placed the flowers on her lap, her arms formed an instinctive cradle around the lifeless, wilting bundle.

"Dead", she rasped, and in the sterile room that one syllable became a hard, white scratch.

At the hospital, they fed us Christmas lunch. I remember pushing sprouts around the plate and watching Cathy look to the imagined horizon outside the window as if she was interrogating it. It was as if the clouds might contain an answer that could make sense of life.

That night the buses stopped early so we walked home. The streetlights caught the early frost, and icy mirrors reflected back petrol rainbows to the neon moons. We moved from light to light like moths with the cold of night caught on our wings. In the high London sky the moon hung, filled with undelivered promise. The echoes of long dead stars made the world seem small and I knew for certain that we held true title to nothing but our memories, and even those are suspect.

Cathy and Frank came back to the flat on Willesden High Road. Frost gave way to spring and wanderlust moved me on. I lost contact.

Some years later, one Sunday afternoon, I observed a family tableau at the end of Bray promenade. A woman leaned to console a small boy whose ice cream had fallen to the ground. Her partner was wearing a conspicuous pair of ox-blood 14-hole Doc Martin's. They had been lovingly burnished with red polish and were on show beneath a pair of rolled-up jeans. It was Frank and Cathy and their young son.

Like accidental tourists, we delighted in the unexpected encounter and rejoiced that life had blessed them both.

As I left them, I couldn't help wondering was Frank still wearing the same pair of Docs. Somehow, I hadn't the heart to enquire.

The Cycle of Life

By Agnes Kimberley

Port Elizabeth, South Africa

Anna was always a good listener and it seemed natural that she would become a social worker ... but she had a dark secret in her own life

"Do you have a son?" The lady in blue yelled at me. It took only a split second of hesitation before she then screamed into my face.

"Obviously, you don't, because if you had a son you would understand what I'm going through."

"Please Mrs.---."

"Don't you dare patronize me." She stormed out of my office then.

Elaine, my assistant, put her head around the door and looked at me.

"Are you okay, Anna?"

I nodded my head, feeling anything but okay. I wanted to be anywhere but here. I saw far too much pain in my job, other people's pain, and I still had so much of my own to try to come to terms with. I could still feel Elaine's eyes upon me.

"I'd love a cup of tea," I said, more to distract her than anything else. She smiled, and left to make the tea.

It's funny really how we have our lives all mapped out. We plan it all out carefully. We finish our education, get a job, then we get married and have two point-four children. We are more or less groomed for it from the moment we are born. If you don't fall into this classical situation you are considered abnormal, a bit of an odd ball. I grimaced at the thought.

My Mum always told me I was such a good child and I went through all the various stages of development at all the right times. I wasn't even such a bad teenager.

"Anna is such a good girl," I used to hear her say to my father when she thought I wasn't listening.

"The apple doesn't fall far from the tree," my father always answered her back. For some reason I hated that expression and always used to think of myself like a little, green apple.

Reading this, you may think I was stuck up, but I wasn't actually. I was popular at school and not for all the wrong reasons either. Kids my own age and even older always used to come to me for advice. They said I was a good listener and that II offered them practical advice. I was never big-headed or smug about anything, and never once did I snitch on another girl. Whatever secrets they unburdened on me stayed with me.

My Mum said it was because I empathized with other people and felt their pain. There wasn't much I could do then but be a shoulder to cry on. Years later, some of them told me I had helped them more than I ever realised.

I'd known Jude then. He was a sad and lonely young man. His father had abandoned the family, and he had been raised by his Mum. Lots of times he came by my house and, when Dad came home, they'd shoot ball together. I could see he missed his Dad very much.

I worked hard at school and got the results I needed to go to university. I became a social worker. It was much harder than I thought it would ever be. I'm not talking about the studying. I had to learn to harden my heart if I was going to be able to help people.

"You allow yourself to get too involved," my supervisor told me.

"If you want to help these people, you have to learn not to get too emotional, Anna."

I nodded my head. She was speaking the truth.

I met Brian, and he asked me to marry him after we had been going out together for nine months. Brian had an honours degree in psychology and was studying for a doctorate. We were two kindred souls out to save the world.

But it didn't turn out that way. Well, maybe it did at the beginning, but things changed and for the worst.

"How can you think you know somebody and then you discover you don't know them at all?" I've asked myself this question at least a million times.

The sweet, loving man I bound myself to was a bully and a tyrant. He was one of the worst kinds, too.

The first time he hit me, I was six months pregnant with twins. He lashed out at me and all because I put too much sugar in his tea. You know when you're pregnant your hormones are all over the place. My memory was hazy and I'd keep forgetting little things. I forgot I had already added the sugar to his tea so I put in another teaspoon.

It was such a surreal moment. At first I thought it was an accident. You try to convince yourself. Then I felt this overwhelming relief that he hadn't hit me in the stomach. The blow was to the side of my head. I staggered against the kitchen cupboard and almost fell over.

He seemed just as shocked as me and, of course, he was sorry afterwards. As it happened, I was seeing my doctor that day and I had an angry welt to the side of my head. I told him I fell over. He told me to be more careful, and I promised him I would.

The next time it happened the twins were four months old. They had cried a lot during the night, and, finally, near dawn I had got the two of them asleep at the same time. Instead of getting back into bed, I had run a hot bath and climbed inside. I can still remember the pure luxury of lying back in the bath and allowing the warm water to cascade over me.

I must have dozed off, as later he was there standing over me, red in the face with temper. I had forgotten to iron his favourite blue shirt and he needed it for work. It didn't matter that he had a dozen other shirts all freshly ironed hanging in his cupboard.

I made the mistake of trying to reason with him. His hand shot out of nowhere. He grabbed my head and pushed me underneath the water. He held it there for several seconds. I was gasping for breath when he finally released me.

"My God. I can't believe I did that. I'm sorry, Anna." He left soon afterwards.

I fell pregnant again when the girls were three years old. I had a boy, and Brian was thrilled. When he was a year old, I went back to work part time. Clara and Nicola were at Nursery School, and my Mum looked after Daniel for me.

Every time I thought the beatings had stopped, some silly misdemeanor would set Brian off again. I say "silly" because he always lashed out after the most inconsequential of things. I was always pathetically grateful that he never did it in front of the kids. What a fool I had been.

My son, Daniel, was 14 when he hit me for the first time. I refused to allow him to go to a party as it was a school night and he had an exam the following day. His father was away at some medical conference. He was known as an expert in his field of psychiatry. He was often invited as a guest speaker to various functions across the country.

"You hit me," I grabbed hold of him and screamed.

"So what!" he sneered right back into my face. "Who are you going to tell? Dad?"

Thankfully, the girls were not there. They were at a friend's house, studying for their upcoming exams.

"What your father does is none of your business," I yelled at him. He'd never seen me so angry because, of course, I'd never been so angry. I grabbed the phone and began dialing.

"Who are you phoning?" Daniel was scared now.

"You're Dad," I hissed at him. "He can come home and sort this out right now. You will never hit me or another woman."

This was my son. I felt torn in two, but I knew if I didn't make a stand right now I never would. The apple doesn't fall far from the tree. I still hated that expression.

"I can't deal with it right now, Anna. Put Daniel on the phone and I'll speak to him."

"You can tell them what you like, Brian, but if you don't come home now and sort this out, I'm going straight to the police station and laying charges."

Daniel paled visibly and disappeared into his room.

Brian arrived home shortly afterwards. I thought he was going to be mad, but he came straight to me and said: "Are you okay, Anna? Did he hurt you?"

I shook my head. "I'm so sorry, Anna." Then he went to speak to his son. I never asked what transpired between the two of them that night. Daniel went to therapy. Brian insisted upon it, and soon the two of them began going together.

The next years passed uneventfully. Brian and his son grew close. Daniel was doing well at school and was planning on going to college to study engineering.

The two of them were in the car together. Daniel had gone to Brian's office to show him his A levels results. I know this because Brian had phoned and told me. Brian was going to take his son for a few drinks to celebrate. Then they would be both home for dinner.

The truck didn't stop at the red light and drove straight into Brian's car killing them both instantly. Brian had one beer that night to celebrate his son's success. His blood alcohol level was normal and, besides, he wasn't much of a drinker.

I buried them both together. They could look after each other for eternity now. I fell apart after that and the grief poured out of me.

"Do you have a son?" The echo of the woman's voice still rings in my ears. How does a mother who has lost her child answer that?

Are you still a mother when your child dies? I can say I'm a widow because Brian died. Everybody understands that. Funny, I'd never thought of it before. What does a mother become when she loses her child? I became obsessed about it

It was Clara who told me about St. Felicity. She is the patron saint of those who've suffered the death of a child. I began praying to her. They say that you get over your grief but do you really? It hurts now just as much as it did that first day.

"Dear St. Felicity," I pray silently though I was never very religious. "Help me."

When Elaine popped her head around the door to see if I wanted anything else, I told her I was going home. Elaine knew when not to say anything, and I was grateful for that.

When I came outside, I stopped and looked all around me for what seemed the first time in weeks. I was amazed to see that the world had moved on without me. Seasons had come and gone and I had been oblivious. There was a definite nip in the air now and I pulled my coat tighter around my body. I looked up in surprise when I heard somebody call my name.

"Anna. Is that really you?"

"Jude. The patron saint of hopeless cases." I had become somewhat of an expert now.

He smiled and took my hand. "I can't believe it's you. It's been so long." He looked at me intently, sensing that there was something wrong.

We rekindled our friendship and, no, nothing romantic has happened yet. I like to think St. Felicity answered my prayers that day and sent me a real live saint instead. Somehow it gets me through the days.

Forsaken Nests

by Clare McAfee
Ballycastle, Co. Antrim

It is an idyllic scene; eldest daughter Sarah does her bit to help with the haymaking in 1905 as her mother is expecting another baby, but she has an ominous feeling of foreboding

" What are you looking at, Sarah?"

Four-year-old Robert's shrill voice cut into Sarah Blair's thoughts as she gazed up at the empty clay nest, plastered on the rafters of the cart shed. Sarah glanced down kindly at her little brother who was holding a dog-lead very tightly. You would have thought he was trying to control a lion instead of their mother's old cocker spaniel, Prince.

"I was just looking at the swallows' nest," she explained, pointing it out to him. "In the autumn the birds fly away to Africa, but they come back to us every summer. People say they bring good luck."

Robert listened solemnly before answering.

"It's summer now. They'll come back any day."

"Maybe they will," his sister murmured, though in her heart she knew that the little migrants should have returned when the celandines bloomed. Now it was July, 1905. Sarah was ten and she could not remember a year when they didn't reappear. Their nests in all the outbuildings of the farm were left undisturbed year after year, waiting for them. She had often heard the old adage: "One swallow doesn't make a summer."

Suddenly, Sarah experienced a feeling of foreboding at the thought of a summer with no swallows. Was it a bad omen?

She tried to shrug off the sense of unease, as they continued their walk, slow as a funeral, towards the meadows, which were full of rich flowers. Big white dog-daisies raised their faces to the sky. There were bright buttercups, purple vetch and yellow dandelions. Without warning, a rabbit darted out from the long grass and scuttled across their path. Prince strained on the lead to be after it and Sarah had to help young Robert to control him.

"We can't let him run through the field with the mowing starting tomorrow. Dad was even complaining about the pheasants trampling the grass!"

They stood staring at the place where the rabbit had vanished from sight.

"Would there be many rabbits in there, Sarah?"

"Yes, I think there would be quite a few," replied his sister thoughtfully.

Above the meadow, flowers, butterflies and bees flitted blithely. However, Sarah knew that deep down in the grass another world existed, full of creatures such as field mice, beetles, frogs and hedgehogs. They were in there now, living their lives, unaware of tomorrow when the mowers' cruel scythes would invade their fragile security. In previous years Sarah had loved harvest time. Now she sighed deeply, feeling a rush of compassion for these innocent victims of the haymaking.

As they passed the cart shed on the return journey, the boy enquired:

"Sarah, where's Africa?"

"It's far, far away."

"Is it farther than Ballymoney?"

"It's much farther than that."

The townland of Drumskea where they lived was the only part of the world either of them knew well. Occasional trips to Ballymoney with their parents in the pony trap were the longest journeys they took.

"How do the swallows know the way to Africa?"

"I suppose God tells them."

This answer seemed to satisfy the small boy as he asked no further questions. In any case, Prince was becoming more difficult to hold back because he had seen his mistress and wanted to run to her. Their mother was standing in the yard with their little sister, Maggie, who was just two years old and toddling about happily among the hens. Sarah observed that their mother was wearing her grey shawl tied about her waist in an attempt to conceal the fact that she was expecting another baby. When the last hen was coaxed home, the door of their shed was closed and made secure against the fox.

Mrs. Blair turned to her eldest child.

"Sarah, go in the house and set the table. The supper's ready and your Da will soon be coming in after milking the cows."

Obediently, the girl set off towards the house where honeysuckle spilled its heady perfume over the porch. Everything seemed normal and good. At the front door stood a pot of orange-yellow marigolds that her mother had planted. Sarah thought their petals were like the sun they would need to dry the hay in the days ahead. Later, as the family sat round the big table in the kitchen, the mother said Grace. Sarah tried to forget her earlier misgivings and strove to believe that no evil would befall them here in their home.

Sarah woke at five o'clock next morning to hear the corncrake making its familiar crek-crek sound. Down in the meadows the mowers were already sharpening their scythes. The dew lay thick over the grass like a blessing. Soon, the rhythmic swish of the scythes filled the air. That afternoon when Sarah returned from school she hurried to the fields. Rabbits, field mice and frogs disturbed by the mowers were fleeing from the scene. Her heart went out to the lost, terrified animals, but at least these ones had survived the onslaught of the shining blades.

In the following days everyone who could be spared from other tasks went out to work in the hayfields. To Sarah's delight she did not have to go to school. Instead, she worked all day at the farm, running errands and helping with the hay. The mowers were now well ahead but the haymakers came after them, forking the grass and spreading it to dry. Sarah used a rake very carefully. The warm sun beat down on the fields, drying the hay. It was thirsty work and Sarah was often called to bring over a drink to her father or some of the other men. Tea and oatmeal water were kept in bottles by the hedge. When the tea was finished, Sarah went back to the house for more.

Inside, it was cool and quiet. Robert and Maggie were not to be seen, and where was mother? Sarah was surprised to find her normally active mother lying down on her bed on top of the patchwork quilt. The woman smiled wanly at the sight of her daughter.

"Where are Robert and Maggie, Mam?"

"I left them with Mrs. Gamble for an hour or two. I just needed a little lie down."

Mrs. Gamble was a widow who lived in a cottage nearby.

"Are you ill, Mam?"

"Not ill, just very tired."

"Is it because of the baby?"

"I suppose it is, but I'll be all right. Have you come back for more tea?"

The woman made an effort to sit upright.

"Don't get up, Mam. I can manage."

"You're a good girl, Sarah. I'll be rising very soon."

She lay back wearily on the pillow. On the wall above her head hung a framed text of the 23rd psalm "The Lord is my Shepherd." It was a hymn she was fond of singing.

When the tea was made, the girl went back to her mother before leaving the house.

"Can I get you anything, Mam? Do you want me to come back and help you?"

"No, no, Sarah. They need you in the fields and, look, I'm getting up now."

With some effort she forced herself to sit up.

"Off you go now. They'll be wanting a drink. I'll bring some food out to them in a little while."

"I don't like to leave you on your own."

"I'm not alone. Prince is with me."

For the first time Sarah noticed the old dog lying patiently on the floor beside his mistress's bed.

Ill at ease, Sarah returned to the fields and the thirsty workers. One man called her over to see a round nest of field-mice which had been uncovered. As she gazed at their tiny, curled-up pink bodies she felt stricken with grief. How vulnerable they looked and where was the mother? Later, she took some comfort from the sight of her own mother walking over the fields with a basket of food, accompanied by her siblings, Robert and

Maggie. The faithful Prince followed at her heels. On the surface all seemed well.

However, the weather was changing and soon the lovely days would be over. The men had most of the fields in cocks, but rain was threatening. Ominous clouds were gathering and moisture could be felt in the air. Everyone was apprehensive, especially Sarah's father.

"I don't like the look of it," he remarked to his wife. "Do you remember the weeks of rain we had three years ago? Good hay turned black in the fields and one field was even left uncut. We had to buy tons of hay to see us through the winter."

"That won't happen this year, Thomas," replied his wife calmly. "The work's nearly finished and I'm coming out to help you to-morrow."

"I won't hear of it . . . in your condition!"

"I'm fine, Thomas. Don't worry about me."

So next morning the younger children, Robert and Maggie, were left in with Mrs. Gamble. Sarah's mother tied her grey shawl around her waist. She and her elder daughter set off to the fields and began helping to secure the haystacks with ropes. As the hours passed, Sarah's arms were aching from twisting the ropes, but she did not complain. She and her mother worked steadily along with the men. Thankfully, the rain held off and around midday there was a short break for food over by the hedge.

The men had gone back to work and Sarah was tidying up the food things. Suddenly, her mother gave a cry and doubled over in obvious pain.

"Sarah, help me back to the house," she whispered urgently.

Before they had taken many steps, another stab of pain stopped the woman in her tracks.

"Sarah, get your Da. Tell him to yoke up the pony and trap and go for the doctor."

The next few hours brought irrevocable change to Sarah's family. A baby brother was born, but her mother was dying.

"Don't leave me, Mam," the girl begged, watching the light fading from the woman in the bed.

"I'll never be far away, Sarah. . . Look after your Da," were the last words the mother uttered in this world. Then she was gone. The pale figure on the bed was no more her mother than a broken egg-shell is the bird it once held. Her spirit had flown.

Numb with shock, Sarah left her stricken father by the bed and wandered to the kitchen. It was not the time to tell the younger ones. Robert was concerned because the old dog, Prince, had not come home, so Sarah took the children out to search for him.

The completed haystacks stood in the silent fields like monuments. The hay had been saved, but at what cost?

"There he is, Sarah . . . over by the hedge!" cried young Robert suddenly.

There indeed was the old dog lying faithfully guarding his mistress's grey shawl which she had left behind her when the pains started. He rose and came towards them warily, sensing there was something wrong. Sarah picked up the shawl and instinctively put it over her head and around her shoulders. Instantly, she felt the warmth of her mother's loving embrace. Strength and courage filled Sarah's whole body.

As the first real drops of rain began to fall, she gathered Maggie up on one arm, covering her with the shawl. Then, taking Robert's hand, she brought them back home. Prince, the dog, followed them back to the nest where the marigolds which their mother had planted still bloomed at the doorway.

CAR THIEF

A Memory from JIMMY KELLY
Raheny, Dublin

*Some youthful escapades that could have had serious
consequences*

I t was never pre-planned nor organised that I should become
a car-thief, but it happened, and I was never caught. This is
the sad part, however, because had I and my companion in
crime been apprehended we probably would have made history.
It all started when I was 15 and got a job in the local garage fixing punctures and washing cars. Not that there were too many
cars to wash. The main business was with farm tractors and lor-
ries, but one of the little extras, as well as wages and tips, was
that I could learn to drive. Way back in 1946 it wasn't necessary
to do a driving test. Any Joe Soap could simply fill in a form and
exchange it for a licence so long as he had reached the age of 17.
I pretended I was older and forged my age.

Probably within six months I could class myself as an excellent
driver. The boss didn't always think so. There was the odd mis-
hap involving smashed mudguards, bumpers, etc. Indeed, there
were a few threats of being fired as a result of damage caused, but
between cover-ups and "blind eyes" we managed to survive.

Helping the mechanics with oil-changes, fitting plugs and
points, carrying out servicing under their supervision taught us a
lot while slightly swelling our heads. Another apprentice worked
there and we spoke of nothing else but brakes, clutches and gear-
boxes all day long. To be honest, we thought we knew it all!

Before I could afford a bike, I used to walk the two miles to
work. Few country roads in those days were tarred, and in a lay-by
close to where my friend, Tommy, lived the local council had placed
a few lorry loads of small stones for filling in pot-holes.

Very shortly there arrived a caravan on wheels which was
used to house workmen. Then a steam roller appeared, both

sure signs that our old dilapidated road was in for some updating. But best of all, the man who operated the roller was the proud owner of an Austin Big Seven.

Readers of a certain age may have come across this type of car. There weren't too many of them built, and all appeared in one colour, black. Cars in those days did not have an ignition key, only a little on/off switch. Car doors did not lock either, and joy riders were unheard of.

The owner of this Austin Big Seven was very careful about his car. At night he would take his bike to the village when he went out for a few pints. Drink-driving was topical even then. Tommy used to meet me coming from work and we started to take an interest in this man's vehicle. My friend couldn't drive but was anxious to learn. One night, after making sure the owner was in the pub, we started her up and went for a little spin. I did the driving. It was the first time I'd driven on the road and I was nervous. Everything went well and we got back safely, even though in those days vehicles had only six-volt batteries so the lights were very poor. We did the same the following night but extended the distance.

Tommy was getting more enthusiastic and ventured out in the car himself, and while he somehow managed to return safely to base, he still couldn't find reverse gear. Heading the little steed homewards involved a lot of manual manoeuvring.

On about five occasions we succumbed to temptation and took the car out for a drive. Then we got worried that the owner would notice the petrol gauge going down. This was solved by my borrowing a can and a piece of hose from work and siphoning petrol from a neighbour's tractor. One night it suddenly dawned on the two of us that the more often the car was taken for a joy-ride the greater were our chances of getting caught. It wasn't as if the police were not on the roads, and to this day we wonder how, given our limited driving experience, we didn't make matchwood of the little car or injure or kill ourselves.

What would have happened had we been caught: jail, heavy fine, reform school? And what would the parents and neighbours think? And wouldn't it be headlines in the local paper?

'Car theft: two appear in court'. Sometimes I wish we had been caught. We might well have qualified as Ireland's first car thieves. Now that would have been some accolade!

Tommy moved to England and it was some sixty years later when we next met. I went to see him in the nursing home and, when he held out his hand to greet me, his first words were: 'Lord, Jimmy, hadn't we the quare crack with your man's oul' car'!

WEDDING DAY

By MYRA DUFFY
Glasgow

Noreen is very concerned about her daughter's wedding plans,
which don't seem to have much in common with Mum's ideas

N oreen tried hard not to think about it during the day.
But at night when she woke up in the early hours her
mind was in turmoil. She had dreamed about this for
so long, had thought about it so often, and now it seemed at last
that her prayers were about to be answered. Her only daughter
had found herself a young man.

Well, a youngish man, if she was being entirely honest, judging by the photo Maura had sent with her last letter. Oh, it was
early days yet, but Maura wasn't the kind of girl to get involved
lightly, and the way she spoke about Alan sent Bridget's heart
racing. Given that her daughter was now not far short of forty,
she had just about given up hope. As one by one all her friends'
daughters found a man and got married, she felt herself becoming more and more anxious.

At one time she had treated it all cautiously, tried hard not to
ask the wrong questions or seem like she was probing, but she
couldn't let it rest. A particularly fraught discussion over dinner
on one of Maura's rare trips home had made her decide to seal
her lips on the subject forever. Or at least for the time being.

She shouldn't be so concerned about it, she rebuked herself.
Both the boys, Aedan and Niall, were married and had several
children between them. She loved her grandchildren dearly and
was on good terms with her daughters-in-law. Well, on good
terms most of the time, though she did have to be careful what
she said when Anna, Niall's wife, let the two-year-old stay up
till all hours of the night.

She sighed. Every time she complained, Kevin said she should
count her blessings. How could he understand? It wasn't the

same as having a daughter married. All the excitement of a white wedding: choosing the long white frock and the head-dress and the lovely sparkly shoes.

Not that she was naïve enough to think that the white dress meant anything nowadays. Maura was so casual about it all when she phoned. That was probably what living in London did for you. They did everything differently there. Nothing was like life in the small village far south of Dublin where Noreen lived.

"We'll probably be getting married at Christmas. It suits Alan best with his work schedule and all."

Noreen could hardly keep the disappointment out of her voice. "A winter wedding, then?" Visions of guests in all their finery trying to contend with rain and wind sprang immediately to Noreen's mind.

"Oh sure," replied Maura, either not picking up the vibes from her mother or deliberately ignoring them.

"And so soon?" Noreen asked tentatively, dreading the answer.

Maura burst out laughing. "No need to worry, Mam. It's not a shotgun wedding."

"It's only that I had thought.........." Noreen let her voice trail off. Her relief that it wasn't a "have to" wedding was short-lived. No point in antagonising her daughter. So many of them now opted for some kind of registry office wedding. And if it was to be held at Christmas all the decorations would still be up. It might even be better than a summer wedding. At least in the winter you could rely on the weather to be bad and dress accordingly.

The thought came to Noreen in the middle of one of her sleepless nights. Where on earth was Maura to be married? Would Father O'Malley at Our Lady of Lourdes be happy to marry them? He hadn't seen Maura since she was a teenager and not often at that.

The long hours of the night dragged past as she tossed and turned. Maybe a wedding in the Cathedral could be arranged? Kevin with all his family connections must be able to help somehow.

Sure his sister was never out of the Church, and wasn't one of their aunts a Sister of Charity? There must be someone who could help. It could all be done through a third person and

would save her the embarrassment of having to meet Father O'
Malley's eagle eye.

"Oh, for goodness sake, Noreen, stop fretting will you."
Kevin was less than sympathetic to her worries. "Maura has
been gone from here for years. Sure, she hardly comes home at
all. She didn't even make it back last Christmas."

"That was her work, Kevin." Noreen was quick to jump to
the defence of her only daughter.

"Queer kind of place that makes people work on Christmas
Day." Kevin was not so easily pacified. "If she wants to get married, then let her. I'm not stumping up for the wedding."

Noreen opened her mouth to speak and then thought better
of it. The secret stash of money she had been accumulating in
the Post Office for this very event had now grown to a sizeable
sum. There had been plenty of years for it to grow, given the
time Maura had taken to find the right person to marry.

Noreen lost no time in telling her friends and started to buy one
of the many "Brides" magazines on sale in the local newsagent's. It
was a way of showing them all this was a serious event.

"When will you be announcing the engagement, Maura?"
Noreen asked next time they spoke on the phone.

"Oh, there's no engagement, Mam," replied Maura loftily.
"A waste of time really at our age."

Noreen felt a little stab of disappointment. It was always
good to have a party and now there would be no opportunity to
show Alan off to the family before the wedding.

Ah well, at least there was the wedding to look forward to.
As soon as the exact date was set, she would have to make up
her mind about an outfit. She could still spend a lot of money on
her outfit. At her age it was entirely justified. There had been a
lovely blue suit in the window at Brown's last time she had been
up in Dublin. The suit would be gone, but maybe they would be
able to get her something in that same colour.

She would ask Cara in the local hairdressers to do her hair
that shade of light blonde with caramel coloured streaks that
you saw in all the magazines. It was supposed to be very flatter-
ing for the older woman.

She frowned. Of course, she would have to consult with Alan's mother. Orla had told her about a wedding she had been to recently where the bride's mother and the groom's mother had turned up in exactly the same outfit, even the same colour. All because they had had some kind of falling out before the wedding. Well, she would make sure that wouldn't happen to her. Though, of course, as the mother of the bride she would have first call.

As the days wore on, it troubled her that Maura was saying so little about the arrangements.

"Why don't you just ask her, woman, if you're so worried?" said Kevin. Just like a man to say that, thought Noreen.

"I wouldn't want to antagonise her at all, Kevin."

"I don't see how you would upset her by asking when the wedding date is." He returned to the sports page of the newspaper. "I might have something else on that day if she doesn't let us know soon."

That evening, as Noreen was getting up the courage to phone, a call came from Maura. Now was her chance. Maura's reply almost caused her to faint.

"Oh, we thought we might get married in Thailand. You know, just the two of us. It would combine a honeymoon with the wedding and be far less expensive."

"Thailand?" Noreen's voice came out in a squeak. If Maura had said the moon, Noreen could not have been more upset. "But I thought you would come back here, back home, to get married."

"Oh, Mam, have a heart. You surely don't think I would want to be having a great big wedding and the meringue dress and all at my age, do you?"

As that was exactly what Noreen had thought, she was too upset to speak.

"Anyway," Maura went on, unaware that every word she spoke was like a dagger in Noreen's heart, "Alan doesn't want a lot of fuss. It's better for a second marriage to be a quiet affair."

A second marriage? Was the man a bigamist or what?

"It's all my fault," she sobbed to Kevin later that night when some of the shock had worn off.

"Nonsense," said Kevin stoutly. "You know that Maura was always headstrong. She left here as soon as she could. She's always pleased herself."

All the same, it was not what Noreen had envisaged as the wedding day for her only daughter. How could she face her friends after boasting to them all these years about Maura and her big job in publishing and her pride in the wedding?

Sleepless night followed sleepless night. She tried to go on with her life as usual, answering questions like "Have they set a date yet?" making excuses about how busy they were, trying to find a "window" from the hurly-burly of their London lives.

She knew that behind her back they were whispering, wondering if poor Noreen had finally lost the plot, no matter how kind they were to her face.

Perhaps she could say to Maura that she and Kevin would come out to the wedding in Thailand. A summer outfit would be good. She wouldn't have to worry about the weather. Even as she imagined herself on the beach in a diaphanous dress of deep blue, she knew Kevin would never agree to go.

The days rolled past and her contact with Maura was limited to the occasional phone call. Noreen couldn't bring herself to mention the wedding again. She would give them a present, of course, but the money languishing in the Post Office would now pay for some new carpets. Instead of wedding magazines, she started to buy "Perfect Home."

She had almost reconciled herself to waiting for the wedding photos when the call came. Maura was calm, but direct. There was to be no wedding.

"It's all off, Mam. Much better like this. I'm going to come back home for a week or two if that's o.k."

Noreen's heart gave a little leap. Then she felt totally ashamed. Her poor daughter, to have this happen so soon before the wedding.

Well, she thought, it wasn't as if they actually knew this Alan. So they couldn't be expected to be sorry about him. And when Maura came home, it would be good if she could get out and about again, meet some proper people.

She thought about Colum who owned the farm across the river. He was a lovely lad and how sad to have been left a widower at such a young age. Perhaps she would invite him over for supper once Maura was home.

It was probably a good thing it hadn't worked out with Alan. There was still plenty of time. Why, you heard of girls, well women, these days getting married and having children when they were well into their forties.

Noreen smiled. There was no substitute for a real wedding. Somehow she would make Maura see her mother was right. And there was plenty of time to get started on that diet.

Julia's Irish Wisdom

By Karen O'Neill

Glencar, Co. Kerry

A woman is comforted by the wisdom of her grandmother as she faces into some big decisions

Every inch of her spoke of mortality: the slight hunch in her back that made her look small and delicately balanced, the deep wrinkles in her skin that dropped from her bones, the small, arthritic hands that were always cold to touch. I saw her indignation at the indecency of modern dress, the reverence she bestowed on the male members of her family, crediting them with almost legendary strength while quietly stating that women these days didn't know how to take care of their men.

I never thought of her as out-dated. Perhaps she was an antiquity, like a chipped porcelain vase in which the ways of olden days could be admired. She was my grandmother, old before I was conceived. Sometimes, I was hard-pressed to think of her as anything but that frail little lady. Even when I was well past my childhood, I hadn't learned to value her wisdom as much as I should have. I was wrong to belittle her as I had done.

Now, bathed in the pale winter light, I stared at a recently discovered picture of her, gripped in my hand like a talisman. My admittance letter lay half-crumpled in the other hand. She had been a strong young woman. My much-envied hair, I realised, was only a dull echo of her shining, raven locks. Her eyes caught my interest, their bright blue colour denied life by the sepia photograph. They looked much like mine, framed by heavy lashes and crinkled with a smile. She had not been what you would call typically beautiful, but her dark colouring and plump figure were contrastingly exotic and homely, a picture of Irish good health. No, I am but a shadow of her, I thought, smiling. And this Ireland is a shadow of hers? Could I willingly leave it behind? What if it all goes wrong?

I stared forlornly at the letter in my hand. It was tauntingly white in the snowy glow from the window - the white an emblem of new beginnings. I looked out over the rugged landscape and grove of gnarled oak trees, loving Ireland with a fervency I had learned from her. I recalled the day she had convinced me that I would not regret leaving home. "Always think of the end as a new beginning," she had said. "That's what my mother used to say. The end of the sunshine brings the rain to start new growth. Even passing away begins your new life with the Lord."

Then she looked out at the sunshine and green fields. "Isn't it lovely out? How I love being this age," she said peacefully. "I used to not have the time to appreciate things. Or if I had the time I was too busy worrying about something or other."

I poured us both a mug of tea and came to sit beside her.

"You're upset," she said astutely. She saw me nod.

"Not upset exactly. Not that. I sent off my application today. To Aberdeen for the history degree."

She turned the cup around in her cramped hands, warming them, and pursed her lips. "Sure, I don't know why you didn't do that years ago, girly, when you finished school. Waiting for someone, are you?" She watched me out of the corner of her eye. I sighed; she was hinting at a man I might have married, but he had left me disillusioned.

"He's not going to change, my dear, and no amount of sighing and praying will change that." She was a straight-forward woman and unnervingly insightful. "I was long enough with Michael to know the truth of it." She seldom spoke of her late husband, so seldom that he was merely a myth to me. I was surprised.

"I know," I said, hiding my astonishment. I patted the tabby cat; it purred quietly and settled before the warm stove.

"No, you don't," she replied brusquely, "but you'll learn. Oh, don't look so glum. I left my mother's side at eighteen, younger than you are now, and I left men, too, believe it or not. I stepped out of our little cottage, and off down the Strickeen path with my case. Little did I know I wouldn't see those handsome hills again for ten years."

Her tone was light, but quieter than it had been. She absently ran a hand through her silvery hair.

"What happened?" I asked, having heard the story before but wanting to gratify her desire to tell it, relive it.

She stood up wordlessly and pulled a leather-bound jewellery case from a shelf beside her. She opened it carefully, setting it on the red lounge between us. "The war happened," she said, "and, try as I might, I couldn't get a ship back from Boston. I was living with this Yank, a nice man. I was the cook and his children's minder. I used to walk the two children home from school and make the tea for them. The mother said I made the best tea in the state! They had a gardener, too, a well-off bunch. I think he was a lawyer, or something official anyway. He didn't give us much time off, but nobody got much those days, especially not the Irish, except for Sunday morning mass. I didn't mind, I always thought the harder I worked, the sooner I'd get back home."

She handed me a handkerchief, carefully and tenderly embroidered with shamrock in emerald thread. "I cried into this for the whole ferry trip. I think the sea was feeling fuller after I got to Boston!"

She laughed her reserved little laugh. "It was very hard for the Irish, going from a countryside to those big cities. I suppose it's much the same these days, hmm?"

Next, she handed me a photograph. It portrayed a sturdily handsome young man astride a battered motorcycle. He wore a soldier's uniform with a rumpled cap protruding from the pocket; his hair was slicked back with grease and it shone. He was grinning broadly. The writing on the back read: "Les. Paris, 1942."

"Les?" I murmured. I had never heard of him before.

"We," she searched for the word, "courted for a while, before he was shipped out. It was a whirlwind romance, not much fibre to it, I'd reckon. He was a nice fellow, all said."

"Did you love him, Nan?"

"I did, but no love was greater than the love I had for my home. I was glad of my time in Boston, though it was hard, but I was gladder still to return to Ireland."

"But you loved Granddad then?" I said, as if trying to bolster my romantic notions.

Her eyes focused on me, her gaze soft. "My children loved me, that's what mattered. And my children's children. You'll understand when you're my age."

I snorted. "I don't think I'll ever understand," I said derisively, leaning forward to pull a photo from the violet lined box. It was a picture of her wearing a simple, dark dress and looking radiant. I turned it over. The words on the back were scribbled out. I could just read: "To Les, with love." She had never given it to him. The American soldier would have made a home for them in Boston, but her loyalty to Ireland was too important to her. She returned home, and even if she didn't love my grandfather to the same degree, she was happy.

"Do you at least understand what I'm telling you now, dear?" she said.

I shook my head like a child. "Not really."

"If I had the chance to go and meet the young girl that walked down that path, and pull the ribbons from her hair and tell her to turn back, to go home and not go to America, I wouldn't take that chance. No one gets to pick the easy parts of life and discard the rest. Don't let fear of life stop you from living."

I was taken aback by her speech. Never before had I known her to be so expressive. She continued: "And never doubt your ability to find love, or for it to find you. It's like spring, it comes around again and again, no matter how hard the winter."

I hugged her gently. "Thanks, Nan." I took the empty cups to the sink and washed them with suds.

"You'll be going to Aberdeen then?" she asked flippantly.

"I guess so," I laughed, "who can argue with such an out pouring of wisdom?" I could picture her rolling her eyes behind me. I turned to sort her tablets, the little pills lined up on the table top almost like a soldier's medals, recognising her struggles and perseverance. I counted them out: this one for bravery, this one sacrifice...

"I seem to gather more of them every day," she commented quietly. I hugged her again and left, too early to hear the rattling cough that signified the unfolding of her new beginning.

She would tell me that I was young enough to think that sand castles last forever, even though the tides of time will always wash them away. But then she would smile and say: "That is no reason not to build them."

I glanced again at the two items in my hand. "I'll go to Aberdeen, Nan. For you," I said, feeling the wind pick up. It blew through the trees and, in the background, through the mountains. The snow fell on the cemetery, drifting down like torn love letters, dancing in the fading light. It coated the tomb stones in reverently gentle fleeces, like a loving mother draping a blanket over a sleeping child. I shivered with the cold, but bent down to clear the grass away from the edges of her grave. I rested the framed picture of her against the cool marble. Every inch of her spoke life: the joyous creases around her eyes, the waves of her hair, her strength. This is how I will remember you, I thought, and turned down the road less travelled.

GRANDA

A Memory from **BERNADETTE BRANAGH HEGARTY**
Cross Douglas Road, Cork.

A warm portrait of a colourful and entertaining man

I remember him as a small man with rounded shoulders and a straggling yard-brush moustache. He wore a dark blue suit with a broad stripe when he was parish entertainer and a waistcoat hanging loose over work trousers and Wellington boots as he ambled around the farmyard talking to the pigs. "My wee pets," he called them, scratching their backs with his stick or giving special attention to a sick turkey and reciting some lines:

"He mended her head with boiling lead
And vinegar and brown paper."

I always assumed this referred to the turkey.

He was "Granda" to myself and my two brothers. He became a grandfather when I was born and he was eighty years old. I was told that my birth was announced in the village by the local doctor, who, when asked where he was all day, answered:

"Today I was making James Branagh a grandfather."

James Branagh was the entertainer at "box socials." He was a raconteur and singer. I remember him at parties held in the parish hall for visiting Americans or "Yanks," as we called them.

Those were great days for us children -lots of lemonade, buns and sweets, and the adults all in good humour and more tolerant of high jinks than usual. Maybe the tolerance had something to do with the bottles of porter, the naggins of whiskey and the genteel glasses of sherry which were liberally provided by some wealthy Irish cousins to fete the Yanks in style.

At some stage of the day my grandfather would take the centre of the floor and sing and tell yarns. One of his jingles which always went down well in those pre-PC days was

"A woman wears a ring which shows

She's got her husband by the nose."

He would sing a song called "That's the way to the zoo," each verse of which ended with

"the monkey house is nearly full but there's room enough for you."

We children would point gleefully to each other at that line.

His brand of entertainment was simple by today's standards. Yet I remember the loud laughter which greeted his every comment. He would not sing until he was the right distance from my grandmother and much entertainment was provided by his shuffling:

"I'm too near, Ellen."

"I'm not near enough, Ellen."

In a country divided by religion and politics, Granda got on well with everyone.

We were lucky grandchildren, because every Friday when Granda got his pension he would go into the local shop and ask the shop woman to make "three parcels" for the children. We would eagerly await his return from the village when he would dig deeply into his pockets and produce three brown paper bags, each containing an apple, an orange and sweets.

On one occasion the parcels contained mouth organs and, however the adults' ears might have suffered, we children got tremendous fun from the noises we produced. Our greatest delight was when our parents went out for the evening and we sat around the fire with Grandad and Granny and he sang to us all our favourite songs.

Granda died aged ninety. He was waked in traditional style. He was laid out in a brown shroud in his coffin in the big bedroom. Huge numbers of mourners filled the house and told stories about him. A non-stop buffet of tea, sandwiches and home-baked cakes and buns was provided and, from time to time, some of the men were invited out the back door to what to us children were very mysterious goings-on in a shed and which involved clinking of bottles and loud laughter.

My two brothers and my father walked as chief mourners behind the hearse. As was traditional, the coffin was carried to the end of Granda's land before being put into the hearse. As a female, I was not allowed to sit in the main body of the church for the funeral mass, but sat in the gallery from where I had a good view of everything. People came in, genuflected and blessed themselves. When the mass was over, the priest stood at the front of the altar to receive the "offerings."

At the back of the church sat a few rows of men who, to my puzzlement, had neither genuflected nor blessed themselves and who all through the mass sat upright with what I new to be "hard hats" on their knees. These were our Protestant neighbours who, like all the rest of the community, had come to pay their respects to a good friend and neighbour.

As the coffin was carried down the church, I saw clearly, from my vantage point above, the writing on the brass plate.

JAMES BRANAGH

R. I.P.

15th. Nov. 1955

And I knew that was my last sight of my beloved Granda.

THE ITINERANT BEEKEEPER

By JOE KEARNEY

Enniskerry, Co. Wicklow.

*I'm not a Buddhist, yet whenever I see a bee trapped against the
windowpane I am compelled to set it free*

The town I came from was a place made for dreaming.
The dreams it evoked frequently involved notions of escape from the grip of its dismal streets. These ambitions
gained strength from stories of the lucky ones, the ones who had
"made it." This is the tale of one such son of this small town, a
man who was lost and eventually found. But, who, according
to himself, and by the very nature of his discovery, became lost
all over again. He was slightly built but, in the small place to
which he returned, you couldn't help noticing him. In a town
where you were considered jaunty sporting a pair of turned-
down wellies, he stood out, if not in stature, then by the nature
of his cowboy hat and hand-tooled, leather boots.

The hat was the distinguishing feature. It was a straw Stetson
with plaited leather band and was the colour of heather honey.
I'd see him in the street, and, over time, established a nodding
acquaintance with him. Someone, I can't remember who, told
me his name was Billy.

In those days, for recreation, I liked to fish the slow waters
of the Suanree, hunting out small, shy trout. This was a grey,
meandering river that drained the fields and split the town in
two before disappearing over a weir on its escape towards the
sea. When these events happened, the season was closing in.
Bunches of moldering blackberries drooped from brambles and
the bracken was bent and brittle along the riverbanks. A path
that glistened like a snail-track in the dew had been beaten beside the water. It marked the passage of lovers and fishermen.
I would sometimes see Billy casting a gossamer line above the
sluggish stream. His casting technique was both graceful and

economic, and I envied his touch. During these near-encounters, he deliberately maintained his distance, shuffling away from me along the bank, but never failing to cover the water with his line and flies as he retreated. There was no mistaking him, the halo of his hat catching the brightness whenever he moved through the checkerboard of darkness and light.

One evening, in low sunshine, I came upon him. He had hooked a salmon using light trout tackle and seemed afraid he might break the line and lose his fish. The rod bent away from his hands and trembled. It was a conduit of energy unifying both man and fish in the life or death struggle played out beneath the water.

Uncharacteristically, he waved me towards him.

"I got no landing net, Buddy. Can you dig me out here?"

The accent was a fusion of Hollywood and Midland Ireland. For the next half hour or so he played that powerful fish. I wet my landing net and positioned it where I could scoop the salmon from the stream. At times the tired creature came tantalizingly close, but the inevitable happened, it broke the line and escaped to live and fight another day.

"I'd have let it go anyway," he drawled and looking at his face, I believed him.

In the closing weeks of that fishing season, we'd meet again, and it was during those odd encounters, on the quiet, confessional riverbank, he drip-fed me with his escape story.

One autumn, he remembered, when the swallows lined the wires, he left. Simple as that, just walked out the door. He had lusted for change, just to do something different, something other than the routine slog of his daily existence. He never suspected what he might do until the day he pulled the hall door shut behind him.

He had been squirreling money away, inside an envelope taped to the back of a drawer in his bedside locker. On the morning he set his face from home, he left a farm, a wife and three small children.

The journey is hazy to him; he thinks he may have blocked out the details. There were days spent in a Dublin guesthouse, getting his papers together. When he stepped through the exit doors in San Francisco airport, he told me how, for the first time, the very first time, in his entire life, he felt alive. The distance he travelled had, in some way, freed him.

When he arrived, the city was in the grip of Flower Power and a Summer of Love. Each day, when the fog burned off, the sun shone and his skin turned brown. He worked in construction until one Sunday, on a casual bus-ride, he discovered the Central Valley and its endless fruit farms. It was like Eden before the fall. He would not have believed that the earth contained such fertility. So he stayed on, working the farms as the seasons allowed and returning to construction when they did not.

"You make your own luck," he told me. "If you want apples to fall into your hand, it pays to spend as much time as possible in an orchard."

Billy's luck arrived on the night he hit the jackpot in a Las Vegas casino.

"I just knew when to quit. I walked out those doors with enough greenbacks in my jeans to make my dream come true."

That was how he "Got into the bees," as he liked to put it.

He bought a truck and a trailer. It took him a year to collect and buy enough hives to mount on the rig and make his enterprise viable. For the next twenty-odd years he transported those colonies of bees from farm to farm across the fruit growing regions of his vast adopted home.

"They got to know me over time, those farmers. I just knew when it was time to show. I'd set up in a field or orchard and stay as long as the blossoms lasted."

From the almond groves of California in January, to the apple orchards of Washington in March, then on to North Dakota and back to his beloved California by November. He hired out his winged workers and in the fall of the year sold their honey.

The river chuckled past us as it heard his tale. These waters, older than time, never lie; all they know is truth.

Billy explained how he took to the wandering life. He liked moving on with the turn of the seasons. That was what had made him unsettled, in the little grey town, that notion of being lost on the fold of a map, stuck in a crease, unable to set his face to the line of the far horizon. The country he found himself in was vast. It was a place of big skies, sunny days and endless blossom.

Billy changed with time, started calling himself Adam.

"Kinda apt, don't you think."

He sometimes found it hard to remember the old life, and eventually developed a liking for country music and Mexican food. The Central Valley offered him the things he grew to love: Burritos, Buck Owens and Jalapeño peppers. There is time to think about the meaning of life in the quiet of an apple orchard. He'd sit in the evening and watch the golden air shimmer and hum with the wings of his homecoming bees. It was his favourite time, watching the slow shadow-creep of dimming light through the cordons of trees. Whenever he felt like company, he unhitched the truck and drove into one of the small towns for a beer and food.

It was here, one night, on the outskirts of Bakersfield, that he sat by the bar watching TV and minding his own business. As he remembers, it was one of those occasions when he might have had a beer or three too many. Certainly, details of the evening are unclear in his head. He recalls being drawn into conversation by a young couple sitting close-by. They were struggling with the choices on the menu. He suspects they might have been honeymooners.

Neither wanted anything too spicy. They asked for Billy's advice, something without chili peppers, perhaps? In the way that the orbits of the roulette wheel had spun in Billy's favour that night in the Las Vegas Casino, the permutations of chance made a similar, improbable rotation in that Bakersfield barroom. Perhaps it was the beer or just the passage of the decades, but Billy failed to heed the man and woman with the bland palates.

He was happy to pose for a photo though, his straw Stetson tilted back, the burnish of the seasons on his cheeks and a smell of bee's wax on his skin. They bought him a bottle of Dos Equos? He listened to the details of their road trip, he told them what he did for a living and that was it. They shook hands and parted.

Seventeen days later, he is very precise about this: seventeen days later, Billy was packing up for the haul north to Washington State when she walked up through the orchard. He saw the woman approaching, watched her get closer and, even with the light at her back, knew who she was.

"Did you ever hear of a thing called the tule fog?" he asks me.

"It's a thing you get in the San Joaquin Valley, after rain, when the humidity is high. It's like a ground fog that creeps along and covers your boots. Kinda spooky the first time you see it. That was what she moved through, like an apparition. Like as if she was floating, not walking."

Billy examines his boots; the toecaps are scuffed, soiled in places by river mud.

"What do you say to someone you haven't seen for twenty-five years, someone who has only visited you in dreams?" He might have been addressing the stones of the river. He has become so lost in his tale I don't exist.

Billy failed to see the links between his life to those of the man and the woman in the Bakersfied bar. In that odd space, with the jute-box pumping a stream of Tex-Mex music and the enchiladas hotter than the purple night, the degrees of separation narrowed and narrowed until they locked into place.

Our small town never forgot Billy. They still talked of the missing man; the one who walked away and never came home. He is as fresh in the lore of the place as if the years had never passed. The returned travellers were happy to share their holiday snaps with friends, family and neighbours, in fact, anyone who would take the time to look. The sharing allowed them to relive the sunny days in California. One member of that willing audience paused with a 6x4 photograph in her hand. Its image showed the inside of a Mexican-themed bar and a man with the sun in his cheeks, a jaunty hat perched on the pole of his head.

"Jasus! That couldn't be Maura Connor's Billy." But it was.

"She never questioned why I went, never asked why I hadn't written or sent money. Just walked up with the fog on her shoes, took my hand and asked me home."

131

Billy sold his bees and rig, withdrew his savings and moved back to the small town.

"The secret of moving bees," he informed me, "is that you must bring them at least two miles from their last location. That way they'll settle and forget where they've been."

Does Billy forget California? He unties the cast of flies, reels in the line and disconnects the three sections of his rod. All about us, bats have started quartering the river.

"Jalapeño peppers" he says, "you can't get Jalapeño peppers in this God-forsaken town."

AUNTIE'S LESSON

By RHODA TWOMBLY
Westport, Co. Mayo

Nerves are severely tested as Emma gets in some driving practice in her aunt's car in preparation for her driving test, accompanied by the aunt's caustic commentary

The air in the car felt buttermilk-thick and my sister Emma bit her lip in concentration as she navigated the road under the tutelage of our Auntie Kate.

It didn't take long for Auntie Kate to find fault. "Should you not keep out a bit more to the right, Emma? Just a small ..." From the car's back seat, I could see our Auntie brace herself, hand pressed white against the dash, spine unnaturally straight, head swivelling. Her bird-like eyes scanned the road for dangers, real and imagined. Judging by her tight lips and deep frown, it seemed she was already regretting letting Emma use her car for a bit of driving practice.

Emma protested: "But you *just* told me to stay to the *left*, Auntie Kate." My sister's flush deepened with each word. "Left, right, middle – what's it to be?" Emma's temper strained against its leash – and we had only been in Auntie's car ten minutes. I told myself I was along strictly as an observer, but deep down knew I might have to protect Emma from Auntie's impatience and irascibility.

"Honestly, Emma, you'll be the death of me – my nerves! You *know* what I meant, child. Keeping away from parked cars doesn't mean you have to drive the middle of the road!" Auntie's hand fell to her lap, leaving finger marks on the padded dash of the '68 Ford. Her eyes didn't leave the road as she retied the dark green paisley headscarf under her chin for the third time.

Emma sucked in her breath. She began to hum softly, tunelessly, no doubt swallowing her reply. I wondered would Emma's acne rage so disastrously had it not been for all the bottled up bile and choked back words banging about inside of her.

Auntie wasn't finished with poor Emma, not yet.

"Get your hair out of your eyes, Emma – no wonder you're all over the road!" My sister's strawberry blond hair was a blessing and a curse: left long and loose, it was impressively thick, curly and unapologetically unruly, but truly beautiful. I flinched as Auntie Kate turned and directed her glinting eyes at me.

"Siobhan, lend your sister those slides you have in your hair – they're not the right colour for you anyway." I foolishly thought the purple plastic slides set off my hazel eyes. "Honestly! Where you girls get these cheap looking bits of tat – EMMA! Watch it! God bless us and save us."

As Auntie Kate's left hand clawed the dash, her right flew in genuflection across her chest. The brakes howled in protest, the wheels locked and the car skidded to the left. Emma barely missed a scraggly marmalade tomcat intent on dancing under the wheels.

"Lord, Emma - you put the heart cross-ways on me! Did you not see that cat?" Auntie tugged on the lapels of her jacket, straightening a non-existent wrinkle. "Siobhan – did you see what your sister did? We were nearly killed for the sake of a *cat*, for pity's sake!"

I straightened myself in the seat. "Give her a chance, Auntie," I said, rubbing my arm where it had banged against the door. "After all, Emma is only learning and driving takes practice. Emma," I gently touched my sister's shoulder, "don't worry, pet – you're doing really well. Just try to relax a bit." Her death grip on the wheel eased and she shrugged the tension from her shoulders.

"That's right, Emma," Auntie added dryly, "It's a known fact that the more relaxed you are at impact, the less damage will be done. If I could doze off, I might stand a chance of surviving your driving!" I sent my sister an encouraging wink as her eyes met mine in the rear-view mirror.

Our father's older sister, Auntie Kate, moved into our house straight after Mother's funeral twelve years ago. Father said wryly that she was a hardy mix of nervous energy and self-discipline. He told us how Kate relished Lent when they were children, foregoing sugar *and* milk in her tea as well as all sweets and cakes.

Before Mother became ill, Auntie Kate's dreaded twice-yearly visits were inescapable. The impending visitations sparked our normally easy-going mother into a housekeeping dervish. Our playmates sent home, Emma and I nervously strove for Sunday-best behaviour for the duration.

News of an impending stay always came in the post, never by phone; like a royal decree, the announcement had to be in writing. Even Walter the postman, deaf as a doorknob but still razor sharp, knew who belonged to the spidery writing on the vellum envelope; always black ink, never blue.

"She's on her way, so?" Walter gathered correctly every time, watching Mother's whole body droop. He'd hand Emma and me a boiled sweet and tweak our noses, delighted at our squeals. "May as well enjoy them while you can, hey girls?" No such thing as sweets and treats when Auntie Kate was about.

At the time I was too young to appreciate the kindness and patience Mother showed Auntie Kate, but sitting in the car with my tense, tight-lipped aunt, I did now. For Emma's sake I had to try to soothe frayed tempers and jangling nerves.

Struggling to keep my tone even, I asked, "Maybe you should have enrolled her in driving school, Auntie Kate? I know lessons aren't cheap (and I know all about the cash you have stashed in the hidey-hole in the dresser, I thought), but wouldn't it be worth it to keep your nerves in one piece?" And keep us all on speaking terms, I added to myself.

I felt sorry for my little sister, remembering all too clearly what Auntie put me through when she attempted to teach me to drive two years ago. After a few hours in the car with her, I smashed open my piggy bank and signed up for proper driving lessons.

Emma was in the hot seat now, getting more frustrated by the minute, ready to burst her seams with temper. I tried to calm her while sending a hint to our aunt that she should do the same. "I'm not saying anything, Em – just concentrate, will you?" I cooed. "You have time before the test and you're doing really well – truly – a bit more practice is all you need. *Right*, Auntie Kate?"

I laid my hand on the bony shoulder, felt her stiffen, then ease. She had that jacket, I swear, from the time she walked into our house. "Buy well and it will stand to you," was her motto. She must have bought very well in her younger days, as I had never seen her come home with anything new.

"Well ... perhaps. She hasn't killed us yet, anyway," Auntie Kate said grudgingly. "Here, girl, take this – wipe your face." She handed Emma one of her own linen handkerchiefs, trimmed in Donegal lace with her initials embroidered in one corner. It was impossibly white, the ironed creases so sharp you'd cut your nose if you had the nerve to do something as silly as blow your nose on it.

Our learner tipped the right-turn indicator, its "clicks" loud in the car. Emma made the turn onto Butcher's Hill. Gears ground and groaned as she shifted up into second. "It's your fault, Auntie!" My sister exclaimed. "Your nerves are contagious."

Emma changed gears to third prematurely and the car jerked, threatened to stall. I winced as she pumped the accelerator and, her body bobbing forward as if this would make the strangled motor gain speed.

"God – the sweat is pumping out of me! My hands are slippery – give us some tissue, will you?" My sister placed the linen hanky on Auntie's lap. "I don't want to ruin this lovely thing." I handed her a wad of Kleenex and she mopped her forehead, then both palms. After Emma dropped the damp tissues to the floor, I noticed she placed her hands in the seven-and-five position. Auntie would not be pleased but I hadn't time for a gentle reminder: Auntie Kate's stern voice headed me off.

"Now Emma, calm down. Just watch the road, please." Auntie Kate's voice shifted from placating to nagging in two seconds flat. "Hands, Emma – your hands! Ten and two – how *many times* ..."

Auntie Kate reached over, caught my sister's left hand and moved it up on the wheel. "Auntie! NO!" We girls shouted simultaneously just as Emma tried to avoid the aftermath of a near accident between a tractor-trailer and a cyclist. In that split-second I reckoned that the tractor must have swerved to avoid hitting the poor old man on his ancient black bicycle. In the process, the trailer became unhooked from the tractor, now stopped at the side of the road. Its teenage driver was chasing the runaway, frantically trying to catch up. It was lucky we were near the top of the hill; the trailer was only trundling along but was picking up speed.

The car filled with horrified shouts. My head brushed Auntie's headrest; my seat belt cut into my chest, but a few bruises are better than a concussion. There was the sickening sound of shattering headlamp, then metal-on-metal as the now slowing trailer scraped along the side of the car. .

A split second of silence, then whimpering from Emma, who was holding her left arm. She had thrown her arm out to stop Auntie Kate from hitting the dashboard and had taken quite a blow to her wrist. Poor Auntie Kate looked like she was in shock. Dead white and silent, she stared straight ahead, her lips moving with no sound coming out.

Emma must have switched to autopilot, managing to steer the wounded car to the left with her good arm so that she crossed the footpath just at Church Lane, at the bottom of which was Lennon's Body Shop.

We limped to a stop just at Charlie Lennon's door as he stood there, mouth open, lit pipe forgotten in his hand. His wife, Maggie, had dropped her wicker basket with surprise, so Charlie's sandwiches, biscuits and flask lay in the gutter, smack-dab in a puddle of water shining with oil.

The cyclist, thankfully untouched and quite spry for his age, coasted to a stop just as the hapless tractor driver caught up with his trailer, gasping and pumping sweat. Miraculously, no one was hurt and the trailer had held on to most of its cargo.

Emma needed a week to calm herself, but went on to do very well with her driving instructor, paid for with some of the money she got from the insurance company for the whiplash. Two months later she passed the test with flying colours, even though the examiner was as cranky as our aunt and twice as pernickety.

As an extra-added bonus, Emma found herself with a new boyfriend. Turns out Charlie Lennon's son, Fergus, was saving for a new car by giving driving lessons. Spotting Emma from an upstairs window the day of the crash, he confided to me after their second date that his first thought was: "Wow! Now that's the girl for me!" He couldn't believe his luck when she rang up looking for lessons.

Auntie Kate? Her shattered nerves mean that she is torturing every taxi driver in town. I hear that one cab company has taken to drawing lots when Auntie Kate rings. The loser is blessed with her company for the hour or so it takes for her shopping trips. The other taxi establishment has permanently designated one driver whenever she orders a cab. He's a lovely fellow, the grandfather of one of my friends. Half-deaf and made immune to nagging by a torment of a wife of forty-eight years, Johnny is the perfect man for the job.

BOOPAW

A Memory from SEAN DOYLE
Santry, Dublin

Portrait of a door-to-door salesman from 60 years ago.

I was a child in the forties, and lately my mind has been drawn back, more and more, to a particular memory of that time. I used to love to accompany my mother whenever she went to answer a ring at our hall door. Through this childish practice I became acquainted with many of the callers to our house. There was the bread man, the butcher, the milkman and the whistling messenger boy from the local grocery shop. But of all the callers, my memory of one man in particular stands out head and shoulders above the rest.

He was basically a door-to-door salesman. He sold polish. All kinds of polish. Boot polish, shoe polish, floor polish, furniture polish, as well as a selection of dyes and creams, brushes, cloths and a host of small household items. All of these he carried in an enormous wooden case, similar in shape and size to an extremely large suitcase.

Tuesday was his day for calling to our house, always in the afternoon. God bless the mark, but he was an odd looking man, with a severe speech impediment and a blank expression on his long face.

In calling to us over the years, his opening sales pitch never changed. "Want any boopaw?" This was his honest attempt at asking: "Want any boot polish?" Consequently, he was known in our house not disrespectfully, I hasten to add, as Boopaw.

My mother always made a point of purchasing something from him, whether or not she needed it at the time. And on occasions when she required a particular item which he did not have, he would promise faithfully to bring it the following week; and he always did.

I think of Boopaw now with a mixture of sadness and admiration. His frantic efforts at times to make himself understood at our hall door, his voice rising sharply from the great effort he was making to articulate his words, was simply heart-rending.

Also, it was a harrowing experience to observe his slow progress going from house to house, being forced frequently by the weight of his wooden case to stop and change arms, the strain all the while etched on his face. Yet one could not but admire his spirit, his resolve and determination not to buckle beneath his difficulties - difficulties which others in a similar plight might have found to be insurmountable.

Regrettably, I concede that he did present a forlorn image to the world. His long threadbare overcoat that reached almost to his ankles, and his boots, though somehow always clean and shiny in spite of showing evidence of much mending, were testament to his poor circumstances. I see him in my mind's eye on a sweltering summer's day setting his case down to catch his breath for a few precious moments, while he mopped the perspiration from his beleaguered brow. Then grasping the handle of his case once more, his stride reduced to a shuffling gait, he continued on his way.

Some onlookers and passers-by were probably amused by the efforts of this brave man to do an honest day's work. Some, I hope, were filled with admiration. Some, alas, may have regarded him as a pathetic figure. Some, I fear, may have scoffed at him from behind their hands. Yet it is my deeply held hope that Boopaw had the last laugh, for who amongst us today can say that he is not now in one of the many mansions in God's heavenly house, adorned in a princely glory that is far beyond our wildest imaginings?

"I Do"

By Liam Mulvin
Godalming, Surrey.

*A couple look forward to their wedding and both have a
burning ambition to do something special for the big day*

"Would you marry me?"

The words ran around in Aisling's head as she gazed
at Sean sitting opposite her across the table. Her dark eyes
watched as a shadow passed over his face. Guiltily, she suddenly
realised.

"He thinks I'm going to say no. Idiot, as if I would."

Her eyes crinkled at him and she nodded her head. Looking
down and wiping her mouth on a fresh hankie, she smiled delightedly at him and nodded again.

Sean visibly relaxed and slumped back in his wheelchair before sitting upright and giving a thumbs up out of the window
beside them.

Aisling turned and looked out in time to see two shadowy fig-
ures sitting in the pub garden get up and head towards the door.
The next moment their two closest friends, Doug and Louise,
burst smiling into the pub and came across to the table.

Louise kissed Sean as Doug kissed Aisling and then, while
the two men were shaking hands and grinning at each other,
she turned towards Aisling and hugged her closely.

"So you're to become an old married couple like us, then, are
you? It's about time."

Aisling picked up the electronic key-pad which never left her
side and tapped a message out on it. She wiped her mouth again
before showing Louise the words typed there.

Louise laughed and nodded.

"Yes. We did know all about it. We've been sitting in the
garden waiting for him to ask you before we could come in for
dinner with you both. And yes, I will be your bridesmaid."

"Sorry to leave you both out there so long," Sean grinned at them both, "I was more nervous than I thought."

"A fine way to greet your best man and the bridesmaid," grinned Doug, punching Sean on the arm. "Still, you paying for the dinner should sort that out. Don't worry now; I'll pay for the champagne."

Aisling watched them all with a small smile across her face. The four of them had been friends since their first days at school. Sean in his wheelchair and her being autistic had brought out the worst in some children and the best in others. They had been together ever since.

She sat quietly watching Sean and the other two animatedly discussing her wedding. She thought of the vows she would be taking. A sudden thought struck her: "I wonder, is it possible for me to learn to say 'I Do' in time for the wedding? Could I do it?"

At best the only sound that Aisling ever made was a grunting sound that meant nothing to anybody. She only wanted to say "I Do". God, she would be so proud at the wedding if she could say that. Imagine how pleased and proud Sean would be. "Yes," she thought, "I will learn to say I do."

She tapped on the keyboard: "Sean, have you any thoughts or ideas for the date of the wedding?"

"I have." He looked a little embarrassed. "I fancy getting married at the beginning of September next year. It's just over ten months away." Aisling typed back, "That's when we all met up. I like that."

Before she could type in anything else, Sean, with a huge grin on his face, dropped a small bombshell amongst them all. "I have been talking to a private physiotherapist and I am going to be visiting him over the next ten months. I intend to stand on my own two feet at the wedding." "Well", said Doug, "I admire your dedication but I hope you haven't bitten off more than you can chew. Good luck with it anyway. Any help needed, just let me know."

Aisling moved her hand away from the keyboard. She could not steal Sean's thunder now. It looked like they would both be attempting something for the wedding; one publicly and one secretly.

"Let's head back now," said Sean. "I would like to get home I think." He called the waiter over and asked to settle the bill.

As soon as this had been achieved, the other three stood and put their coats on. Sean, too, pulled his coat on, and with a thrust of his powerful arms, propelled himself towards the door. The other three followed him out into the night and all four of them headed along the street to his bungalow.

On the way, Aisling thought about what Sean had said. She hoped he would be able to do it. She decided not to tell anybody her own plans. Both she and Sean could try to do this extra thing, but she would keep hers a secret. She wasn't even sure why she wanted it kept as a secret, but she was going to keep it none the less. From the very beginning, Sean was told he would probably never stand on his own two feet, but he confidently set out to prove people wrong. As the countdown to the wedding continued, the young couple - one in secret and one in public - put every effort into their chosen quests.

Once a week, Sean went through a tough series of manipulation and exercise. The physiotherapist felt less than hopeful, as the wasting disease that Sean was suffering from had become quite advanced before it had stopped. He would give him all the help he could, but he felt it his duty to warn him he would in all probability fail. Sean refused to believe this and the sessions continued.

Every time Sean went off to his weekly sessions, Aisling would go to her speech therapist. An over-anxious and doting set of parents had ensured that Aisling would be well schooled and looked after, but, unfortunately, she missed out on the mainstream speech therapy which might have helped her at a younger and more responsive age. She was now trying to fight years of neglect to her unused voice box and throat muscles as she attempted to say "I Do."

A visit to the local priest had put Aisling at her ease over one thing. She would be able to tap out her responses on her keyboard and Louise, her bridesmaid, would be able to repeat them for all to hear. This also applied to her vows as well. She was pleased as this meant she had a plan to fall back on if things didn't work out.

With two months to go until the wedding, Sean was no nearer standing on his own two feet than he was at the beginning.

His frustration was getting plain to see and he was becoming more irritable as the date approached.

Doug was working out in the gymnasium one afternoon and encouraging Sean as best he could. The physiotherapist was still valiantly trying to toughen and strengthen the muscles in the wasted legs. Sean had still found that he was unable to move his legs on his own and was getting annoyed with everyone.

"I'm sure the muscles have got stronger. They have got to have built up enough to let me stand," he shouted. "Help me up and I will show you both."

"It won't work, Sean," said the physiotherapist. "The strength just isn't there yet."

"Don't tell me that," Sean yelled. "Come here, both of you, help me stand."

Doug put down the weights he was using and came across. "Steady Sean," he said, "this guy is the expert. If he says you can't do it, don't fight him."

"That's easy for you to say, Doug. Don't you let me down as well."

The proud and angry man looked up at his friend. "Please, Doug", his voice softened, "Let's give it a go."

Doug looked at the physiotherapist, who shrugged his shoulders resignedly, then nodded acceptance. He and Doug picked Sean up under the arms and stood him up. As soon as the weight transferred itself to Sean's legs and they let go, he buckled straight away. Four times they did this, with the same result.

In the end Sean growled, "O.K. Put me back in my chair." He breathed heavily and his heart pounded. He felt stupid. "Sorry," he muttered. "Just keep doing as you're told," said Doug, "it's your only chance, old friend." "I know," said Sean, "I know".

As for Aisling; her perseverance was paying off. Against all the odds, she was making two recognisable sounds "I Do." Not clear, but recognisable. She practiced constantly and she could hear the improvement herself. The most surprised person was the speech therapist.

Aisling was sitting on her own, ten days before the wedding, when Louise called round. "Hi ya," she smiled as she sat beside her. "Hey. I hope people don't think it's me marrying Sean when I repeat all your responses for you."

Aisling looked at her best friend for a moment and then tapped out a message on her keyboard. Louise read the message and her eyes grew wide. "Go on, then," she said, "say I do". Aisling shook her head and wrote: "Not today. The day I say 'I Do' will be on my wedding day, not before". She smiled happily at her friend. Louise could only grin back: "Is it a secret?"

Aisling nodded.

The day of the wedding dawned brightly. Aisling had spent the night at the hotel with Louise. Doug had gone over to the bungalow and had spent the night with Sean.

Aisling had decided to walk to the church as it was only just along the road. Her father was whiling away the last few minutes by having a quick puff on his pipe on the veranda.

The two young women sat in the hotel foyer waiting for the moment to arrive. Aisling was troubled. Sean had been noticeably quiet all the previous evening at the small drinks party held at the hotel. He had looked at his two closest friends and the woman he loved more than life itself and in an anguished voice had blurted out: "I couldn't do it, Aisling. I couldn't stand. For ten months I have tried everything and I just couldn't do it. I tried so hard but I couldn't make it. I can't stand at all. I let you down. I'm sorry."

Aisling had rushed to him, put her arms around him, and held him close. She had gently stroked his face. Words had been unimportant. She certainly hadn't felt let down. He looked a lot better when he and Doug had left. He looked happier than he had for some time.

Her thoughts returned to the here and now and she wiped her mouth. She picked up the keyboard. She held it so that Louise could read it as she wrote. "I can't say my response at the church, Louise. Sean has tried and struggled for ten months to stand, and he couldn't do it. It would go so hard on him if I speak my response. I can't do it. I know he would be so proud of me, but he would feel so hurt as well. The blow to his pride would be tremendous. Please, Louise, will you do my responses as the priest said. Please?" Louise looked at the troubled face in front of her.

"If that's what you want, of course I will. You definitely want me to say all the responses and the vows," she confirmed. Aisling nodded and a quiet smile played across her lips, a smile brought on by a feeling of peace with herself.

Again Louise spoke. "This could be your finest achievement and in front of all your family and friends, too. Do you understand what you are giving up?"

Aisling's beautiful face lit up as she looked at her friend. She wiped her mouth, and slowly and clearly said: "I do".

THE LANGUAGE OF FLOWERS

By MARTIN MALONE
Rathbride Road, Kildare Town

*A mother is unhappy that her 30 years old son has decided to
become a priest*

O f one thing she was sure: she needed help. She had no
close friends in whom she could confide; her trustable
friends were on holidays, the ones she could rely upon
not to bring her news to the pub or the whist club.

Veronica Molloy was a thin, quiet woman, ill at ease at social functions, and inclined to worry too much. For many years
she had waitressed in the town's best restaurant, a necessity
forced upon by her by premature widowhood: her husband Ed
was killed in a traffic accident when she was twenty-four and
carrying their first child.

There'd been another man a few years ago, when she had
turned fifty and the loneliness was biting at her – seeing her
friends enjoying themselves with their families used to leave
her feeling envious of them. But the relationship didn't last: he
wanted a cook, a cleaner, and to spend too much time in a pub,
while she wanted a companion.

In the last while she had taken to examining her life – she
had joined a hiking club and spent her Sundays trekking over
fairly rugged terrain. She loved the open air, the lake scenery,
the feel good factor in having tired limbs after healthy exercise.
And she was slowly making new friends; it had taken a deal of
courage for her to pick up the phone and make that initial in-
quiry to the hiking club.

"We're not elitists," a soft voice told her, "and we have a
beginners..."

She drove into the grounds of the church and reversed into a
space shaded from the scorching sun by the branches of an overhanging tree. She stared through the windscreen at the flank

of the church, noting its lancet windows, the scaffolding that reached to the eaves. Veronica was not a religious woman: she did not attend church, she didn't believe in a just and forgiving god. In her mind she thought that a person was born, went from A to Z, and died. That was it.

When Ed died she had found no solace in her faith; it broke her heart to lie to her son: she had told him he was in heaven and to pray for his soul; she hated herself for lying. Her lies, she told herself, had merely served to encourage him.

Veronica entered the church, stood in the vestibule, joining a queue. The double doors were open; a long line of people down the aisle were waiting their turn to touch the glass encasing the saint's relics. The last time she had been in a church was for Michael's confirmation; a long, long time ago.

As a small child he used to love going to Mass; she was glad when he became an altar server and started going to Mass by himself – when he hit his teens he was like her: he didn't bother with church. It was merely an austere edifice where people went to pray, to confess sins, to marry, to receive the last blessings before burial. Many times she had declined offers to attend weddings and christenings and as for those who died whom she liked and respected, she visited their graves a day or so after their burial.

She broke from the queue to sit in a pew. Sunlight dappled the walls and floor with beautiful reds and gold of the garb and halos worn by the saints depicted in the stained-glass; a spill of gold touched the altar. She turned her eyes to the casket: people touched the glass, touched red roses to it. She felt a great sadness which came close to overwhelming her.

None of it is true, she said, none of it.

An old man who had been to the casket, was returning along the side aisle, a corridor so narrow a person had to almost walk sideways. Their eyes fell to one another; he smiled and proffered her a flower. She couldn't very well refuse. She smiled her thanks and sat with the flower on her lap. On the walls looking down upon her were framed black and white photographs of the young saint with her sister, another of her by herself, another with her parents. There were others but she couldn't make them out, her eyesight not as good as it used to be, not even with the spectacles she should be wearing but had forgotten to bring.

Father Matthew had said he would be here at this time. She had called him yesterday and said she needed to speak with him urgently. He said he was busy and asked if she could wait a day or so, but she insisted and so he relented.

There was no sign of him. She glanced at her watch. The scent of the flower carried to her nostrils and she brushed a petal lightly with her fingertips. I'll go home, she thought. What could he tell me anyway – probably only rubbish; I can just imagine: God's will, mysterious ways, all that. The usual spin.

Still, he was the only one who could help her. The priest was also of her native town in the south of the country – they'd been childhood friends and it was this reminder that had softened his stance about the appointment. In fact, he was delighted and was all talk about old times and neighbours; his "busy" forgotten about.

When she looked up, she saw him. She had seen him around town a few times but had not announced herself to him: she had little regard for the clergy – their world was all about power and power corrupts and the country had witnessed the truth of this. He was looking at the faces, the pews and then saw her. He excused himself from the company he was in and went to join her, rubbing his large hands together. He was stout, grey-haired, and had a sheen of happiness in his large round face.

"Veronica?" he said, sitting in beside her, "it's been so long."

He had a shaving nick to the angle of his jaw.

She nodded, and he took her hand and squeezed.

"How are you?" he said.

She looked at him and he saw the hurt in her and suggested they go into the parochial house. Then he said: "I'm afraid every square inch of the house is taken up because of," he indicated with his hand, "but let's go outside ..."

He walked with her to her car and they stood beside it. She held the rose in her hand, down by her side.

"It's about my son, Michael," she said, wading into the heart of the matter after some preamble concerning their shared childhood memories.

He said nothing. There was a knitting of his eyebrows, a folding of his arms.

"He's studying to become a priest," she said.

Still, he remained silent.

She narrowed her eyes a fraction to show she expected a response.

"Veronica, what's the problem?"

"I've just said it."

"That's no problem. In fact, you should be proud of him."

"Well, I'm not. He's too young."

"How young?"

"Thirty."

"Not so young – he'd obviously thought hard and long about it."

"Neither hard nor long enough."

A look of complete bewilderment crossed his face.

He said: "What do you want me to do?"

"Talk to him."

"About?"

"The life he'll have for himself – lonely, no friends, in a world that's been sullied by..."

He looked away. Oh, the pain caused by those of our cloth who erred greatly – the wash of time might work but not for my generation nor I suspect for others after us, he thought.

"I don't mean you," she said.

"Ah, that's what everyone says; we don't mean you, Father."

"But you know what I'm talking about – he'd have no life."

"I'm not lonely," he said, "I have friends. I believe in my God, even if you don't. That's not to say I don't have problems – I have. I can't help you with your son. I feel sure he's at the right age to make a good decision. Haven't you expressed your thoughts to him?"

"Yes."

"And?"

"He won't change his mind."

Father Matthew sighed and said: "You've no faith, Veronica."

"Is it that easy to tell?"

"Yes."

"I can think what I want."

"It's strange, isn't it? A mother has no belief, her only son has – if anything it's usually the other way round."

He smiled.

"I see no humour in all this, Father."

"No," he said, the smile withering, "but I don't know what to say. I've no influence with your son...I'm sorry."

"If you could talk to him or someone like you could talk to him –"

"Do you really think that they haven't?"

"He said they told him all the pitfalls."

"Well then?"

"He's no more a priest than..."

He showed her the palms of his hands and said he had to be going; that she could see the day of it – there were many pilgrims coming to visit the relics of a saint who had died young, who in spite of her own personal pain had not failed to believe. He wanted to be with people who were like him, who believed. And if she didn't want to lose her son, then she was to find a way to reach a compromise.

"I've already lost him," she said.

He put his hands to his lips in a gesture of prayer and then brought them away: "Was he living at home with you when he made this decision?"

"No."

"How often were you getting to see each other?"

She didn't answer: once every six to eight weeks with the occasional phone call in-between.

"So you were getting on with each other's lives. Where's the change there. Veronica, give him your blessing and let things be."

"I won't go to his ordination," she said stubbornly.

"That's your choice. Not his."

For moments neither spoke. She should have known better than to try to enlist the help of a priest – everyone knew there was hardly anyone joining the priesthood; they'd be glad to have Michael in their ranks; someone honest, dependable, straight-talking like his father had been.

"His father?" Father Matthew said, as though he had read her mind.

"He was killed in a car accident."

"Have you prayed for him to help?"

"No. He's dead."

"Well, he's alive in the next world."

"You *are* so sure of yourself."

"It's time I was going Veronica – we could fall into argument and I don't want that to happen on this day of all days."

"Yes, I don't want that either."

He was about to walk away when he paused, and said: "I'll pray that you'll receive guidance and some acknowledgement that the world is much more than the two colours you think it is."

She watched him walk to the church, climb the steps and go inside.

Black and white? It isn't, Father – I walk the mountains and see the heather, the granite boulders, the black lakes, the red deer, the red kites – I see the colours of the world.

She got into the car and drove home, bringing the rose with her and putting it in the vase along with the carnations she had bought in Lidl's earlier that morning. That night she went to bed: she had to get up early and eat a good breakfast before heading off to join her hiking party in Wicklow. In the morning she went downstairs to the chimes of the cuckoo clock. After passing through the hall into the kitchen, she retraced her steps to look at something that had belatedly struck her as peculiar Her eyes fastened on the flowers in the vase, at the yellow rose looking out at her.

THRESHOLDS

A Memory from BREDA JOYCE

Knocklofty, Co. Tipperary

Revisiting an old childhood holiday home revives memories

I took the road to Drum and I time-travelled thirty-three years. I was a child again heading to my grandfather's for the summer holidays. So when I entered the house where my mother was born, it was the smells of the scullery that my nose sniffed out. The yellow cream Aga was still there ageing quietly in the corner. The little window in the kitchen looked out on to the Barrack Yard.

At the opposite end, the ever-open door led into my grandfather's drapery shop cum small pub where he treated us to Nash's red lemonade on a heavy brown panelled counter while we listened to farmers slobber stories like porter. The Garibaldi biscuits, hidden in a big cardboard box under brown grease-proof paper, were a fair-day speciality, a vain attempt to keep some customers sober.

Eileen, my late uncle's wife, kindly offered me tea. Her quiet voice and sense of style were as ageless as the chair next to the Aga. We reminisced over slices of rhubarb tart and talked about how it was back then.

I asked her if I could wander around for a while. Next door, the living-room exhaled ancestral voices. Ghostly faces peered out from between the yellowed panels and sat around the polished parlour table. Cards found fingers dealing long into the night.

Someone sat knitting by the open fire. The housekeeper perhaps. A framed face looked out at me from the mantle-piece over her head - my cousin, Kevin, so serious and proud in his graduation gown. But I was looking at the face of a six-year-old blond-haired boy, gold-framed spectacles gilding the light in his eyes. Hard to believe those eyes are closed now, shrouding his secret suffering behind a strained smile.

The statue was still there in the glass cabinet - Saint Teresa of Avila offering flowers to perfume the stale air. Dark mahogany panelling lightened as I ascended the narrow stairs. My footsteps warned old ghosts of my arrival. The door lay ajar into the bedroom on the right and I half expected to see my uncle smiling back at me, tucked up in his coral-red candlewick bedspread.

I loved this house as a child. The steps reached further and further still into sprawling rooms and spidery alcoves. I made straight for the big room where the sash window looked out on the square. The gramophone had disappeared under the dust of years; the little dog no longer able to announce "his master's voice."

The attic stairs was hidden round another corner. I boldly took the steps I was banned from taking as a child. The broken door was no longer able to hide treasures. Old broken mannequins, books breathing in the dust of years, Ladybirds lined up beside old L.P.s.

The massive brown trunk in the corner caught my eye. Yes, I remembered it now. It was the one my grandfather had used to carry his samples from drapery shop to drapery shop. I smiled, recalling the story of him leaving his suitcase outside Todds in Limerick and causing a "pedestrian obstruction." I wondered if it was this same suitcase that cost him the shameful one shilling fine in court seventy-five years ago.

On a high shelf a dilapidated angel statue still guarded her young charges, but even she could not rescue their childhood now.

As I descended the attic stairs I looked back at the lonely clock. Cobwebs cloaked the broken face of time.

The final doorway led to the store room. I loved the suddenness of entering new rooms, new worlds, experiencing new smells, and hearing new voices that transported me in seconds across thresholds of time.

THE GIFT OF WISDOM

By MARY HEARNE
Castlebridge, Co. Wexford.

This story of Ireland in the 1960s reveals how a childish prank had far-reaching and unforeseen consequences

They are opening up old railway lines again, old tracks where briars and weeds have flourished for decades. And whenever I read in the papers or hear on the radio or television about the prospect of trains running again where only the silence of fields has reigned for so many years, I think of Nonie Sullivan. And I think of her father, Tommy, opening and closing the gates at the level crossing two fields up from our place. I picture again the lights moving across our fields in the darkness and Sullivan's cottage at Carrigossera where the tracks left our land and crossed the Mahon road.

Nonie Sullivan worked on our small farm when I was a child. She came to us when my mother was left a widow and I was barely out of infancy. She worked inside and outside, in field and yard and house. She was small in stature, but her solid frame made her stronger and better able to do the heavy work than my tall slender mother.

All through my early childhood one of the first sounds I'd hear in the morning was the noise of an empty milk can clattering against the handlebars of Nonie's bicycle as she cycled into the yard.

On weekdays she dressed in a crossover apron and a pair of Wellington boots with the tops cut off. And always she wore the same headscarf loosely tied around a tangle of unruly frizzy hair. For Sundays she depended on two seasonal items of clothing. If the weather was cold, she turned out in a tweed coat my mother's aunt had sent home from America, and in good weather she wore a red cardigan that came in the same parcel. But the pride of her meagre wardrobe was a pair of white shoes, bought after long saving in a shop in town. On Saturdays she painted the shoes with some sort of whitener and left them to dry out in the little shed at the back of the cottage.

Nonie's family had always been gatekeepers, but when I was a child there was only herself and her father, Tommy. Her mother had died the same year as my own father and I was too young then to remember either of them.

She could hear the sound of the trains before any of us. I can see her still, standing in the dairy on churning day, the handle of the butter barrel held at mid-turn, her head tilted, listening. "There's a goods," she might say, "coming up Schach Hill." Or she might be helping my mother bring feed to the cattle in the fields, and even on windy days she could tell when a downward train was approaching the crossing.

For years, Nonie had been going out with a fellow who worked on a big farm in the next townland. My mother never liked him. He was shifty, she used to say, you only had to look at the way he wore the cap down over his eyes. His name was Sean Gallivan and Nonie was stone mad about him.

On Sundays she used to cycle down to Rosses Bridge to meet him, flying past our gate in her red cardigan and white shoes.

Many harsh words passed between my mother and Nonie over Sean Gallivan. My mother would say he wasn't good enough for her, that he was only using her and she shouldn't be wasting her time. Nonie would shout back that it was easy for my mother to talk and that she should mind her own business.

Afterwards, we might not see Nonie for a few days, but I was always sure she'd come back. I suppose even as a child I sensed that those two women depended on each other. And I depended on Nonie, too. As an only child, I was lost for company most of the time. Nonie brought life into the house, and laughter, too, when she was in good humour.

After those rows I would be sent up to the cottage in the evening with the milk. I loved going up there, loved to wander freely in and out of the two little rooms - one above and the other below the kitchen - or to play cabby in the grove of trees at the back. But the real treat for me was when Nonie gave me a spin on one of the railway gates, me standing on an upper rung, swishing through the air while she pushed the big gate, running backwards and forwards as fast as she could.

One Saturday evening after my mother and Nonie had words the day before, I was sent up with the milk. Tommy was outside cutting furze bushes. He straightened up when he saw me.

"She's within," he said, winking and nodding at the open door. Nonie was sitting on a low stool in the kitchen, painting her shoes for Sunday. I sat by the fire and looked on. Beside her on the floor was a bag of white powder and a jam pot in which she had mixed some of the powder with water. One shoe was nearly done, the other was lying on the floor.

"Nonie," I said, "will you give me a swing on the gates when you have the shoes finished."

"I will not," she said. "You'd better be running off home, you'll be having your wash for tomorrow."

I kept on pestering her while she did the other shoe, but she refused to give in and, after a while, I went outside. Down by the grove I had stored a collection of chainies in a crevice in the ditch. I took them out and played for a while, laying out different colour patterns on a flat stone. Nonie came around the side of the house with the shoes in her hand and went into the shed.

"Will you do it now, will you give me a swing on the gate," I called up to her when she came out of the shed.

"I said I won't," she shouted back, "go home, its going to rain." She closed the door and went back into the house.

I put my chainies away and placed a stone at the mouth of the crevice. I went over to the shed and opened the door. The shoes were on a box in the middle of the clay floor, two white ghosts in the darkness. I picked them up and carried them outside and closed the door. I walked down to the end of the grove and hid the shoes behind an ash tree. I wiped my hands on the damp grass. Large drops of rain were beginning to fall.

Tommy was throwing bits of furze bushes on the fire when I put my head around the door.

"I'm goin' home now," I said.

"Tell your mother we're thankful for the milk," he replied.

Nonie came up from the room. "I might be down on Monday," she said.

By the time I got home it was pouring rain. My mother filled the zinc bath and made me take off all my clothes and wash myself. Next morning there was no sign of Nonie at Mass.

"I wonder what's wrong with herself today," my mother said on the way out. "No doubt she'll be better by this evening, well enough to doll herself up and go down to the bridge to meet that fellow."

Nonie didn't come down on Monday, and in the afternoon when I went up with the milk she was sitting at the fire. Without the headscarf, her hair looked wild

"Why did you destroy my shoes," she said.

"I only hid them," I said, "for a joke."

She got up and turned on me, and caught me by the shoulders, her hard fingers pressing into my bones.

"You little rip," she shouted, shaking me, "you put my shoes out in the rain. I couldn't go anywhere yesterday, you destroyed the only pair of shoes I have." She let go and put her hands over her face and started to cry. I turned and ran out the door.

I ran through the fields. It was autumn, the ditches were thick with briars. By the time I got in home my hands and legs were scratched and bleeding, my dress was torn. I told my mother I had fallen into the thorns.

Nonie did not arrive next morning. In the evening when my mother told me to bring the milk up to the cottage, I had to tell her about the shoes. I said I was afraid in case Nonie might still be cross with me. My mother went up with the milk herself, and during that week she went down to Rosses Bridge and got the bus into town and bought a new pair of white shoes in Nonie's size. Before she brought them up to the cottage, she took them out of the box and tried them on, they looked like boats on her small feet.

Nonie came back to us for a few weeks. Everything was different. I kept out of her way as much as I could. There were no more rows between my mother and herself over Sean Gallivan. From bits of conversation overheard I learned that he had been seen at Rosses Bridge the Sunday night she had no shoes, but that when she cycled down the following Sunday there was no sign of him, though she waited a long time. There was no sign of him the following week either. Coming out from Mass one Sunday, I heard a neighbour telling my mother that it was rumoured he had taken up with a girl from over that side.

In October, Tommy Sullivan had to go into hospital in town. Nonie stayed at home to mind the crossing, so my mother had to take on a boy who had left school that summer. Tommy died on the last day of the month. I remember the date - he was prayed for at mass on All Saints' Day. I never again went up to the cottage. The boy brought up the milk on his way home in the evenings.

For about eight years after her father died, Nonie minded the crossing, opening and closing the gates for the trains. I used to see her at mass on Sundays, over at the other side of the church. After my Confirmation I went away to boarding school.

In the early nineteen sixties they shut down the railway line. I was just out of secretarial college and in my first job in Dublin when I learned in a letter from my mother that Nonie had gone to England.

"What in God's name is she going to do over there, at this hour of her life," my mother wrote. I was too taken up with my own life and the dizzy taste of freedom to give Nonie a second thought.

It wasn't until long afterwards, in the depths of despair and feeling the deep pain of love and loss for the first time - I thought of Nonie: was this how she felt, too, all those years ago? The memory of her face at the other side of the church began to haunt my dreams. Tormented by guilt, I went to confession. I told the priest about how, through a silly childish prank I changed the course of another person's life.

The priest listened while I poured out my story, then he blessed me and told me to go in peace. A loving God does not require us to ask for forgiveness in adult life for the innocent acts of childhood, he said. And even though at ten years of age I had attained the age of reason, I had not been confirmed and therefore had not yet received the gift of wisdom.

Bed & Breakfast

By Helen Bennett
Conna, Co. Cork

Nan lost her husband to a German torpedo in World War 2 but she battled on and raised her family through her B&B business

The click of the hall light signalled the end of another long day. Nan shuffled down the well-worn carpet to wind the grandfather clock which had stood in the same place for the past fifty years, never losing a minute.

She made her way slowly to her little sitting-room at the back of the house - the guests had their own one just inside the front door, but this was her haven, here she could leave her paper open, her knitting on the coffee table and not have to tidy it away.

The old ginger cat, Ralph, languished on the sofa, basking in the evening sun, now sinking behind the heather-covered hills that surrounded Sleepy Lodge, Nan's bed and breakfast.

To-night was no different to any of the other nights over the past fifty years since she had first opened her doors to paying guests, except for one thing: it was her last night of business. To-morrow there would be no breakfasts to make, or beds to change, or guests to meet and welcome. She had not made the decision lightly and would miss the friendly banter at breakfast time, the house slowly coming alive with guests ready to head out on their daily excursions.

What she wouldn't miss was the endless work, nearly eighty she was now, and she felt she had earned the rest. After she had closed the door for the last time when the final guest left, she was looking forward to a few hours in front of the television in her old worn brown armchair, its stuffing pushing through the worn places and the pattern almost indistinguishable.

Nan's eyes grew heavy and began to droop, the paper slipped from her hands to lie in a crumpled heap at her feet. She slept.

A sleep of memories enveloped her, drawing her back to when she had first decided to open the bed and breakfast. She remembered all the people who had passed through her doors, and sometimes her heart, in those years. Her children and what they had achieved were all jumbled together in her sleepy memories.

Her dreams took her back to when she first opened her doors to the public, a decision not made lightly, but out of necessity at the time when she had just lost her beloved husband, Edmond. It was 1942 and a cold February day when word had come that his boat had been torpedoed off the coast of France. The only words she remembered were "no survivors."

He had been honoured for his service to his country, but little good were fancy medals on a wall to a girl of twenty-two with a baby of a year old and another on the way and no means except a meagre army pension. So the decision was made to open her own bed and breakfast and hope to become an independent woman and not have to rely on her family to put food in her children's mouths.

Oh, her mother had been strongly opposed to the idea, horrified even at the thought of her, a young girl, inviting strangers into her home.

"It's no way for a young widow to be carrying on," she had stated when told of her daughter's plans. "In God's name, what will the neighbours think?"

"I'm not really bothered what they think", Nan had replied, displaying a confidence she was far from feeling, "I have a family to feed and feed them I will, by whatever means are available to me, and you can either support me or oppose me, but, one way or the other, I'm doing it."

She had never spoken to her mother in that way before, but her survival instinct had taken over and from that she gained courage.

Her mother had mellowed a bit then and said: "You know your father and I will not see you short and we will provide for the babies as well, won't we Jack?"

Her father was replacing the wick in the oil lamp on the kitchen table.

"Sure, she knows that, Mag, but I can see the girl's mind is made up." And then he added: "We'll try to help you out as best we can, love, don't worry."

"Of course we will, Jack," Mags said, "but I still think you're taking on too much, Nan, especially in your condition, but if your mind is made up, we'll do our best to help you out. We just worry about you, don't we Jack?"

Nan and her father had always been close and she knew she could rely on his support.

So, shortly after that, Sleepy Lodge had opened its doors. Nan's thoughts shifted, and another dream enveloped her from the far recesses of her mind. It was the day her son, Jackie, had started school. The image of his dead father, with jet black curls and dimpled cheeks, Jackie had danced happily along beside her as he headed towards St. Francis National School in the village.

But it was a very despondent little boy who returned that afternoon. "All the other boys and girls say you're a bad woman," he said. "They said we have strange men living in our house, and they said they're not allowed to play with me," he said as he sobbed into Nan's skirt.

Nan was heartbroken and angry all at the same time. She had spent the last four years doing her best to try and build up her little business and had become well-known in the area for her wonderful baking. All it took was a few bigots in the village who were always quick to point the finger and say she was nothing more than a hussy when she ran a perfectly respectable business. Well, she'd show them.

On Sunday morning she dressed the boys in their Sunday best and walked briskly down the hill to the village church. She made her way to her usual seat and waited. When old Fr. Murphy had concluded the sermon, she stood up, walked to the altar, and told the entire village exactly what she thought of their narrow-minded, spiteful gossiping.

"You call yourself Christians," she said, "sitting here in God's house and trying to deny a young widow a decent living for herself and her children. You're nothing but a bunch of hypocrites."

Then, taking her boys by the hand, and, with her head held high, she left the church. Fr. Murphy had called to the house that afternoon and had been very upset by her actions, but as she told him:

"I only did what I had to do, Father, and I'm sorry if I offended anyone, but I'm sick of people talking about me and pointing the finger. I'm a good, clean-living person."

He hadn't been able to deny that and they had parted on good terms.

Nan had no more trouble after that and her business grew and thrived.

Ralph stirred on Nan's knee. He shifted position and so did her dream, to the time when Jackie had fallen down the well. If it hadn't been for the two salesmen who were staying at the time, he might never have been found. He was a very lucky little boy to escape unscathed by the experience. They were lovely fellows, those salesmen, but a bit picky about their food, didn't like eggs or brown bread, but nice lads nonetheless.

Then there was the newly-married couple who had spent their honeymoon with her in Sleepy Lodge, and had returned every year for thirty years. She had gotten to know many couples like that who returned year after year. She had gotten to know when their children were born and what they did as they grew up. Now most of the young couples who had stayed were grandparents themselves and often brought photos of their grandchildren to show Nan.

Her business had grown and so had Sleepy Lodge. She had had to build on extra rooms and had seen many interesting and unusual people over her fifty years. As her son, Jackie, once said to her:

"Mam, do you know that all human life passes through this house," and he laughed for he knew his mother loved every minute of it, even though she often complained about the workload.

Her reply was: "Some of them not so human, Jackie," and they had laughed together at the thought of it.

Jackie was now grown up and running a successful garage business in the village. Her other son, Dermot, had emigrated to Australia. Her plan was to visit him when she retired.

Her boys had grown up to be a great help to her and had spent their summers taking bookings and running the little kitchen shop she had opened to sell her preserves, jams, breads and homemade cakes to visitors and guests. They were good boys and never gave her any trouble. Dermot was only a year younger than Jackie and they did everything together. So she was naturally very upset when Dermot told her of his plans to move to Australia.

"It's the other side of the world," she said, "I'll never see you again."

"Don't be daft," Dermot said, "it's only a day away on the plane and it's 1970, Mam. I'm twenty-eight years old and if I don't go now I never will."

So, with heavy heart, she had waved him off on the bus to Dublin, to get his flight which would take him first to London and then to Singapore where he would spend two weeks before boarding a flight for Sydney. Dermot was a sensible boy and an excellent carpenter, who should have no problem finding work, but she would miss him and so would his brother. At least she had Jackie nearby and his wife, Maria, who was a great help to Nan during the busy season. They had a little girl, Libby, Nan's first grandchild.

So Dermot had left, and Nan and Jackie had continued to work in the village. Nan was still providing the best bed and breakfast in the area. The years had slipped by. Dermot would be fifty now. He had been born the year she had opened Sleepy Lodge, and Jackie was fifty one. Her grand-daughter, Libby, often helped out in the bed and breakfast and had grown into a beautiful young woman, and her sisters, Carol, who was eighteen, and Stacey, who was fifteen, kept the kitchen shop going. Carol was a wonderful cook and did most of the baking these days, but Nan still liked to meet her guests and see them off when their visit was over.

All these thoughts and memories rambled through her sleepy mind as night closed around her. With Ralph dozing comfortably on her knee, she dreamed she could see her long dead husband, Edmond, walking towards her and she reached out her arms to him. Maybe it was time to meet him again, maybe she had achieved all she had planned to do now and she could rest.

The dawn chorus started at five-thirty in the morning around Sleepy Lodge and by six Nan would normally be up and ready to greet the first guests as they came down for her wonderful home-cooked breakfast, but not to-day. To-day Nan could rest, she could sleep, she could dream.

When Jackie called at ten o clock that morning to see how her first day as a lady of leisure was going, he found her still in her chair. Ralph was pacing up and down the window sill waiting to be fed and let out into the garden. Nan's rest was now eternal and, sad though it was, Jackie felt she deserved it.

FISHING FOR MEMORIES

A Memory from DERMOT LANE

Tyrellstown, Dublin

Recalling the first time he went fishing with his dad as a young boy

We walked hand in hand, Daddy and I, down past Hazel Hill, over the big steel gate and on past the cowshed where every day Uncle Tom coaxed the frothy milk from nervous cows.

As we crossed the Rushy Field the ground underfoot grew more marshy, but I didn't care as I squelched happily along in my Wellington boots, swishing the purple heads off the overgrown thistles with my new fishing rod, bought earlier that day in Broderick's Home Store on High Street.

Closer to the river we had to fight our way through a thicket of giant plants. Daddy said they were giant rhubarb and they certainly were big, some of them towering ominously over my head. But I felt safe and proud to be here alone with my dad. After all, my big sister Margaret hadn't been allowed to come and had to stay at home with Granny. Fishing is not for girls; Granny had tried to console her, as Daddy and I crossed Davit's yard heading towards the river. She stood in the middle of the road, forlornly watching us go.

When we reached the river Daddy said it was a good evening for it, but it didn't look too good to me. What had started out as a fine warm summer's evening, with the smell of fresh mown hay floating on the breeze, had taken a sudden turn for the worse and now the drizzle was starting.

The river looked huge to me and the black water seemed to run and swirl in slow motion compared to the stream at the back of Granny's haggart, which tumbled fast and noisily under the low hanging trees.

Daddy pinched a worm from the jam-jar and put him squirming onto the hook. I felt sorry for the poor worm but Daddy said not to as worms didn't feel pain. He let me cast the line, and it took me a few attempts before I got the hang of it, but soon I was casting and recasting like an expert, at least that's what Daddy said.

When the line got tangled in some weed Daddy had to cut it with his penknife, and re-hook it. This time, when he let me put the wriggling worm on the hook, I was glad that worms didn't feel any pain.

We didn't catch any fish but that was probably because every time I felt a nibble on the line I would jump with fright and excitement, which Daddy found hilarious and the fish found to be a little off putting.

I must have been getting tired, for my expert casting soon started to go astray, and by the time Daddy patiently disentangled the line from an overhanging branch for the third time, he said it was time to head back.

It was growing dark and the rain grew heavier as we made our way home. Granny must have heard us crunching across the gravel out front, because she was standing over the Aga when we walked in bedraggled and soaked to the skin. I can still see her in her blue housecoat, waiting with an expression of mock expectation on her face and the big black skillet at the ready. All we caught was a cold, was all Daddy said.

Margaret had already gone to bed and after a big slice of crusty soda bread and a mug of fresh creamy milk, it was off to bed for me too. I didn't mind that night as I was tired after all the excitement and exertions of my first fishing trip. After I said my prayers with Granny, kneeling on the cold linoleum floor, I hopped happily into bed and snuggled down beneath the covers. I drifted off to sleep to the comforting tick of the old brass alarm clock and the sound of the wind blowing in the trees outside the bedroom window, two of my favourite sounds in the world to this day.

All is changed now of course. Broderick's Home Store is a branch of some chain store or another, the river is polluted with industrial effluent and Daddy and Granny have since passed on.

My children had no interest in learning the simple pleasures of fishing, but I will never forget that special day long ago when my dad and I made our way to the river and spent a special evening together. All we caught was a cold? I don't believe it for a minute, we caught something else that evening, something special, which I hope neither of us ever forgot.

And I hope that when my time comes to pass they will be waiting for me, Daddy with a brand new rod from Broderick's Home Store and Granny with a big black frying pan sizzling on the hob.

Shoes of Exceptional Quality

By Brian Dinan
Ennis, Co. Clare

The O'Donnell children have the tough job of thinning and weeding turnips for their father. Liza endures the work because she has a definite target for her earnings

No, this year Liza would buy her own shoes! She had decided months ago, before all this slavery had begun, that she wanted something of quality; shoes that would have fine leather soles, shoes with good strong stitching, shoes with a wide strap and shiny buckle, shoes that would last all year, and still look good.

The shoes that she would buy would not be worn in the turnip field where they would be torn to shreds amongst the stony drills. She had decided on that, no matter how much Daddy would insist. They would be red patent shoes of the finest quality, in fact they would be the very shoes in Corrigan's window, priced at thirty-five shillings.

Liza O'Donnell kept her eyes firmly shut against the dampness of that May morning. The Transit van jarred their cold bodies as it bounced wickedly over the potholes of the Old Ridge Road. The one thought that lifted her spirits was that it was the last day of the week and also their last day in the turnip field for now.

'No longer will I scratch my feet and fingers to the bone! At the end of this day I shall have enough money for my new shoes. Tomorrow I'll catch the bus into Derryvale and walk straight into Corrigan's Shoe Emporium, and buy those red shoes.'

In her mind's eye she could see the gleaming red shoes holding centre stage in Corrigan's window. When she had tried them on a month ago, Miss Corrigan was emphatic that they were made for her. With her fluttering eyelashes and haughty demeanour she assured Liza that she would 'hold' the shoes for her.

The Transit lurched to a halt at the turnip field. Mary and Josephine, older sisters with their grown-up superiority, snapped out of their drowsiness. Tony, a year older, and Eddie at two years younger, both of whom could easily outstrip Liza in the turnip drills, knocked against her as they tumbled through the double doors. Tony jibed, "Come on, 'weeding machine,' you don't want to get left behind do you?" That got a good laugh.

Liza was reluctant to open her eyes, for she knew what would assail them. Row after row of turnips, or *Brassica rapa*, a vulgar and common vegetable as she reminded her siblings when they boasted of their prowess in thinning them.

Her father slammed the driver's door and came round to the gate. "We need to finish up today," he said. "It'll be hard going, but it can be done." They made no comment. Liza felt guilty, knowing how slow she was at the thinning. But she would do her best for Daddy; and of course, to earn enough money to pay for the shoes. She prayed that she would not need to do the final thinning in June.

She pulled on her sun bonnet while stumbling over the drills to where she had left off on the previous day. The cooing of pigeons filled her ears, and she wondered why she never saw them. Black crows flew over the turnip field, cawing incessantly, and swirling in great clumps round their rookeries in the headland elms.

Liza folded the burlap sack and placed it between the drills. She dropped to her knees to begin the toil that would tear at her shoes, skin her fingers to the bone, and wedge dirt under her finger nails.

Each one laboured at their own speed. Daddy was halfway up the hill when Liza looked up—and he doing two drills together! Even Eddie pulled ahead of her. Liza felt more at home in the classroom than in the fields, a bit like Mammy in that regard.

She had always found schoolwork manageable. Her classmates liked her because they found her company refreshing. She wasn't so smart as to be scholarship material or anything like that, but good enough to be appreciated by the teachers.

One of her acknowledged attributes was her ability to speak in front of a large group. Occasionally she had been called upon to say the address of welcome when dignitaries visited their school.

Lost in thought while pulling stubborn weeds from the rough ground, a piercing whistle from father startled her. Although happy that it signalled time for their morning tea break, she could not help muttering, "Oh, Daddy, do stop whistling at us as if we were sheep dogs. Surely, there is a better way to call a tea break!"

The warm tea tasted as good as it did in Mammy's kitchen. The lads joked about the work, about who was doing best and who was slacking. Then her father interrupted, "Come on, let ye. There's plenty more thinnin' to be done."

When her father whistled for the mid-day break they ran like suckling calves to the van at the bottom of the field. Daddy soon had the kettle singing on the Primus stove. Without waiting for the tea to brew, they tore into their sandwiches. Liza loved Mammy's delicious ham sandwiches, but even better was the slice of rich fruit cake she carefully unwrapped from the greaseproof paper.

After the meal they lazed under the shade of the van, dozing in the drowsy midday air. Now and then a fly would land on Liza, causing her to jerk from her drowsiness to swish them away. A wasp buzzed her, which made her jump up with fright. She dusted herself down and muttered, "Pesky insects! Why can't they mind their own business?"

Her father came round to the side of the van, puffing on his pipe. "Right so," he said. "let's get going. Liza, you will have to pull up your socks if you hope to make today's shilling. You are almost half a drill behind Eddie—and we all know how slow he is."

They laughed as they trudged back to finish the work.

Out in the drills they resumed in earnest. Nobody wanted to have to work on Saturday, least of all Liza, who planned to spend the day in Derryvale buying her new shoes. At the end of the day Liza practically collapsed on her face at the drill's end, down in the hollow near the hazel wood; but she had made up the lost ground from the morning.

"Come on!" her brothers and sisters shouted down to her from the crest of the hill. "Come on, Daddy is paying out. You're holding us up!"

She trudged down the hill to the van where she gratefully accepted the five shillings for her week's work. At last, that brought her savings to thirty-five shillings, just what she needed to buy her shoes.

That following morning, Mary and Josephine accompanied Liza on the bus to Derryvale. While the bus lumbered along the regional road, Liza gazed absentmindedly through the window. The tilled fields whizzed by, reminding her of the turnip field and how she had laboured there. She hoped never to have to go back to weeding turnips. When the time came to graduate from school, she would go on and study to be a fashion designer. She just loved fashion.

The bus drew up outside The Savoy Hotel. "Oh, let's go in for a coffee," Mary spurted, "But, of course, maybe Miss Prim has better things to do."

"As a matter of fact I do," said Liza. "At least I have better things to spend my hard-earned money on."

"Oh," said Josephine, "buying fancy shoes? Tyler's will hardly be good enough for you. It'll be Corrigan's I suppose—whatever next!"

Liza looked down at the plain brogues she wore. They were lacerated from scratching in the turnip field. She had polished them up as best she could, but no amount of polish could hide the scarred leather. It saddened her to see shoes treated so.

"I think new shoes are somewhat overdue," she said simply.

Before entering the shop she glanced in the window. She was horrified to see that her shoes were not there. Had Miss Corrigan done the unthinkable and sold them?

Liza flung herself at the entrance door with such vigour that the chime bell almost clattered from its moorings. Miss Corrigan turned from a customer with a look that froze Liza.

"I'll be with you in a moment, Miss O'Donnell," Miss Corrigan said.

While waiting, Liza fidgeted about the shop. She stared vacantly at shoes that held no interest for her. She went to back to the window to see if she had been mistaken about the red shoes.

Miss Corrigan said to the customer... "and be sure to break them in gently—the heels are rather high you know."

At last she came free. "Miss O'Donnell, how can I help you?"

"My shoes, Miss Corrigan! They are not in the window. What has happened to them?"

"Oh, the red patents, ah yes."

"Yes, the red patents, Miss Corrigan. You promised you would hold them for me. I have the money now."

"They were not of the most enduring quality, Miss O'Donnell. Not at all your style I fancied, especially when these wonderful *Sacreenis* came in from Milan..."

"But I can't afford..."

"Oh, do try them on, and then let us talk further."

Liza slipped her foot into the soft but durable-looking shoes that were so stylish they took her very breath away.

When she stood up in them, she at once acknowledged that they were not the bright and brassy red of the patents. Their colour was rich and suggestive of wine, trailing to Burgundy, which swept round the heels. There was a subtle hint of black at the seams where the colours sort of melted into each other, and the black stitching was so cleverly camouflaged. Liza felt exhilarated, standing there in those stylish *Sacreenis* from Milan.

"A classic style in Chamois leather from the Alps," Miss Corrigan said, as she slipped the forty-nine shilling shoe box beneath the counter, and drew up the thirty-five shilling box to take its place.

"They are shoes of exceptional quality. We were fortunate to receive them at a special trial price, Miss O'Donnell," Miss Corrigan added. "Thirty five shillings, very good value. I believe it is within your budget."

Liza could hardly believe her luck. She said yes, oh yes of course she would take them. She repeatedly thanked Miss Corrigan for thinking of her.

"Not at all, my dear," Miss Corrigan chirped as she tied a string around the shoebox. Liza handed over the thirty-five shillings.

"And how is the turnip harvesting going, Miss O'Donnell?"

"I believe the worst is over," Liza told her. "But it brings its own benefits."

"I'm sure it does, Miss O'Donnell. I'm quite sure it does. Good day, now. Thank you for your valued custom."

All the way home on the bus Mary and Josephine did their utmost to get Liza to show them her new shoes. She refused to open the shoebox until she got home. When she paraded up and down the kitchen, her family were all 'uuhs' and 'ahhs' in admiration, especially Mummy who loved fashionable things.

"Now that you have a fine strong pair of new shoes you'll be able to help us with the final thinning in June," her father remarked from behind his newspaper.

Liza looked down at her beautiful Milan shoes, then towards her father. "No, Daddy, she said flatly. "I don't think so."

"And why not?" Her father wore a look of surprised bemusement.

"Because," she answered, "I don't believe that shoes of such exceptional quality should be worn in a turnip field."

THE BLACK SHEEP

By BOB DENNIS

Templecourt, Derry

Bernie and Jack were childhood friends but Jack hit the bottle and fell in with a bad crowd. He asked Bernie to marry him and then disappeared ... now it seems he is back in town

As she sat on the bench just along from her mother's grave, Bernie was deep in thought. She liked spending time here, away from the hustle and bustle of the doctor's surgery where she worked as a receptionist. She loved her job dearly and didn't mind hearing people she grew up with discuss their health and other little problems. But every so often she would make time to visit the grave with fresh flowers and sit on this bench and think.

She always thought about the same things, her childhood and growing up in a small town. How her mum had ignored the lump on her breast and when she did go to the doctors how it was too late. How her Dad was totally devastated when mum had died and he passed away himself within six weeks, some said of a broken heart.

She remembered how Jack had left without saying anything. Jack, whom she had known since he was 12 and who had moved into his granny's house just across the road. How they had enjoyed each other's company, laughed and played together, shared each other's dreams.

He used to show her his father's Hunter watch, the only thing he had that belonged to his parents who had both died in a road accident - the reason he had moved in with his granny. She recalled how he had first kissed her when she was 14 and how there had been a certain awkwardness afterwards until he told her that since she had allowed him to kiss her, they were now officially boyfriend and girlfriend.

But all that had changed when he was 17. His granny was taken into hospital and died unexpectedly a few days later. Jack was devastated. Worse still, the house was rented and as Jack had just left school and was not working, he found himself homeless. Jack was unable to cope and took to hanging out with a bad crowd and started drinking and getting into trouble with the Gardai. Very soon he was up in front of the courts and being threatened with prison.

Then came the event that she would never forget.

Her mum was ill at the time from the effects of the chemotherapy and spent most of the day resting in bed. Jack paid one of his visits and seemed to be very upbeat. He said that with the help of his Probation Officer, he had been booked into an Alcoholics Anonymous group. He was determined to give up the drink for good. She was delighted for him and then he took her completely by surprise by handing her an engagement ring and asking her to marry him. She had been so taken aback that she was speechless. He said that she didn't have to answer straight away, he promised to call back in a few days.

That was the last time she had seen him.

As Bernie entered the surgery car park, Sinead, the district nurse saw her and said, "You've had a visitor. Came marching into the surgery as though he owned the place and wanted to know where you were."

"Sinead, what are you talking about. Who wanted to know where I was?" said Bernie.

Sinead looked at her, hesitated, and then said "Jack. Jack O'Reilly. The cheek of the man! You haven't set eyes on him for over 10 years, and he comes along expecting me to pass on his messages for him."

"Message", said Bernie still slightly dazed, "what message?"

"Only that he would be in town for a few days and that he wanted to speak to your good self. Ha! Anyway, I have to go on my rounds. I'll catch up with you later. Bye."

Bernie tried to think straight but her thoughts were too jumbled. After a little while, she decided what she would do. She would agree to see him and tell him exactly what she thought of him. I'll show him, she thought. I'll show him that he can't just disappear without a word and come waltzing back into my life after all this time. I'll show him!

Bernie was glad that she had taken a few days off work. Next morning she followed her usual routine and went to the local shop. As she turned into her street she noticed someone outside the Delaney house, up for sale now for almost a year. As she walked towards her house, the man turned, smiled at her and said "Hi Bernie. How have you been?"

She stopped in her tracks and was aware that her mouth had fallen open. It was him. He had filled out, was taller than she remembered, but his eyes were still the same, those deep grey eyes that she used to love about him. His hair was neat and tidy and there were flecks of grey through it. He still had those high cheekbones and his teeth were pearly white against his tanned skin.

"Hello" she found herself saying, "where have you been, I mean how have you been? What are you doing here? I'm sorry... that's none of my business...it's just that you've shocked me."

"I know", he said, "and I'm sorry. I didn't mean to. I visited the surgery yesterday, but that snotty district nurse more or less told me to get lost."

"So, what brings you back here?"

"This house. I was thinking of buying it. Have you ever been in the Delaney house?" he asked,

"When I was younger, yes. But that was a long time ago."

"Would you like to see inside it again? I would love to hear a woman's opinion. Now where's the harm in that?" he said as he stared intently into her eyes.

"Well," she could feel herself weakening, "just for a minute because I have other things to do today."

The large hall was dark and dusty and a pile of letters and leaflets littered the floor. The bedrooms were big and spacious and as he measured them, he made some notes in a little book. She saw the big Aga Stove and memories of Mrs. Delaney's cooking came flooding back to her.

"Well, I've seen enough, Bernie. What do you think?"

"It's just as I remembered it. It's a beautiful house. So, will you be buying it?" and then added in spite of herself, "your wife will love it."

Jack looked at her and said, "But Bernie, I don't want it to live in. If I do buy it, I will turn it into bed-sits and rent them out. That's what I do, I am a property developer".

"What?" she was shocked. "You are going to turn this beautiful Victorian house into bed sits. How could you? I won't let you. I'll...I'll object to the council and they will stop you. How dare you? How dare you?" she could feel the tears welling up in her eyes. She didn't want him to see her crying, so she turned and ran out of the house. She didn't stop running until she got home and locked the door behind her. She was sitting in the kitchen drinking a cup of tea when the doorbell rang. As she opened the door, Jack was standing there.

"Are you O.K.? I didn't mean to upset you. Can I come in?" he asked.

She pursed her lips and said, "You can come in but I want the truth Jack. I want the truth about why you disappeared all those years ago and why you have suddenly come back. The truth Jack, otherwise you don't get through the door."

"That's why I'm here, Bernie. No lies. But if I do tell you what happened you must promise not to interrupt me. Let me finish. Deal?"

"Come in", said Bernie.

He sat at the kitchen table. "Where to start. You remember I gave you the ring and I said I would give you time to think about it. Well I couldn't wait and I came round to your house later that day. The doctor had been visiting your mum as I arrived at the door and he let me in. I shouted out your name but it was your mum who answered. She called me to come up stairs, as she wanted to speak to me. I went up and she was lying in bed. She didn't look at all well. She asked me if it was true that I had given you the engagement ring and I said it was.

"She was silent for a while looking out the window. Then she turned to me and told me that I wasn't the right man for you

Bernie. She said that I would never make you happy. She asked me to promise her that I would leave the town and not come back. I was stunned, so stunned that I just nodded my head left your house, went home, packed my bag and made my way to England. "When I got there I managed to get a job as an apprentice electrician. I went to night school and qualified. I saved my money, went into partnership with two other Irishmen and we started buying derelict houses, doing them up and letting them to students. The business really took off and I am now in a position to take things easy. I came back a few days ago to visit an old neighbour in hospital. We got talking and she mentioned that you were working at the surgery and here I am."

Bernie sat for some minutes, letting what Jack had said sink in. She was still trying to understand what had happened

"Bernie, your mum was right. I was drinking hard, going nowhere fast. I would have given you a life of Hell. Don't blame your mum, she was doing what she thought was best for you."

"So why didn't you get in touch. My mum died a month after you went. You could have come back."

"I didn't find out about your mum until about a year later and by then I was going to night school and working during the day. Anyway, I assumed that you would have been married by then."

"Another thing my mum said was that you must have stolen the engagement ring. Did you?"

Jack went quiet for a few seconds and said very quietly, "No, I didn't steal it."

Bernie quickly said, "You didn't have a job and you were spending all your money on drink. So how could you afford a ring, tell me that", her voice rising.

Jack lowered his eyes and said, "I pawned my dad's Hunter watch."

Bernie was stunned. She knew he was telling the truth. She didn't know what to say. There was a long silence. Bernie cleared her throat and said, "And what about the Delaney's house. Are you going to buy it and turn it into bed sits?"

Jack smiled and said, "Yes and no."

Bernie looked at him quizzically and said, "What do you mean?"

179

Jack said "Yes, I am going to buy the house but I am not going to turn it into bedsits. I am going to turn it into a family home and live in it. Of course I am going to need a local expert, just to keep an eye on things. Do you fancy the job?"

Bernie didn't quite understand what he meant but then it dawned on her. "Are you asking me to marry you?"

Jack got up slowly from his chair, his eyes never leaving Bernie's. He stood in front of her and said, "Well, will you Bernie? Will you marry me?"

Bernie got slowly up and her lips met his. They kissed, tenderly at first and then harder. Tears were running down her face as she whispered "Yes, Jack. Oh yes."

CLOSE ENCOUNTER

A Memory from TONY WHELAN
Tonbridge, Kent

All about surviving a battle with tuberculosis

In 1947 I was nineteen years old. The war had just ended and the world was still in a state of turmoil. My own situation was not too good either. After one futile and depressing year I had dropped out of university where I was hoping to qualify as a teacher. There were good reasons but that is another story.

Now I needed to find a job. As there seemed no prospect of employment in Ireland I decided to head for England where apparently private schools were willing to take on staff without formal qualifications. My two sisters were already living in England. Rita was a nurse in London and Jean, who was married and living in Hampshire, offered me accommodation. It was hard enough leaving my parents and there was something else that worried me. For some weeks, I had been troubled by mysterious stabbing pains in my upper back. Nonetheless I set out full of hope.

Once I had settled in at my sister's I began to apply for jobs. Early on there were a couple of interviews that came to nothing and after a few frustrating weeks I could see it would be a long haul. Fortunately I found some employment in a local college which provided me with a small income.

But now my health began to deteriorate. The back pains became more severe and gradually new symptoms would emerge, severe headaches, bouts of fever and a dramatic loss of weight and energy. The local doctors did not take my condition seriously and would usually prescribe codeine. As my condition grew worse my sisters became very worried and Rita arranged for me to be admitted to the private hospital where she worked so that my illness could be properly diagnosed.

181

One of the doctors there examined me and I was then sent to the local clinic for a chest X-ray. The result was not good. I had advanced tuberculosis in both lungs. The doctor at the clinic, a kind young man, not surprisingly found it difficult to break the news. Dramatic though it might now seem, he was pronouncing a death sentence.

At the time tuberculosis was a deadly and widely prevalent disease and hospitals and sanatoria that treated the illness were overflowing. Even if I could have found a place there appeared to be no cure for someone in my advanced condition. My only option was to go home and make the best of what remained of my life.

I wrote to tell my parents who no doubt were distraught. Rita, who would accompany me home, booked seats on the train and berths on the ferry. We would take a taxi to Euston.

On the morning of our departure something strange happened. If I were a more devout person I would call it a miracle. This was the set up. The taxi had arrived outside the hospital and just as we were going through the door the telephone in the office rang. The call was for Rita. It was from the doctor in the clinic. He had found a bed for me in Colindale Hospital in North London, a hospital that was pioneering new treatments for tuberculosis. Was I willing to go there?

It was not a difficult question to answer. I owe so much to this Englishman who did not know me and whose name I do not even remember. He had been moved by my plight and had gone to a great deal of trouble to find me a place in a hospital. I doubt if I even thanked him properly.

Colindale Hospital, which would be my home for a year, was one of only two institutions in England trying out Streptomycin, a new drug for treating tuberculosis that had just been discovered in the United States, where it was reported to have been remarkably successful in advanced cases. I was one of those selected for the treatment that involved an injection every six hours. After a short time my condition improved dramatically and at the end of the six months course I felt once more like a normal healthy person. Although I had a lengthy convalescence

I had been cured and throughout my long life never had a recurrence.

Not everyone was so fortunate. A great writer, George Orwell, then at the height of his powers, had also contracted tuberculosis and was in another London hospital during my time in Colindale. Wealthy friends helped him to import some Streptomycin from America but the treatment did not work for him and he died a year after I was discharged. Why was I one of those to be cured? Over the past sixty years I have often asked myself that question. I have never found the answer.

OBSESSION

By FRANK MCDONALD
FINGLAS, DUBLIN

Land has always been a powerful and emotive subject in Ireland,
and Donal O'Neill is determined to buy back his grandfather's farm

The sky was blue and cotton-ball clouds drifted across it-
Down in the valley, farm buildings nestled in the shade of
some sycamore trees. A little girl played in a field close
to the buildings. As Donal O'Neill gazed down on the homely
scene, he felt sadness engulf him. He was leaning against a gate
and he bent his face onto his forearm, shutting out the view.
But although he shut out the view he could still see it in his
head. That was the way he had been seeing it for the past five
months. Five bitter months in a grey prison.

He raised his head and looked out across the field. That should
be his field. That farm should be his. It had been in his family for
generations. Hard times had forced his grandfather to sell it. His
father had spent a lifetime trying to get it back, saving like a miser,
pleadings with bankers, all to no avail. He died without achieving
his goal.

As the only son, Donal had to take up the challenge, which he
did willingly. He was the only member of the family alive, his
mother having died some years previously. But as a young man, he
set about his lonely task with even greater determination than his
father. He waited patiently and he watched his opportunity.

The owner of the farm at that time was a man called Owen
Healy. By a stroke of luck Donal learned in a conversation with a
relative of Healy's that Owen was thinking of retiring and was going to sell the farm. Donal sensed his opportunity.

Long years of hard saving had built the O'Neill's a good reputation with the bank. Donal felt that he could depend on it for some
support to supplement his savings. As he drove out to the Healy's
farm he allowed himself a small feeling of optimism. Perhaps! Per-

haps his hour had come. He parked the car on the roadside and strolled slowly towards the house. He gazed almost reverentially around. This was his. His and his family's. He heard a noise from the direction of the red barn and he strolled slowly towards it. As he did so Owen Healy emerged from the barn.

"Donal O'Neill is it?" Healy sounded a little surprised. "And pray, what brings you here?"

Donal was taken aback. He had hoped to get to the business in hand a little more circuitously. Still, he had come to do business and he would do it.

"I'm sure you know that me and my father before me had, and have, a great interest in this farm," he began hesitantly. " I'm sure you know the history. My grandfather had to sell it but we always had the hope that one day we would get it back." He paused watching Healy's face, hoping to get a clue as to what he was thinking. But Healy gave nothing away.

"I won't beat about the bush, Owen," Donal said. "I want to make you an offer for the farm. Are you open to that?"

Healy gave him a surprised look and Donal felt that he had regained the initiative. Healy rubbed his chin and nodded.

"I'm listening,,." he said. Donal mentioned a figure and waited every nerve in his body tingling as he tried to read Healy's face.

There was a long pause and finally Healy said, "Look, I need a while to think about it . It's not the sort of a decision a fella would want to rush into."

"Okay." Donal couldn't argue with that. He hadn't expected to leave with the whole deal signed and sealed. He was happy that his offer was being taken seriously.

For three weeks Donal's head was in a turmoil. He could not sleep at night. Thoughts of the farm consumed him during the day. He didn't want to appear too anxious but the uncertainty was driving him mad. He decided to drive out to see Healy. As he parked on the roadside Healy drove into the yard on a tractor. He climbed down from the tractor and greeted Donal.

"Well, Donal," he said. His voice was cheerful but he looked uncomfortable.

"Owen," Donal said"I was wondering if you had given any thought to our discussion about the farm."

Looking awkward, Owen said, "I did Donal." He paused, "The situation is that I've received an offer from a man called Robert Costello.It's way in excess of yours, Donal. Don't ask how much. I'm sure neither you nor anyone else around here could match it. And even if you could, I'm sure he would up his offer. He seems determined to have the farm. He's the sort of fella that usually gets his way. He farms in a big way. He has two other farms outside the county."

The words crashed like an avalanche on Donal's ears. They pounded in his ears until he thought his head would burst. He could not think coherently.

"Owen! You can't do this to me.," he almost sobbed. "It's my farm - ours, the O'Neill's."

Owen Healy squirmed with embarrassment. "Donal, I'm sorry. I'm really sorry. But I couldn't turn down his offer. I need it for my retirement."

"Our farm-our farm. Going to a fella with two farms outside the county!" He almost crooned the words. "It's not right. It's not right." He turned and half staggered away.

"Donal! Donal!" Owen hurried after him and tried to detain him but Donal tore himself away. He reached the car and flung himself into the driving seat. Bitter disappointment churned his insides. He sat in the car, his mind a blur. Somewhere in the blur was the overriding thought that he had failed.

After a while he started the car and turned it towards town, his mind working on auto pilot. In the town he stopped outside Molloy's pub. He sat in the car for some minutes staring into space. Then he dragged himself out of the car and went into the pub. There was a man seated at the bar and a few others scattered around. The man at the bar nodded to him and the barman passed a comment on the weather but Donal did not seem to notice these overtures. He took his pint back to a table and sat down, seemingly oblivious to all around him.

After a while the man at the bar stood up and bade the barman "good day".

"Good day, Mr. Costello," the barman replied.

The name cut through the fog that was Donal's brain like a searchlight. Costello! That was the name of the man who had taken his farm. He stood up and as the man reached the door he caught him by the sleeve.

"Are you Robert Costello?" His voice was hoarse.

Costello stared at his agitated face and wild eyes. "Yes, I am."

"The fella that owns two farms outside the county and wants to grab another one here," His words burst out in fury.

"Yes, I am buying a farm near here, if it's any of your business." Costello tried to pull his arm away but Donal held on. Alarm reddened Costello's face as he stared into Donal's fierce eyes.

"That farm is mine," Donal snarled. "It belonged to my family for four generations. You've no right to it."

"I've paid good money for it. Of course I've a right to it."

"My family"- Almost incoherent, he ground out the words. "It was a tradition. Four generations."

Costello got his arm free and had regained some of his composure. "Traditions begin and traditions end," he snapped. "Your tradition has ended. I'm starting a new one." He emphasised his words by stabbing a finger at Donal.

It was a mistake. All the pent-up, irrational, bitterness and anger in Donal's mind exploded and he lashed out at Costello. His fist caught the man on the cheek and sent him crashing to the floor amid the ruins of a broken table and some glasses. He lay still on the floor.

Whatever conversation was going on stopped and there was a shocked silence for about ten seconds. Then the few customers rushed to help Costello who seemed to be unconscious.

"You get yourself out of here, O'Neill," the barman shouted. "The police will be talking to you."

Donal stared at the hostile faces before him. He walked out to his car in a daze. He was still seated in the car sometime later when the sergeant and another garda came and brought him to the station.

He went through all that followed in a daze. His arrest, being charged, his day in court, the unforgiving judge. Mr. Costello had

had his cheekbone fractured and had been unconscious for a while. No excuses, six months in jail.

Donal raised his head once more and gazed at the idyllic scene. A heavy sense of loss pressed down on him. He had failed.He turned away and leaned against the gate.

"Are you not well?"

It was the little girl he had seen playing in the field. He hadn't noticed her approach he had been so self-absorbed.

He managed a smile. "No, I'm fine, thank you."

With her fair hair and blue eyes and pink, summer dress she complemented the scene beautifully. She gazed at Donal, her eyes filled with childish curiosity.

"Are you looking for my dad?"

"No, I was just admiring the farm," he replied.

"I live there. I think it's the best place in the world to live."

Donal felt a lump in his throat. "I think so too. You're a very lucky girl," he told her.

A car came along the road and pulled up suddenly where Donal was standing.

"Here's my dad," the girl shouted.

Robert Costello got out of the car warily, his eyes on Donal. For a few seconds neither man spoke. At last Costello said, "I hope you're not here to punch me again."

Donal shook his head. "Neither am I going to try to buy your farm. I'm just here for a last--to tell you the truth I don't know why I'm here."

There was an awkward silence. "Your daughter seems to like it here. Part of the new tradition."

He turned to the child and waved. "Goodbye."

She waved back.

"Where will you go now?" Costello asked as he turned away.

"Far away," he replied. " Australia or America, perhaps. Obsession can destroy a man. Mine nearly destroyed me. So the farther I get away the better."

Robert Costello held out his hand. "Good luck to you."

Donal took his hand. "Good luck to you too. I'm sorry about--" He turned away and headed down the empty road.

NEVER A BRIDESMAID

By CATHERINE SLATER
Stevenage, Herts, England.

*Bridget Flanagan remembers the excitement when her friend Katie
Walsh asked her to be bridesmaid at her surprisingly
suddenly announced wedding*

I sat on a bench in the village Main Street enjoying an ice-cream.
It was a glorious sunny day in midsummer, and I was glad that
I had reduced my working hours at the supermarket by half,
allowing me lots of free time to enjoy lovely moments like this one.
A wedding party was posing for photographs at the church across
the road, and I noticed that the bridesmaids' dresses were excep-
tionally pretty in an unusual shade of deep pink. I reflected that I
had never been a bridesmaid, and, at fifty-nine years of age, I never
would be. I chuckled at the thought.

Then, I continued enjoying my ice-cream, as my thoughts wandered back nearly forty years to when my friend, Katie Walsh, asked
me to be her bridesmaid.

Katie and I had been friends all our lives. She was actually a
fortnight older than me, and we both lived in a row of houses called
"The Block." The trains ran directly past our houses. We were
three miles from the village. The proper name for our terrace was
"Railway View", but it was always called "The Block."

Katie lived three doors away from me. We played together as
toddlers, we started at National School on the same day, and we
started work in the village on the same day - Katie at Kelly's, the
bakers, and me at McCarthy's, the grocers.

After leaving school we still spent time together, but saw other
people as well. A crowd of us from the village and its surroundings
used to go dancing together, or to the pictures, or evening classes at
the village Technical School, or just go for long walks through the
beautiful countryside of south-east Ireland.

One wet evening in April, I walked along to Katie's house to listen to her records. Her uncle, who was also her Godfather, had come down from Dublin and treated her to a gramophone and she had bought her first couple of records the previous week. I hadn't seen her for a few days and was looking forward to a good chat.

As I approached her house, she came flying out of the front door, without a coat or umbrella, despite the rain. Her cheeks were very pink, her eyes sparkling, and her light brown curls were wet and dishevelled.

"Oh, Bridget! Bridget!" she called my name, hugging me when we met. Then she stood back and asked: "Will you be my bridesmaid?"

I stared at her, astounded. "Are you serious, Katie," I asked. Being such close friends, I thought I would have known if she had a boyfriend.

She nodded her head vigorously. "Very serious," she affirmed.

Still stunned, I, in turn, nodded my head. "I'll be delighted," I said, "and thank you for asking me. But who's the bridegroom?"

"Come inside," she invited, suddenly becoming aware of the rain, "and I'll tell you all about it."

Katie's parents were in the kitchen listening to a play on the radio. Her mother gave us tea and apple cake, and sent us into the parlour out of the way.

"Now," I said facing Katie squarely, "who is he?"

A coy expression came over her face and she blushed again Then she took a deep breath, looked me in the eye, and said: "Mick Costello."

"I...er...Mick Costello..." I repeated, gobsmacked and croaking.

"Yes," she confirmed, sitting up straight. "And I'm aware he's only eighteen." Katie and myself were now twenty-two. Mick Costello was indeed only eighteen, the youngest of three boys. I couldn't imagine that their doting mother would be pleased at one of her sons getting married so young.

"But," I continued, "I didn't even know that you were seeing each other. It must have happened very quickly."

Katie nodded happily. "Over the last couple of days," she informed me. "Mr and Mrs. Kelly were away and I was on my own in the shop. Mick was doing some odd jobs for them and we got talking. We got on really well together. You know how I've always wanted to get married and have a family - well, Mick wants that too. The fact that I'm four years older than him makes no difference at all."

It was true that Katie was a born wife and mother. Small, pretty, neat and slightly plump, she was good at all the domestic stuff - sewing, knitting, cooking and cleaning - the exact opposite of me. I was taller, with dark hair that didn't stay tidy for five minutes, even after I had been to the hairdressers. I always looked casual and untidy, but I would make a big effort to look good on the wedding day. I hugged Katie. "I'm very pleased for you and Mick," I said, "and I wish you both lots of happiness -and thanks for asking me to be your bridesmaid."

"Who else would I ask?" she said. Katie and myself were both only children. If she had a sister I would have no chance to be bridesmaid. I went home soon after that, I wanted to catch my parents before they went to bed to tell them Katie's news. They were both extremely surprised.

There was no rain the following evening. I walked to the post-box to post a few letters for my mother. While I was posting them, Mick Costello came cycling along.

"Hey, Bridget Flanagan," he called. "What do you think of my new bicycle?"

It was a very smart-looking bicycle, but I was surprised that he seemed more interested in it than in his forthcoming marriage. "I've been saving up for it since I started work," he went on proudly. He was an assistant to Pat Crowley, the village's general handyman. Tall and blond, he was very good-looking, but very young as he stood there holding the bicycle. Having given the bicycle a suitable amount of admiration, I asked him: "Are you on your way to see Katie?"

"Katie Walsh?"

"Well, of course Katie Walsh."

"Do you think she'd be interested to see the bicycle tonight? I might see her around tomorrow."

I gave him a playful punch. "Oh, you're the limit," I told him. "But congratulations anyway -I wish you both lots of happiness. And I'm delighted to be your bridesmaid."

He laughed out loud. "Bridget, what are you talking about?"

"You and Katie, of course. She told me all about it last night."

His face changed. All of a sudden, he looked very serious. "All about what?"

"About the two of you getting married," I mumbled.

"What...whatever gave her that idea?" He looked even younger - and he looked frightened.

"Well," I said hesitantly, "she said it was all arranged when you were doing some work at the bakers..."

His face was ashen. "Oh, no - she didn't take it seriously. We were fooling around, pretending to be an old married couple. I'm too young - for at least another ten years....."

"I'm so sorry, Mick," I said. "I shouldn't have said anything."

"No, I'm glad you did," Mick assured me. Then, some colour returned to his face and he said determinedly: "I must get it sorted out straight away. I'll go and see Katie now." And without waiting for an answer from me, he got on to the bicycle and started pedalling.

I walked slowly home. When I reached Katie's house, her parents were sitting out enjoying the warm evening. They told me that Katie had gone for a walk with Mick Costello. "Planning the wedding, I suppose," her mother said.

I saw her mother again the next morning as I set out for work. She looked pale and upset. "Bridget," she called from the front door as I passed their house.

"Hello Mrs Walsh," I answered.

"Would you do us a favour and tell Mrs. Kelly that Katie won't be at work today - she's not feeling well."

"Of course I will," I promised. "I hope Katie will soon feel better - is there anything I can do to help?"

She squeezed my arm. "Not at present, Bridget - but I'm sure she'll speak to you this evening."

Mrs. Kelly, the baker's wife, was none too pleased when I told her Katie wasn't coming into work.

"Just when I wanted to go to town," she exploded. "Now I'll have to stay in the shop. As if things weren't bad enough already with that young Mick Costello being off sick as well. He was going to do some deliveries for us. I suppose our old bicycle isn't good enough for him now he has his posh new one."

I walked slowly next door to McCarthy's, the grocers, where I worked. As I took off my jacket and put on my overall, I wished I hadn't said anything to Mick Costello the previous evening. I was the cause of all the trouble, even though I had acted in all innocence. Katie had been so happy - over the moon. How must she be feeling now?

Halfway through the morning, a couple of delivery vans arrived, and Mr. and Mrs. McCarthy went to the back room to check the new stock, so I was alone in the shop when who should walk in but Mick Costello.

"Hello, Mick," I greeted him. "Are you feeling better? Mrs. Kelly said you were sick."

He sighed. "Not really sick, Bridget, but very upset. Katie took things very badly last night, and I couldn't face seeing her at Kelly's today."

I told him that she was off sick as well.

"Well, I'm off to work now anyway. I decided to face up to things. I was going to go to England. Aidan Sweeney is going tonight and I was going to go on the boat train to Dublin with him. Then I decided that running away wouldn't solve anything."

"That's the spirit," I said admiringly. "Was poor Katie really badly upset?"

"Bridget, it was terrible. I thought she'd never stop crying." Then he bought some cigarettes and went next door to Kellys.

As I was walking home from work, I met Katie half-a-mile down the road. She was waiting for me, but did not want Mrs Kelly to see her out when she was supposed to be off sick. She was quite smartly dressed, with more make-up than usual, but she still looked a bit pale and shaky. Then she told me that it was she, not Mick, who had finished things between them. She was trying to speak steadily, but her voice kept wobbling. She said she felt they were not suited, and that he was too young.

I put my arm around her. "You'll meet someone else," I said comfortingly.

And so she did - we both met someone. We met two brothers from the next county at a dance and we had a double wedding. They had two sisters and we had one each as a bridesmaid. Katie always kept up her story that it was she who had finished with Mick, and he was a gentleman and never told the truth. He took over as the village handyman when Pat Crowley retired and ended up marrying Pat's daughter - and I never had another chance to be a bridesmaid.

BEWARE THE DOG

A Memory from JOE SPEARIN
Newtown, Clonlara, Co. Clare

Bruno had a scary reputation but was it fully deserved?

Watch out for Bruno! That was the advice I got from one of my colleagues when I took up duty as a postman in a new estate in Limerick in 1967. In that sprawling working class suburb almost every household had a dog. Any cats in the locality were either tourists or else they were hardened survivors. One or two of these veterans had shortened tails, legacies of frantic chases through hedges and alleyways.

In those days the laws relating to the control of dogs were not as strict as they are now and postmen's ankles were fair game for territorial canines.

Approach each animal with caution, we were told. Maintain eye contact at all times and don't smile. The sight of your teeth will be interpreted as a sign of aggression and may provoke the dog into having a go at you.

Small dogs were usually the most unpredictable and I was painfully aware that their bite was definitely always a lot worse than their bark.

My predecessor on that particular postal delivery didn't like dogs at all and he had singled out this black Labrador called Bruno as his least favourite animal. "He's scary," he told me.

Bruno's owner was an old age pensioner named Peadar. Peadar rarely got any mail so it was difficult for me to get an idea as to what sort of person he might be. I liked to know all the people on the route. Some would be chatty, others not so forthcoming. Some of his neighbours said that Peadar was a loner and that children avoided his house at Hallowe'en because they were afraid of his dog.

Fair enough, I thought. If Peadar was something of a recluse, then Bruno might not be the friendliest dog on the planet. Dogs sometimes reflected the personalities of their owners. But I had never come across a bad-tempered Labrador before.

My big test came when Peadar's ESB bill arrived. I was half hoping that the dog might be tied up, but no such luck. Bruno was stretched out on a mat in front of the doorway. His tongue flopped sideways from his huge mouth and he was drooling saliva. He stood up when I pushed in the gate and I heard him growling. It wasn't a snarling bare-toothed type of growl. It sounded more like a low, almost human-like grumble. I had often thought what a pity it was that dogs like Bruno hadn't been given the gift of speech by the Creator. It would have made the postman's job a lot easier.

I called Bruno by his name and urged him to move out of the way, but he just stood there in front of me. He was a handsome dog, probably a thoroughbred, but right now he was standing between me and the front door. I had some corned beef sandwiches in my mailbag, my lunch for later on, and Bruno's eyes brightened as I took them out. I threw one of them into the garden and he went after it. This was my chance to move and the letterbox rattled as I delivered the bill.

When I turned around, Bruno was there in front of me again, his jaws still chomping on the sandwich. My hand went back into the mailbag for the rest of my lunch, the bribe that would distract him and allow me to make my exit.

Then a strange thing happened. Bruno sat back on his haunches and raised himself upright, his front paws extended. He was begging.

The door behind me opened and a voice called out: "I think he likes you, Mister Postman." It was Peadar. "I saw you givin' him the bread. He's lookin' for more now. Hold it near his mouth. He won't bite your hand."

I took Peadar's word for it and I was amazed at how gently the dog took the sandwich.

"He's really an old softie," Peadar told me. "The neighbours are afraid of him.... I dunno why, but it doesn't bother me. We like to be left alone. Don't we, Bruno?"

I could tell by the way Peadar spoke that there was a strong bond between himself and his dog.

"Look," said Peadar. "I'll show you what he can do."

He gave the dog a series of commands. "Sit...Lie down... Stand." Bruno obeyed each order. When Peadar asked him to say hello to the postman, Bruno opened his mouth and growled softly, exactly the same way that he had growled at me when I had pushed the gate open on my way in.

THE VISIT

By DENIS O'SULLIVAN
Newtownabbey, Co. Antrim.

*Jack and Marie had defied convention but lived together
happily in their mixed marriage. Marie is unwell and Jack visits
her in the foreign environs of a Belfast hospital*

Jack didn't bother putting on the light. The fire had died
to almost nothing. The flickering shadows that usually
pirouetted around the walls of the cottage had long since
subsided. The gloom had gradually crept into the centre of the
room. He barely noticed the damp evening chill that sunk into
his old bones. He sat immobile, cap still on his head, left hand
cupping his chin, hiding the line of his mouth, his eyes black
hollows in an otherwise featureless face.

He had been sitting there since arriving back from the hospital in the late afternoon. That morning, he had locked the
door of the cottage just as the last peal of the church bell,
summoning people to ten o'clock Mass, was fading. It was a
brisk fifteen-minute walk to the village where he caught the
10.30 bus to Belfast. He hated being late, better to sit around
waiting for a little while rather than risk being late for visiting
at the Royal.

The city bustle confused him. When he came out of the
Europa bus station, he could never work out which direction
to take to get to the red buses at the City Hall. And when he
got there, he found it difficult to pick out the bus he needed.
He was still uncertain about how to get to the hospital even
though it wasn't his first visit. Invariably, he had to ask someone. People were always anxious to help. But sometimes he
didn't quite catch what was said. They talked so fast and pro-
nounced some of the street names differently from the way he
would have expected. He didn't like to put them to any trouble
by asking again so he just said thanks and raised his cap.

Today, he had been lucky. The woman he had asked was from Ballymena, close to where he lived. He had no difficulty understanding her. It meant he arrived at the Royal before visiting time had started. He didn't mind the short wait. At the shop in the foyer, he thought about what to buy for his wife. He knew she would enjoy the fresh strawberries he had picked from the cottage garden that morning, but he wondered if she would like a magazine or, perhaps, something to drink. In the end, he settled for a bottle of Lucozade. He had heard that invalids liked that. Then he went along to the café and bought a cup of tea.

He had never got used to hospitals, lack of experience, perhaps. Apart from a short spell his mother had spent in the Braid, he had had no reason to visit. His father had dropped dead while out working the high field and been carried back to the cottage on a gate. Jack had been fifteen at the time, suddenly thrown into adulthood and responsibility for the man's work on a farm that produced barely enough to support him and his grieving mother. She had been forty-two years old when she married his father just as she thought her chance had gone. He had been born a year later, a miracle in his parents' eyes, an opportunity for many of their strait-laced neighbours to tut tut and raise their eyebrows at their carry-on. Imagine, at their age!

His mother never really got over his father's death. She went about her household tasks automatically, cleaning, baking, cooking, churning the milk for butter, tending the cottage garden, feeding the hens. But her heart wasn't in it. She lived on with a constant desire to be reunited with her husband and she prayed earnestly to be released from her earthly bondage. Twenty years later, her prayers were finally answered.

It was only when a decent interval had passed that Jack and Marie got married. They had known for the previous ten years that they couldn't possibly get married while Jack's mother was still alive. The very thought of her only son marrying a Catholic would have caused his mother too much grief. He and Marie knew they could not add to the pain of the loss of her husband. Marie's parents hadn't been too happy about her marrying a

Presbyterian, but they had five other married sons and daughters and a pack of grandchildren to worry about so they gave in with a bad grace.

Marie became the new mistress of Woodbine Cottage after a simple ceremony at the local parish church, attended only by her reluctant parents, her brothers and sisters and a few close friends. The reception at the local hotel was a muted affair, but Jack and Marie barely noticed, so enthralled were they with each other's company.

Marie was a practiced housekeeper. The eldest daughter of a large family, she had been doing household chores since she was big enough to kneel on a stool at the kitchen sink to peel potatoes, or wash dishes. As a second mother to three brothers and two sisters, her new role as Jack's wife was, in many ways, much easier than she had been accustomed to. And as well, whatever she did was for a man that she loved deeply and who loved her deeply in return. Their only regret was that they had not had any children of their own.

Jack looked around the hospital café at the other visitors. He found it hard to understand how they could be so cheerful in this place where loved ones were sick, some fighting for life, rigged up to tubes and lines, others just fading away wishing to be out of it.

There were young children sucking coke through straws, chasing one another around the tables, their parents eating burgers and sausage rolls and sticky buns, preparing themselves, perhaps, for a future role as inpatients.

He couldn't imagine why the hospital allowed patients and visitors to congregate at the hospital entrance smoking and talking like they were in an hotel or the local pub. He didn't like the idea of having to walk through all that smoke and the accumulation of discarded cigarette ends. It made him feel that the hospital wasn't really serious about keeping the place clean. And he got angry thinking that it might somehow get in the way of Marie getting better.

When the time came to make his way to the ward, he walked slowly along the seemingly endless corridors ignoring the gaudy pictures that were meant, no doubt, to raise the spirits. Marie was sitting up in bed, her hair newly brushed. She smiled tiredly and, as he bent to kiss her, he could feel the wastage in her muscles through the thin fabric of her nightgown.

"Jack, you look tired. I hope you're feeding yourself properly. You'll need to be fit and strong to take care of me when I get back home, you know."

He forced a smile.

"Ach, don't you worry, love. I'm fit and well. You can rely on me."

He knew that whatever happened, he would do everything in his power to make Marie happy. For him, the reason for his whole existence was now as clear to him as the dawning of each new day. And the time when he would have to put himself to the ultimate test of loyalty between man and wife was fast approaching.

Jack shuffled his feet uneasily. He was not a good hospital visitor. He didn't know where to put his hands, his feet, where to look or not to look. He was embarrassed when he caught himself wondering what was the matter with the woman in the bed next to Marie's. She never moved, seemed always to be asleep, only the gentle rise and fall of the bedclothes confirming that she was still breathing. Marie said the woman had undergone surgery just four days ago and was still sedated for pain relief which was why she slept so much.

The mention of surgery made Jack's blood run cold. The very thought of the sharp scalpel being drawn across Marie's white flesh tracing a line of red in its wake was enough to make his mind shut down. The doctors hadn't decided yet whether or not to operate on Marie. There were test results to come back.

He asked: "Have you heard any more yet about the test results?" His voice was gruff in spite of his attempt to sound casual.

Marie jiggled about in the bed trying to get more comfortable. The exertion was too much for her. Jack jumped to his feet to adjust the pillows, a lump forming in his throat when she smiled her thanks. She tightened her grip on his hand and closed her eyes.

"They haven't told me anything yet. I don't know if that's good or bad. But we'll know soon enough."

In that moment, he knew she was expecting the worst. Marie had always kept bad news from him, as if he wasn't strong enough to deal with it. When she did it, she always looked away or closed her eyes, as if exasperated with him. He usually just smiled and let her have the satisfaction of feeling good about protecting him. It had never mattered much before. This time, it did matter. But he couldn't press Marie about it. She needed every ounce of her strength to fight whatever it was that was wrong with her and get well again. He wasn't going to bother her with any more questions. There would be plenty of time for that later.

When visiting time ended, he went to the nursing station on the ward. There were several people in different coloured uniforms behind the desk, but he didn't seem to be able to attract anyone's attention. They all seemed to be busy gazing at computer screens, shuffling papers or talking to others. He coughed quietly and, when no one paid any attention, a little more loudly. A woman in a dark blue uniform looked sharply at him over the rims of her glasses.

"Can I help you, sir?" she said, busying herself with a pile of papers.

"I was wondering if you can tell me what is going to happen to Marie, to my wife."

She looked at him questioningly. And then, as if a sudden recognition dawned, her face softened and she smiled.

"Oh! You're Mr. Johnston, is that right?" He nodded, already regretting that he had asked.

"Yes," he said. "I was wondering if there have been any results yet from her tests. She seems very tired. I was just wondering."

The nurse fiddled with her papers again. Then she went to the computer keyboard and pressed a few keys. Jack could not see the screen, just the faint blue illumination reflected in the lenses of the nurse's spectacles. He watched her face as if expecting to read the results in a change of expression or a sharp intake of breath. But there was no such clue. She read the screen and tapped again.

When she turned to him, she said:

"Mr. Johnston. There is a note here that Mr. Simms, your wife's consultant, would like to meet you to discuss your wife's condition and advise you of her future treatment. Unfortunately, he's in theatre at present and won't be free until late this evening. I can call his secretary and make an appointment for tomorrow around two o'clock. Can you come back then?"

Jack stumbled from the hospital and somehow found his way back to the bus station. The journey back home was a blur. He didn't remember the walk from the village to the cottage or taking the key from under the flat stone beside the water butt.

And now, he sat immobile, cap still on his head, left hand cupping his chin, hiding the line of his mouth, his eyes black hollows in an otherwise featureless face.

LOSING GRANNY

A Memory from LIZ WALLACE
Coachford, Co. Cork

*The children are shocked to hear of their granny's death when it is
announced at the local Mission*

My grandmother lived with us and was part of our lives.
She seemed very old to us – a small, stout woman
with grey hair in a long plait woven into a knot at the
back of her head, wearing a cross-over overall with tiny flower
patterns. She knew the right words to comfort a cut knee or set
the world right when we'd been scolded, and she had a broad
comfortable lap to sit on. She was never cross.

We loved to hear her singing as she rocked back and forth in
front of the turf fire with one of us on her knee. She passed her
love of music on to us and taught me to sing Nóreen Báwn. She
knew the names of every wild plant and herb and laughed like
a girl when she found field mushrooms that she would cook in
butter on the kitchen range.

She'd "watch the postman" for a letter from our aunt in London, walking with the help of a blackthorn stick my father had
fashioned for her, down the lane to the road, the quicker to get
the letter when it came. She'd read it and put it into her ample
bosom to be re-read many times.

She liked to listen to the news on the radio and, spectacles
perched on her nose, she scanned the death notices in the Anglo
Celt in case anyone she knew had died.

She had been widowed young and reared six children on a
small farm in Cavan. Now they all had families of their own,
some of them living in London and Glasgow. She was always on
hand to go where needed when new babies arrived or someone
was sick. She'd pack her old battered suitcase that she told us
had once been to America through Ellis Island, and she would
send my father to town to get her a sailing ticket.

One evening, when I was twelve, my cousin and I were going to a Mission in town.

Granny had spent the afternoon planting wallflowers.

"We'll have them to look forward to next spring, please God," she smiled, standing back, hands clasped behind her back, admiring the job she had done.

Now she was resting on the bed in her room off the kitchen, rosary beads in her hands. We tapped on the window and waved to her as we passed. She smiled and waved back.

"Be careful," she called.

At the end of the ceremony, Father Tully turned to the congregation.

"Your prayers are asked for Mary O'Callaghan who just died suddenly."

My cousin and I exchanged shocked looks. I felt myself going cold. She couldn't possibly be dead – we'd seen her an hour ago. My Granny wouldn't be dead. Hadn't she planted wallflowers for next spring?

All eyes in the pews around us were on us. The priest said a decade of the rosary and we answered in a daze. Somehow we got out of the church and found our bicycles.

Some of our friends cycled along the three-mile journey with us. We all agreed it must be a mistake. She'd be there as usual when we got home.

But she wasn't there as usual and we saw the cars and bicycles lined up in the yard, and my father, crying. I never saw my father crying before. The kitchen was full and people were going to, and coming from, her room. The table was laden with sandwiches and brown bread. Crates of porter and lemonade sat in the corner.

My brothers were sobbing and my cousin and I were crying now, too. My mother was bustling about making tea and buttering bread, her eyes filled with tears.

I wanted to see Granny, but I was afraid. My father took my cousin and me by the hand and led us into her room.

She lay there, beads folded in her joined hands, as if she were asleep. A candle and crucifix sat on a table. I touched her hand. It was as cold as stone.

The next few days went in a daze. One by one, we said good-bye before the lid was closed on her coffin and she was lost to us forever in this world. Our hearts were breaking.

We missed her terribly, the rocking chair by the fire a lonely reminder of our loss.

The wallflowers were in splendid bloom for her first anniversary. Their fragrance filled the evening air and I could sense her standing there, hands clasped behind her back, smiling.

I wish I'd been old enough to ask her about her life – her time in America; her early childhood in poverty-stricken Ireland and how she coped as a young widow with six children.

May her gentle soul be at rest.

Sonny's Da

By Neil Brosnan

Feale Drive, Listowel, Co. Kerry.

Sonny lived in a world of his own, a mental sanctuary from the harsh reality of his true origins, but when the truth comes out, it is very surprising

" Oh, 'tis Da's!" Sonny had said when I'd first asked about the long-barrelled rifle that hung above the mantelpiece in his parlour.

"Da fought in The War of Independence. Oh yeah, The War of Independence. Da was a hero, so he was... oh yeah, a hero. If that old gun could only talk!"

"As harmless as Sonny Lynch," was an expression much hackneyed in our village. Even now, decades later, I'd be hard put to name a less offensive soul than the bachelor who'd run the grocery next door to our family home. Whenever I'd relate one of Sonny's tales to my parents, they'd exchange a knowing nod.

"Ah, that's Sonny for you!" Was my father's usual comment, to which my mother would invariably add: "Ah sure, God help us!"

To the average villager, Sonny was more to be pitied than laughed at, a pity that undoubtedly helped his business to survive the arrival of an all-in-one post office, grocery and petrol pumps to the village and a new supermarket to the nearby town. Most villagers accepted that Sonny lived in a world of his own, a mental sanctuary from the harsh reality of his true origins.

Though nobody would say it to his face, everybody knew that Sonny had come to the Lynch household, at the age of about eight months, from the orphanage in the city. "True Christians" was how the locals had regarded Jerry and Maud Lynch, for their selflessness in opening their hearts, home and livelihood to an unwanted waif of unknown lineage.

Although both Jerry and Maud had gone to their reward before I was born, I can never remember a time when Sonny wasn't part of my life. I still wonder at his intimate knowledge of his stock and his energetic efficiency in conjuring the most unusual of items from the most unlikely of hiding places. Sonny was a nervous little ferret of a man, with an unruly shock of spiky white hair above a pair of constantly flitting dark eyes. Paraffin oil, turkey ration, home-cured bacon and boiled sweets were all dispensed with an unmentioned extra ingredient: a fine dusting of grey ash from the Sweet Afton cigarette that seemed to be perpetually smouldering in the corner of Sonny's mouth.

Tobacco smoke was just one of the aromas that constantly permeated the little shop. From the time Sonny had found himself alone in the world, he had stoically added cooking to his growing list of chores. Depending on the day of week and time of year, customers could be greeted by the smells of frying fish, boiling bacon or stewing steak, wafting from the kitchen at the rear of the shop.

Over the years, Sonny's stomach had been conditioned to expect dinner at midday, five hours after breakfast and four hours before an afternoon tea break that bisected the eight-hour wait until supper. All of Sonny's cooking was done on the rings of his electric cooker, the only modern convenience he had embraced since the demise of his elders. He never owned a motorcar, washing machine or television set, although he did take full advantage when a food supplier had insisted on installing a fridge-freezer in the interests of both products and shoppers alike.

As time passed, it seemed that Sonny became a natural extension of our family: he was a perennial Christmas dinner guest. During the GAA championship season, he would join my father and listen to match broadcasts on the radio and, on the rare occasions when my parents had a night out together, Sonny proved a willing and capable childminder. I suppose that was how my regard for Sonny grew and strengthened from childhood to boyhood, through adolescence to middle age.

To the village, it seemed that Sonny's life revolved around his shop. From Monday to Friday, his working day began with early deliveries of bread, milk and newspapers, and continued until the eighth chime of his grandfather clock released him to finally bolt his door.

On Saturdays, he would close at 6 p.m., but, on Sundays, wearing his best suit instead of his brown shop-coat, he would open after ten o'clock Mass for about an hour; or less, if the day's newspapers had sold out. Newsprint was Sonny's lifeline to the outside world. Every paper, periodical and magazine, whether English, Irish or local, would be digested between mouthfuls of food and the demands of the public.

I was well into my teens before I gained further insight into Sonny's reading habits. With adolescent curiosity, I mouthed names like Tolstoy, Hemingway and Hardy who, along with Joyce, Wilde and Shaw, vied for shelf space with the short story collections of O'Connor, O'Faoláin and O'Flaherty. Sonny's library was extensive and occupied one entire wall of his parlour; the blind wall that secreted the mysteries of his private world from the mundane predictability of ours.

Unlike Jerry and Maud, Sonny held learning in high regard. He deeply regretted his own lack of formal education and would constantly encourage me to avail of every opportunity that came my way. He once told me how his primary school principal had summoned Jerry to discuss Sonny's difficulties with algebra.

"I never learned algebra and I'm one of the richest men in the parish," Jerry had said. "Teach him his prayers and a few sums and save the rest for them that don't have a business to walk into."

I'd been based in New York for about ten years when a phone-call from home conveyed news of the break-in at Sonny's. After a few days of manic re-scheduling, I visited Sonny on the following Saturday morning, the first Saturday that Sonny hadn't opened for business in over half a century. As I had since childhood, I approached Sonny's through his backyard and was mildly surprised to find the scullery door unlocked.

"It's Mark!" I sang out from between the jambs.

"Oh, Mark, is it yourself; back from America? I'm in the parlour. Come in, Mark; come in and welcome." Sonny sat on the ancient tattered sofa, under a pall of smoke, half-submerged in a sea of sepia photographs.

"Sonny, how are you? I was so sorry to hear about the robbery. Did they get much?" After a firm handshake, Sonny lit a fresh cigarette before replying.

"They got a lesson, Mark, oh yeah. They got a lesson and that's all they got. I got a lesson too, Mark, oh yeah...a timely lesson. Oh, there 'tis. Oh yeah!" He selected a print and eyed it for a few moments before handing it to me. "That's me with Ma." While I'd never known Maud, I'd been midway through secondary school when Nora, their housekeeper, had died. Nodding, I bit my tongue, thinking that my elders had been correct regarding Sonny's grasp of reality.

"What age were you then, Sonny," I asked, deciding to detour my curiosity via the scenic route.

"I don't know; a few weeks?" I studied the photo again. I was no great judge of babies, but this one did look more like a newborn than an eight-month-old.

"I never knew your mother, Sonny. I can see that she was a fine looking woman." To my astonishment, Sonny guffawed scornfully before grabbing my right bicep with a ferocity that belied his frame.

"I'm sorry, Mark, sure 'tisn't your fault for believing the same as the rest of them, and 'twasn't their fault that the old people did things the way they did. God help us, Mark, they were hard times – hard and cruel – and it's the times that mould the people in them. I'm going to tell you something now, Mark, something that I've never shared with a living soul, but I think we'd better have a drink first."

The mention of drink only further compounded my state of incredulity. Anybody you'd ask in the village would have sworn that Sonny was teetotal.

"What'll you take, Mark," he asked, opening the twin doors of his sideboard to reveal a stock of spirits to rival either of the village pubs.

"Whatever you're having," I said, not trusting myself to make any kind of decision.

"There was no orphanage, Mark." Shaking his head, he handed me a neat Paddy whiskey. "People are strange, Mark, they'll believe anything if they hear it often enough.

"The truth is this: after fifteen years of a barren marriage, things weren't great between Da and Maud. At some time around then, Maud's nerves kicked-up and she went back over the mountain to her own people. Da advertised for a housekeeper and Nora came from the west to take the job. After about six months, Maud got herself together and came back, only to discover that Nora was pregnant with me. There must have been some tatter-ah in this house before they finally settled on the orphanage story.

"Nora disappeared and Maud and Da let it be known that they intended to adopt. I arrived in due course, with Nora re-employed as housekeeper. Look at that, Mark!" He handed me an open manila envelope. Inside was a birth certificate stating that Jeremiah Michael Lynch, shopkeeper, and Nora Mary Collins, spinster, were the parents of Jeremiah Patrick Lynch.

"That's you?" I gasped. His expression spoke volumes.

"Don't be too quick to judge, Mark. This world is for the people in it and that little deception worked out well for all concerned. When push comes to shove, Mark, isn't that all that matters? Ah yeah, that's all that matters!"

Sighing, Sonny freshened our glasses. As we toasted in silence, I became aware of a monumental change in his demeanour. Sighing, he stretched full-length on the couch as though a huge weight had been lifted from his shoulders. The haunted glare had left his eyes, replaced by a glow of calm contentment.

"Oh yeah; it's a funny old world, Mark; a funny old world!" He extinguished his cigarette and grinned boyishly, revealing a set of even dentures.

"Tell me about the break-in." I thought it time to change the subject.

"Well 'twas like this: I usually have a few drinks on a Sunday evening, before going to bed early in order to be fresh for the start of the week. I must have had one too many that evening and nodded off here – on the sofa. The noise woke me. 'Twas dark, very dark. I grabbed the gun, sneaked to the kitchen door and turned on the light. They got some fright, oh yeah, their hands shot straight up in the air. They were only young lads. I felt half-sorry for them. I made them empty their pockets – they had nearly fifty quid between them – 'twill go in the basket to-morrow at Mass. 'Go now, go while ye can,' I said. They went all right, oh yeah. They went a lot faster than they came."

"They got more than they bargained for, so." I was genuinely impressed. This was a side of Sonny that I would never have im-agined. "Just like your da in The War of Independence - when you came under attack, you responded like a true hero!"

Sonny was grinning again. "Da under attack in The War of Independence? Hah, under the bed more like! Da never even saw that gun. He'd been dead for years when I bought it, at old Wilkinson's auction. That's the strange thing about people, Mark. While I could never tell anyone about Nora, thanks to my yarns, most of the village now believes that Jerry Lynch was a freedom fighter, a Republican hero. They were lies, Mark, all lies, but 'twas the lies that people believed, not the truth: that he was my Da."

GOING TO THE CREAMERY

A Memory from ANN GARDINER

Burncourt, Cahir, Co. Tipperary

A vital daily farm task and only a bad farmer was late for the creamery. It was almost as bad as being late for Mass!

I have an abiding memory of riding to school on the back of the old creamery cart.This was drawn by Dolly, our beloved white mare. How I enjoyed watching the tarred road disappearing beneath my dangling feet, which would be spared the two-mile walk for once. If I'd made the effort, I could have availed of this lift every morning and been on time for school. However, the lad who was driving the cart delighted in giving me the slip.

In those far-off days, going to the creamery was undoubtedly the most important daily task. Collecting and straining the milk and filling the scalded churns were all part of the laborious preparations. The other possibilities of the milk churns were also explored. I liked the nice echo effect I got when I stuck my head into the mouth of the churn and did my Bridie Gallagher impersonation.

My father built a stand in the front yard under a large shady tree to facilitate the manoeuvring of the churns on to the cart. Beside it was a water trough, into which the churns were dropped, to keep the milk cool. Donkey and cart, or horse and cart were the mode of transport to the creamery and you could tell a farmer's financial standing by the number of churns. On arrival at the creamery, which in our case was Kilbehenny, the farmers lined up in an orderly queue. They chatted to their neighbours while they waited. Even the animals turned their heads and played whickering and snorting games with each other.

When your turn came, the creamery assistant lifted in and weighed the "new" milk and replaced it in the churn with "back" milk. This skimmed milk was a great boon to my father for feeding calves and pigs and it also had its uses in the kitchen.

Women rarely took the milk to the creamery. It was considered a man's job and if a husband was sick, a charitable neighbour would usually step into the breach. Only a very brave, or forward, woman would chance going into this male dominated arena -unless she didn't mind being the talk of the parish.

The creamery book was sacred and carefully minded. It was handed in each morning to the creamery manager – a god-like creature who was addressed as "Sir." He recorded the number of gallons of milk received and the amount of butter and animal feed given out. It was like a transaction card. Ours had a green cover and was kept on the ledge of the front window of the kitchen. Once, as a child, I dared to scribble with a black crayon on its grainy whiteness. The manager was not amused and questioned this violation and I got a telling off from my father. The monthly creamery cheque was eagerly awaited and kept us ticking over.

This, more or less, constituted the official creamery business. But there was the equally important social side to consider. Here was a glorious opportunity to exchange ideas and gossip with your neighbour. All human life was discussed, from politics and distant world events to salacious local scandals.

Stories, rumours, innuendo, scheming and double dealings were all grist to the mill.Weddings, funerals, christenings and murders were discussed and pondered over.Sheep and cattle prices were debated. You got to hear of upcoming events like gambles, threshings, pioneer excursions to Tramore and pilgrimages to Knock.

Free legal aid was generously dispensed at the creamery regarding trespassing and rights-of-way. You could get information on where to locate a reliable thatcher, a good bottle of poteen or a young gander. Some farmers also purchased household commodities at the local shop before returning home to a welcoming cup of tea and a wife agog with curiosity for all the latest news.

It was no mean task to have the milk ready and on time for the creamery each morning. My parents would be up very early during the summer months, milking the cows and regulating the milk. We had a young lad helping on the farm who "did" the creamery. One morning, he overslept and rushed madly to be on time. About a mile from Kilbehenny, he tied the donkey to a bush and ran the rest of the way to the village to see if the creamery was still open.

My father had another story. A neighbour of ours had an extremely well-trained donkey that managed the creamery on its own. The farmer loaded up the cart, pointed the ass in the direction of the creamery and off it went. It stood in line with the other horses and carts and when the man in charge had completed the business, he turned the animal for home, gave him a slap on the backside and it trotted back to his own yard.

In later years, tractors and trailers and motor cars were used for transporting milk as donkeys and horses passed into history. Farming methods became revolutionised and updated beyond recognition. These days milk is collected from the farms by a motorised "bulk tank." This sounded the death knell for many small farmers who could no longer compete with stringent testing, milk coolers, quotas and red tape.

When we were growing up, we thought creameries were there for good. We could never imagine that such a vital facet of country life, with all the attendant fun and social interaction, would, like so many other things, become a victim of progress.

WISE WOMAN

By ANNE MARIE MADDEN
Glasgow

A mother is worried about her daughter's plans to become
engaged to a young lad who has been fostered from a broken home

I had known the young couple for a few years. Sandra lived
with her family in the cottage next to mine and Jim lived
in the next village with the Thomsons, the people who had
fostered him from about the age of twelve.

Betty, Sandra's mother, used to come in once or twice a
week usually to take a letter to the post for me or to hand
in some home baking. I think she liked to relax in one of my
easy chairs and enjoy a break from the noise and busyness
of her own large family.

I looked forward to her visits, as my arthritis meant I
couldn't get about as much as I'd have liked to, and I counted myself lucky to have such helpful neighbours. If I thought
there was a chance of Betty or Sandra calling in, I often did
some baking of my own for them to take home with them.
I didn't want always to be on the receiving end of kindness,
after all. Betty was a woman who lived for her family and
Walter, in his own quiet way, seemed much the same.

Money was a bit tight, I knew, and Betty had confided
that she and Walter had been relieved when Sandra had been
able to find herself a job as soon as she left school. The
younger daughter, Eleanor, had just started a college course
and to have one child in work - though Sandra's wages as
an office worker could not have been high - was at least a
welcome contribution to the family budget. The three boys
had still not decided what they wanted to do when their time
came to leave school.

Lately, Betty's conversation had been all about Sandra
and her boyfriend.

"It's not that I don't like Jim," Betty had said more than once to me, "and Walter thinks he is a nice enough lad, too, but he seems awfully keen on our Sandra and it worries me."

I had learned from past experience that there was little need to ask questions when Betty was in a confiding mood.

She continued: "They're far too young to be this serious about each other. I wouldn't be surprised if they started talking about getting engaged soon. Sandra has already dropped some hints. I've just pretended to let it go in one ear and out the other."

"Would that be so awful then if they did want to get engaged? After all, weren't you yourself married by Sandra's age, Betty?"

"Yes, I was," admitted Betty, "which is why I know how much of a struggle it is. I want something better for Sandra. I don't mean Walter isn't a good husband. He is - maybe a bit quiet, but a good, hardworking man."

"Well and why should Jim be any different? He could make just as good a husband to Sandra as Walter has to you."

"No, no, you're forgetting one thing, Nancy."

"And what's that?" I asked.

"Just this. Walter and I knew each other from primary school. His grandparents and my grandparents lived next door to each other. By the time Walter and I got married, we knew everything there was to know about each other. There were no unpleasant surprises waiting to jump out at us when we got married."

"So?" I queried.

"So? Just this, Jim is fostered, or at least, he was. He was taken in by the Thomsons when he was about twelve. He'd been dumped in a children's home before that. I heard the social workers couldn't get a family to take all of the children together so they were split up in the end and the Thomsons took Jim. From what I've heard, it wasn't plain sailing. He used to get really wild when something upset him and the Thomsons thought they'd have to give up and send him back."

"To his parents," I asked.

"No, not to his parents. Back into care is what I mean. As for his parents, I know nothing but bad about them - drink, drugs, debt, fighting, prison. You name it, they've done it all."

217

"Did the Thomsons tell you this," I asked.

"Not the Thomsons, no - in fact, when I asked them, all they would say was that it was up to Jim to tell us about his background if he wanted to."

"So how do you know about Jim's parents," I asked.

"I know because my sister still lives on the council estate where Jim's real family used to live. They're not there now - got evicted, put into homeless accommodation. Next thing my sister heard is that they had dumped the children into care and then disappeared. No one knew where they went but, wherever it was, they left all their children behind, didn't even take the baby."

She paused for breath and I took the opportunity to suggest: "Even if Jim's parents are like that, or were like that, it's not Jim's fault. All I can say is that he looks a nice clean lad, good looking too; polite and, as far as I can see, he absolutely dotes on your Sandra. I've heard they think the world of Jim at the joinery firm. My grandson gets work done there and he's always pleased if the job is allocated to Jim."

"Well, that's as may be, and I don't want to do the lad down, but you know what they say -'blood will out'."

"Look, Betty, it's none of my business, but do you think the Thomsons would still be giving Jim a home if he'd shown any signs of turning out like his parents? The Thomsons are a nice family. Their own children have all done well, as far as I've ever heard, and I really think Jim is likely to follow their way of going about things. And as for his parents, I've heard a bit about them, too. They were very young themselves when they had all those problems.You never can tell, Betty, they may have changed over the years and become more responsible."

"Pigs might fly," was Betty's retort. "It really would surprise me. Jim's never had a birthday or Christmas card from them since the day he was left in the Social Services Office. I know because I've asked him. Say what you like, Nancy, Jim's background would be enough to make any decent family worry."

A week passed before I saw any of the neighbours again. My son and his wife, who live abroad now, paid me a week's visit so, what with my time being taken up with Peter and Jenny,

I hardly noticed that I had not seen Sandra or her mother for several days.

The day after my visitors had gone, there was a knock at the back door and then Sandra, looking somewhat dejected, let herself in.

"My mum sent me in to ask if you need any shopping, Mrs McAllister."

"No, no dear. Peter and Jenny stocked up my cupboards before they left. I don't think I'll need anything for a few months."

She laughed, but the worried look persisted.

"Is there anything wrong, Sandra," I asked. "It's just that you don't look very happy today."

"Mrs McAllister, can I just run in next door and tell mum you don't need anything brought from the shops, then can I come back in and talk to you?"

"Of course, dear," I could guess what was coming.

In a moment, Sandra was back. She refused the offer of a cup of tea.

"Mrs McAllister," she began, "you know Jim and you like him, don't you?"

"Yes," I said, "I do."

"Everyone likes him," continued Sandra, "but mum is against us getting engaged even though she says she likes him, too. Dad always goes along with mum so unless she changes her mind about us getting engaged, dad will be against us, too."

"And that's what you both want to do - get engaged? You're awfully young, Sandra, and Jim's only two years older. You can't blame your parents for feeling a bit worried. It's because they love you, you know."

"Oh yes, I know that," said Sandra. "But they were married by the time mum was my age and they get along fine. It's not our age, Mrs McAllister, whatever mum says. I know the real reason for her being against it is because she's heard bad things from my Aunt Tracey about Jim's real parents. She thinks Jim won't be able to cope with responsibility, that he'll turn out like his mum and dad. It's so unfair holding it against Jim that he comes from that kind of background." Here Sandra bursts into tears.

I sat quietly till she stopped crying.

"As far as I know about you and Jim, I mean from what I've seen for myself and what I've heard about you both, you seem very down to earth, hard-working and sensible young people for your age. Maybe your parents just need time to come around to the idea, Sandra. You can't blame them for wanting to do what's best for you."

"No," answered Sandra slowly, "and I know that, Mrs McAllister, but Jim and I have known each other since we started secondary school. I know the Thomsons, they like me, but Jim feels, and so do I, that we'd like to start saving for a place of our own. We want to be with each other, really be with each other. Do you know what I mean, Mrs McAllister?"

"I do know what you mean, dear. I remember feeling that way myself. I wish I could say something to help."

"Well, you can," said Sandra quickly, the words tumbling out. "My mum thinks very highly of you, Mrs McAllister. She's always quoting you to Aunt Tracy and to dad. She thinks you know everything, if you ask me. I've heard her tell my dad that you're "wise" and I've never heard her say that about anyone else."

I was taken aback at this, flattered too. "Well, I never!"

Sandra continued: "Do you think you could maybe put in a good word for Jim? Mum listens to you, even if she doesn't listen to many people."

"I'll try, Sandra," I promised, "as long as you realise that I don't know Jim as well as I know you and I can't see into the future. But what I can do, I will do."

After Sandra had gone, I had an idea. I went into the hall and searched around in the cupboard there until I found what I was looking for. I took them into the sitting room and laid them on the coffee table. There they stayed until Betty's next visit, a day or so later. As she sat sipping her tea, Betty noticed them.

"Don't mind, Nancy, if I have a look, do you?"

There was a little knot of something - anxiety perhaps - in my stomach, but I said as nonchalantly as I could: "Of course not, Betty."

She picked up the oldest of the photographs. From it a lanky young man and a very overweight woman stared sulkily at the photographer.

"Who are these," asked Betty.

"My parents," I answered briefly.

"Oh." Betty returned the photograph to the coffee table. I could tell she had not been favourably impressed.

"And these," She asked, picking up the second photograph.

"They're my parents."

Betty looked nonplussed. She picked up the first photograph again and held both photographs side by side where she could compare them. "They don't look anything like themselves when they were younger. In fact," she commented, "they look like different people."

"They are," I agreed.

"This one," as I held up the snapshot of the young couple, "is of my birth parents. And this one," as I held up the second, "is of the people who adopted me when I was twelve."

A fortnight later, Jim and Sandra's engagement was announced. That was eleven years ago now. They have been married for the last nine years and you would have to look very far to find as happy a couple.

THE HOLIDAY SUMMERS

A Memory from ALLIE MURRAY

Rathcormac, Co. Cork.

Recalling the sights, sounds and smells of holidays on the farm

I was eight when I spent the first of many holidays in the Nire, Co. Waterford, with Auntie Alice, her husband, Tommy Brazil, and my older cousins, Jim and Alice. There was no question of bringing along my own toys and books on these trips - we'd always find plenty to do, playing and helping on their farm. Auntie Alice kept a few old storybooks in a press beside the fireplace for those rare moments when we'd get bored. I remember one day she gave us a box of old beads, bracelets and trinkets to play with - it was as if Santa had landed in her kitchen, we were that delighted.

Each morning, we'd wake up to the smell of porridge cooking and to the sound of pigeons cooing, cocks crowing and the cows making their way through the yard adjoining the farmhouse. My sister, Cannie, and I used to love going for the cows in the evening. We'd take Fanny the dog and walk the few miles up a quiet country road. I'll always remember the fragrant smell of honeysuckle on that stretch of boreen.

Without so much as a whistle of instruction, Fanny would round up each and every cow and direct them to the gate where we'd wait. We'd always be amazed that she never missed one, she was so well-bred and well-trained. Small wonder that Tommy's favourite programme was One Man and His Dog. I often think he wouldn't have owned a TV were it not for that programme.

The fields next to the farmhouse sloped steeply down to a small river. I can still hear the sound of it rushing over the rocks and stones. We loved playing there - rolling down the hill, hopping across the boulders and throwing pebbles into the dashing current. We used to follow the river through several fields, over styles and across a footbridge to the Nire village which boasts the now-renowned Hanora's Cottage Guesthouse and Restaurant.

I recall coming back from the village through the fields one dusky evening. I was seventeen at the time and was furiously sucking mints to camouflage the smell of an illicit cigarette. I took a wrong turn, got lost and panicked for some time before I finally, with much relief, found my way back to the farmhouse. I climbed in through the bathroom window to brush my teeth before facing Auntie Alice, who was blissfully ignorant, both of the lateness of my return and the fact of my smoking.

The highlight of my summer at the Brazils was the shearing. Early in the morning, Tommy, Jim and their dogs would bring the sheep in from the mountains. The Penders, Walls and other local families would come by to help for the entire day. Cannie invariably got the job of raddling and I was left to pack the wool into large, coarse bags. By the end of the day, the backs of my fingers would be raw and bleeding from pressing the fleece down deep into the sacks.

I recall the craic and the banter traded among the men. They were often goaded by my older sister, Anne, who could never resist stirring up the long-standing football rivalry between the Nire and its half-parish, Touraneena, where my own family live.

At various intervals, the shearers' wives and daughters, who'd work tirelessly in the kitchen all day, would bring refreshments in the form of large bottles of Guinness or Smithwicks and the occasional drop of whiskey. That evening, we'd all troop in for dinner - worn, weary and ravenous after our hard day. No meal before or since ever tasted as good as that bacon, cabbage and mashed potatoes. The night would be rounded off with a session of singing and story-telling into the small hours.

Of course, Auntie Alice always tipped us generously for our help. But one summer she really surpassed herself. After the shearing was over, I stayed on for a few extra days to whitewash the out-houses and re-paint the gates. Tommy was very particular about keeping the farmyard spic and span. When Dad came to take me home, Auntie Alice handed me a cheque for £100 -

an incredible amount of money for a young teenager in the early 80s. I can still remember the stunned faces of my older siblings when I proudly showed them my earnings.

I have taken many holidays at home and abroad over the years, but none compares even remotely with my time spent as a child in the Nire. The total sense of peace combined with the smell of honeysuckle, the taste of Milky Moos, the sound of the river, and the sight of the mountains guarantee everlasting and fond memories of my childhood summers.

THE MYSTERY OF THE PINK COLLAR

By MARTINA RUTHERFORD

Tramore, Co. Waterford

*A cat disappears for days at a time and comes home with a flashy
new collar ... a mystery that needs to be checked out*

“ Have you seen the cat today? She's been missing now for three days.”

“Uh uh!” came the reply from 17-year-old Jane as her hands worked furiously texting on her mobile.

“Jane,” said Andrew irritably.

“What, dad? Sorry, I wasn't listening.”

“The cat, have you seen Molly?”

“Oh, no, I haven't seen her. The dog is here, though.”

“I know the dog is here. I walk the bloody dog twice a day, with no help from you! Listen, we'll talk later. Get yourself off to school. I will see you at six.”

Jane picked up her lunchbox, her bottle of water and threw them in her rucksack. She was out the door in one minute flat.

Andrew sighed: “Teenagers - they paid no attention nowadays to anything that didn't have a button on it to press.” He continued to stack the dishwasher and then set the timer on the washing machine for a six-hour delay so it would be ready to hang up when he got home. As he put his own lunch in a bag, he called for Bran and put him out in the kennel for the day.

He was just about to lock the front door when he remembered he hadn't taken the Bolognese sauce out of the freezer for dinner that night. Oh well, would it be a take-away or his pasta? His better self won - pasta. He walked back through the hall into the sunlit kitchen and found the sauce in the second shelf of the freezer. As the door sucked shut, he heard a noise. He looked up to see his recalcitrant cat on the window-sill.

“Well, well, well, who have we here?”

He opened the kitchen window and let her in. "Welcome home, Molly, we've been missing you."

Molly snuggled in against Andrew and purred. Then she jumped down and wandered off to the utility room for a drink of water from Bran's bowl.

"Love is being taken for granted," mused Andrew. That was a line he knew well. He had been a single parent now for four and a half years since his wife, Liz, had left for a successful accountant in a suit! She said she couldn't bear him any longer or the stupid house, the stupid dog, or the stupid cat. She found handling a self-centred teenager a trial and had left for a "better life."

She now lived 30 miles away and Jane saw her every two weeks, or less if she could manage it. She had always been a "daddy's girl" and had insisted on continuing to live with her father. Andrew glanced in the hall mirror. At forty-two and recently divorced, he was still in good shape even if the grey was creeping in at his temples. Molly meowed beside him: "You will never leave me though, even if you have gone missing, you bad girl, you!"

It was then that the tinkle caught his attention.

"A bell," said Andrew. "Since when did you have a bell?" On closer inspection, he realised that Molly now wore a brand-new pink leather collar with a tiny silver bell.

"My, oh my, who's been a busy girl? Who gave you this, I wonder?"

Molly's answer was to curl up on the chair.

I need to be on the road, he thought. This would have to wait till later.

Andrew was a medical representative for a drug company and his job was to call on pharmacies.

It had been the one stable thing in his life when Liz had left him and for that he was eternally grateful. The regular routine had been a comfort.

That evening over spaghetti Bolognese, he asked Jane about the new collar.

"Not anything to do with me," came the reply.

That night as he sat watching TV and stroking Molly, he got an idea about how to solve the mystery. Over the next few weeks Molly came and went as usual and sure enough some times she went missing for two or three days.

"Well," thought Andrew "I'm not losing any more of my family. I am going to find out where you're going, young lady, no matter what.'

Over the next few weekends he walked round the neighbourhood in ever increasing circles hoping to catch sight of Molly at some other house. Luck was not on his side until one March day, which started like a May Day, and suddenly became a January one, he got caught in a shower of rain and hail without a jacket.

As he took shelter under a large oak tree, he heard the familiar tinkle. Instinct made him turn round, and there she was, his beautiful white cat, crying at the door of the house behind him.

As she pawed at the door, a tall dark woman opened it and swept Molly up in her arms. "You poor wet darling," he overheard her say as the door closed. He took her in, the whole captivating look of her, in an instant.

For ten seconds or more, he felt rooted to the spot. Then he was through the garden gate, up the short path and knocking at the door before he realized that he hadn't thought through a plan.

The door opened and "hi" just stumbled out of his mouth as rain continued to pour down on him. He thought: "God, I fancy you."

"Hi"? Came back the questioning reply.

He gathered himself up, smiled and pointed past her. "The white cat."

"Camilla?" said the woman.

"Who?" said Andrew.

"Camilla, the cat," said the increasingly sceptical woman, now folding her arms and being none too sure of this wet, though not unattractive man, on her doorstep.

"What about her?"

227

"Well, she's mine," said Andrew. "Well, she belongs to my daughter and me really."

The woman pushed a few strands of her shiny shoulder-length dark hair behind her ear and looked quizzically at him.

"I can prove it," said Andrew quickly.

"Oh," she replied, "now that has to be interesting. You had better come in before you drown out there."

"Claire Downey," she said as she put her hand out to welcome him into the hall.

"Andrew Bolster - pleased to meet you."

As he walked behind her, he noticed long legs in denim jeans and a shapely figure. He followed her into the warm old-style kitchen with a cream Aga on one wall and one wet cat curled up in a basket beside it.

"Here Milly, Milly," called Claire, and Andrew watched as the cat came over to her.

"You called her Milly?"

"Short for Camilla," she said, as she nuzzled the cat into her shoulder.

"We call her Molly," he said quietly.

"Well on to the proof of the matter," he said, remembering the task at hand.

"If you remove that beautiful pink collar, which shows great taste, I might add, you will find a phone number on the inside."

Claire removed the collar and sure enough there was a number.

"Call it," asked Andrew, "please"?.

Claire picked up her mobile phone and dialled. Two seconds later Andrew's Nokia began to beep.

He answered it in front of her, saying: "Believe me now?"

They both burst out laughing as Milly/Molly slipped back to her warm nest.

"I think that calls for a cup of tea," said Claire. "I must pay recompense for surreptitiously adopting your cat."

"Great idea," replied Andrew. "I could murder a cup of tea," he said, as he pushed his dripping hair back off his face.

She put the kettle on the Aga and excused herself from the kitchen. Moments later, she handed him a blue University sweatshirt and a small towel.

" It's my son's," she said. "He is away at college. Hopefully, it will fit. You can change in the cloakroom, first door on the left. I can't have you catching cold on me."

Andrew dried off and tried not to get too excited as he changed. As he looked in the mirror he said to himself ... take it slowly... don't go rushing it ... man, she is gorgeous, just bloody gorgeous.

He calmed himself and came back to find Claire scalding the teapot and making a full pot of tea. She had already put scones, butter, jam and biscuits on the table. Suddenly, he felt starving. As she poured, he observed her more closely. She had strong slender hands, no rings. Her face radiated calm and yet there was energy there, like someone who is always on the go. He liked the green blue colour of her eyes. Yes, he had to admit it; he felt deeply attracted to her. God, he could take her to bed right now.

"This is wonderful," he murmured, smiling broadly.

She sat opposite, her hands cradling the mug: "So where do you live, not too far by the sound of it?"

Andrew explained and they worked out that by cat walk it was less than half a mile, a bit longer by road. Claire talked about her son being away, her job as a librarian, their move to the area twelve months earlier and the divorce that had prompted these changes.

As he listened, he noticed the brightness in her face and the way that her mouth turned up more on the right side when she smiled. She spoke in long relaxed sentences and, to him, she oozed honesty, practicality and kindness. She'd been through challenges, but they didn't hang round her like chains. She had moved on. He was in awe of this lovely, confident, relaxed woman in front of him.

Having finished two scones, he started talking about his own situation, daughter in the last year of school, job on the road and his newly-acquired divorce status.

There was ease between them that felt good. Eventually, with his hair nearly dry, he felt obliged to start making an effort to leave. He hadn't spent such a lovely hour in female company for a long time. Standing up to go, he said: "Well, it seems like we are going to have to share this cat!"

Claire put the dishes in the sink and turned round to face him "I'm sure we can come to some arrangement," she said with a grin.

"Listen," he said, "as a way of saying thank you for taking such good care of my cat, our cat, can I please take you out to dinner?"

"You choose," he said in a rush, "Italian, Chinese, Thai, French, whatever you fancy." He felt he was holding his breath until she answered.

"Thai would be great."

"When," she asked, now putting him on the spot.

"Is tonight too soon," he asked, as he put on what he hoped was his most winning smile.

She laughed a big deep warm laugh and replied: "That would also be great."

He wanted to hug her there and then, gather her into him, smell her hair, kiss the nape of her neck, but he had learned one thing and that was not to rush things. He didn't want to scare away this wonderful woman. They made plans to meet at seven and, as he waved goodbye and started to walk home, he felt spring in the air, the signs of new beginnings in the wet streets. He looked forward to letting his ex know that she had been wrong all along - they didn't have a stupid cat!

JOHN DEVLIN'S SHOP

A Memory from BRIAN DONAGHY
Pennyburn Court, Derry

*Recalling the much-loved old-fashioned country shop of
fifty and more years ago*

When you go to Ballyliffin now you wouldn't know John Devlin's shop ever existed. Worse; there is not a trace of John himself. There was a time when that name and that shop spelt magic to us children when we savoured those endless summers in Pollan Bay, just a short walk from Ballyliffin village in Inishowen.

The weeks of eager waiting over, we'd cram into Moran's taxi and chat excitedly with childish exuberance as we passed the familiar signposts in English and Irish along the way. Past Bridgend, Lisfannon, Buncrana, Clonmany and Ballyliffin. And there it was – Pollan - stretching before us. We were restive now and when we stopped where road and sand meet, out we'd jump, remove our shoes and socks, and career headlong along the beach, the seaweed-scented air filling our lungs and nostrils.

But back to John Devlin and that never-to-be-forgotten shop. We didn't use the front door much. The rear entrance, just across from the Oratory, seemed cosier, more intimate, almost our private access. The latch announced your arrival with a tinkling and you made your way in, past sacks of coal, drums of oil, brushes for yard-work and ones to be used in the kitchen. There was an array of tools: picks, spades, big broad-mouthed shovels, hoes, all lounging at various angles up against the rough walls of the hallway leading to the shop proper.

As I remember him, John Devlin was a middle-sized man, a little stout on it, but not fat. He wore small, round Sean O'Casey glasses and his face was cheery, roundish and pink. In fact, he looked quite Dickensian. John moved slowly - mostly because of his total disregard for time. But also his eyesight wasn't so good and he'd often pull his glasses down on his nose and look over them to read a label or to find the appropriate jar of sweets or whatever. And he'd often offer us a sweet from a jar.

John was a kindly man. You'd hear his soft, friendly voice as you entered his domain. He was seldom alone. Usually, there were a few ould characters in for a powwow, talking much and buying little. A pipe or two might be in evidence - what delicious tobacco smells! And the aroma of paraffin oil pervaded the shop, vying with the pungent turf-smoke smells from the clothes of the customers.

Sacks of clayey potatoes lay open, alongside barrels of salt herring, Indian meal, for home baking and porridge; loose sugar, white-mouthed bags of flour, sturdy steel buckets, fishing rods and nets. Southwesters and Wellingtons hung from hooks on the rafters, and there, too, you'd find Tilley lamps, saucepans and kettles.

It was that kind of shop with everything you'd ever want and a child's delight to be in - watching, smelling, listening. I loved to see John weighing out the snuff for some woman from the village. He'd reach for a small square of tissue paper already set aside for the job. Then, with the deftness of a craftsman, he would magically create a poke in a matter of seconds. As he removed the lid from the big Grant's snuff tin, he'd beam at "usins" and, with his little metal scoop, would transfer the sweet-smelling powder to the wee poke. Tiny brass weights were ritually placed in position on the scales and then the master's coup de grace: he'd place his thumbs astride the precious poke and adroitly seal it before handing it over.

The teeth-destroying penny bars were the favourite of the children during those long summer months, year in, year out. They were toffee, hard to break and kept you chewing for ages. Other gems John sold were: "nickey" cakes - square, sweet and thick, and great value biscuity-bread treats at 1d each. Pink and white clove rock and (unwrapped) brandy balls we loved and ate frequently. John must have been getting a back-hander from the dentists of Derry!

He could have been written off as a bit of a dodderer by those who didn't know him, but the same John was nobody's fool. He knew the name of every one of his customers and had a personal word for each. He belonged to an era when there was time "to stand and stare" and when the personal touch in business was valued. At some stage - around the early 1960s I think - John suffered a stroke and the shop was closed, never to reopen.

To this day, we refer to the house on the site of the shop as "John Devlin's." And so it will always remain for us children of the 'fifties who knew happier, more innocent, carefree times in a country where people were individuals and were not just data on a computer screen.

THEIR BLUE CHIP SHARES

By P. FOLEY-Ó CLÉRIGH,
Port Mearnóg, Co. Dublin

A topical story brings home the impact of the banking and economic crisis on ordinary people who felt their retirement was secure

Although it was the end of July Brian felt cold. The weather forecaster said that it would be three or four degrees colder than was normal for the time of the year. He put the electric blanket to all night use before retiring after lunch and slept much longer than usual. It was late afternoon before he finally awoke and lay on the bed enjoying the even warmth and the cosy feeling of being completely sheltered from the world outside. Through their wide bedroom window he could see the tops of wet walls and rain dripping from garages across the road. Further back were the drenched green leaves of heavy, soaking trees.

Their blackcurrants were over ripe but too wet to pick. Esther made excellent jam. Some years they got as many as forty pots from the harvest of berries on their two trees, enough to give a pot of blackcurrant jam to each son and daughter and to the families of his wife's sisters and brothers. What was left over always saw them through the winter.

Esther had told him that the price of labels, waxed discs and cellophane covers had increased. She had searched the town for those she was accustomed to use, but strangely enough, stores did not seem to stock them anymore. The new packages cost almost three Euro for ten covers, whereas the year before she bought them for half the price. Besides, the older packages contained twice as many rubber bands, labels and waxed discs as the colourful new covers. One would have thought that there would be more home jam makers than ever during the present economic crisis, but then perhaps those dependant on welfare could not afford the ingredients for making jam.

He once watched his wife at work. She cooked a kilo of fruit, then added a kilo of sugar. When she thought the mixture had boiled sufficiently she put a tablespoon of it on a very cold saucer. In the space of a few minutes a skin appeared on the surface which wrinkled at the touch of her finger. The wrinkling was an indication that the jam was ready for potting.

She always opened a still warm pot of the deliciously fresh jam for tea.

Esther had spent her whole married life of fifty one years as a home carer. Although she was seventy-two, few people knew she was not entitled to an individual old age pension of her own while her husband lived. He had been a middle-ranking Civil Servant.

The day after he he retired Brian cleared the last three payments on the house loan with his lump sum cheque and traded in his old car for a Honda Civic. Esther accepted a new outfit, a new handbag, a new pair of shoes and a share in a few prize-bonds from the Post Office.

She was delighted.

On their return from a mid-week break a banker managed to persuade Brian to invest the remainder of his lump sum in Ordinary Shares that were as safe as houses and would earn him a tidy dividend every year. In all probability they would increase in value and, although only a very small shareholder of the bank, he would be entitled to attend the annual Court.

In time the bank dividends became almost like a biannual nest egg with which they could buy presents for each of their seven grandchildren when First Holy Communions were celebrated, birthday anniversaries came around or when the children triumphed at sports events.

Brian had always been curious to know how shareholders meetings were conducted at the bank and was comforted to meet other small shareholders like himself at his first AGM. The Chairman of the Board of directors reminded the crowded hall that all shareholders were equally welcome. It was true, the dapper chairman said, that several hundred people held just one Ordinary Share of the bank's stock but they were as welcome to the meeting as those whose holdings exceeded a hundred thousand shares. Moreover, the repast that each shareholder present would enjoy after the meeting exceeded the current value of their single shareholding!

But the most extraordinary discovery Brian made concerned the compensation which the directors awarded themselves. Their fees were enormous. Some top executives of the company were paid in one year more than he had earned in his entire working life. Occasionally desultory murmurings of dissatisfaction were voiced from the floor, but while the shares held their value these murmurings were ignored by the executive.

Then this very year the blue chip Ordinary Shares crashed to the floor and his annual dividends were discontinued. What was absolutely outrageous as far as the shareholders were concerned was that the board of directors continued to pay themselves obscene fees. And so, when the Governor invited comments and questions at the Court he too raised his hand.

At least ten times his raised hand was ignored. Finally, the mike was passed to him. Brian had never once spoken in public and he was amazed at the sound of his own voice alluding to specific pages of the Report.

Their venerable institution had been known for altruism down through the years. But nothing in the report suggested that this altruism extended to troisieme aged people like himself. Elderly shareholders also had dreams, hopes and ambitions," he pointed out.

On the radio he had heard a former executive admit that the bank's imprudent decisions had been driven by shareholders' relentless demand for more and more profits on their holdings.

Now he would like it to be put on record that most if not all the private

investors entrusted their savings to the Bank in the hope of modest dividends and steady if unspectacular growth. Had they wished to gamble they would have speculated on African or Australian ventures. Because of the reckless conduct of the executive he and thousands of elderly people like him had been devastated financially.

He sat down to tumultuous applause.

The Governor acknowledged the support in the body of the hall for the sentiments he expressed so eloquently, but also intimated that, though he deeply regretted the fall in value of the shares and the loss of dividends, there could be no change in the banks' priorities.

The directors held all the cards, it appeared.

As a direct result of this calamitous fall in value of their Ordinary Shares Brian and Esther's little world was in upheaval. Frugal though their style of living had been, there was now an urgent need to re-assess the annual household expenditure. Government levies and taxes already were biting deeply into the sole pension on which both he and Esther depended. The direct and immediate consequence of this banking crisis was that their disposable income had shrunk to practically nothing. Where could they make the necessary cuts in the household budget?

Neither he nor Esther smoked, neither of them frequented pubs. Their new reality was that they would have to examine closely the cost of entertainment, holidays and even the food on the table. And they would be obliged to look again at what was unbegrudgingly given to their children and their young families.

Maybe they would have to consider cutting down on the frequent presents bought for the grandchildren. The cost of keeping young children of the new millenium satisfied amazed him since the day he had entered The Pink Emporium in the city centre when Sinéad, his beloved granddaughter, was three or four years of age. In the huge store he was dumbfounded to find four-storey-high shelving packed with every conceivable type of doll, toy or game for little girls.

Sinéad was in her element, of course.

"Can I really have anything I want, Granny?" she asked.

"Anything you fancy," Esther repeated, wrongly assuming that a doll or Teddybear would be the young lady's choice.

Not so. Little Sinéad chose a beautiful, life-like Cinderella complete with magnificent coach and four. It was an exquisite plastic creation made in China. When Sinead's father saw the gift he was both angry and mortified. What kind of a greedy rascal was he rearing?

"But Granny said I could have anything I fancied," Sinéad protested with admirable and inexorable logic. Needless to say, the beautiful plastic creation was cast aside within a week.

"Yes, we might easily save a couple of hundred Euro on presents," Brian thought. But he dismissed the notion from his mind almost immediately as he well knew that Esther would deprive herself of some basic necessity rather than curtail their spending on her adorable grandchildren. Brian next turned his attention to their vacations. During the years that their own children were at school and college they were lucky if they could visit some Irish resort every other year or spend a week abroad once in five years. But ever since he had retired and their grown up children had started their own careers they holidayed in a different European city each year. They spent happy times in Paris, London, Amsterdam and Munich but would need another lifetime to visit all the cities on their mental itinerary. Rome, Prague, Lisbon, Madrid and Stockholm were the next cities to see, provided they survived and remained in good health.

Esther, in particular, had come to enjoy these short holidays immensely. She spent the month before each visit reading up on the culture, art and music of their chosen city. And she delighted in mastering some sentences and phrases of the local language. Whenever her efforts were understood in shops and restaurants she was thrilled.

Having relived their foreign adventures for a quarter of an hour Brian decided that savings in this area should be made only as a last resort. Economising, it seemed, was much more difficult than he had imagined!

Finally, he focussed on entertainment and eating out in the city. Concerts, public recitals, theatre and Sunday games had been abandoned years before this crisis. It was not that he did not enjoy the activities, but they were now completely beyond his means.

The twice monthly visit to the International Film Centre was one indulgence he knew both of them would be reluctant to give up. Restaurants were offering bargain meals for Early B irds and they could still eat out twice monthly at places like Mona Lisa before or after viewing films. If further savings were necessary they could always try a main course with coffee or go to a pancake place. One thing was certain: pub grub was on option which he knew would not be welcomed by Esther.

Brian heard the scraping and plop of post in the hall and immediately rose to investigate. There were some bills and a letter franked with the address Kilorglin, Co.Kerry. His heart pounded for he realised that this meant a Prize Bond win of at least €75.

He tore open the letter and read Comhghairdeachas! You have just won €10,000! "Wonderful. We can forget about scrimping and scraping for another little while," he exclaimed and called down to Esther to relate the marvellous news.

Esther who had been phoning their children shook her head. "We'll need every cent of that win, Brian. Poor Harry has been put on a three-day week and Liam's wife has just telephoned that their old boiler is kaput and needs to be replaced without delay."

They were back to square one.

Hiding his dismay, Brian turned to his ageing wife: "Esther, sure aren't we blessed to be able to help them again?" Then he added: "But to-night, let us go out for one good meal and see a film!"

Religious Invasion

A *Memory from* BRIDGET COKER

Tramore, Co. Waterford

The yearly influx of holidaying clerics and nuns to the local seaside resort was a bonus for some

My brothers were altar boys when they were young in the early 1960s. They performed their duties well all year round, but it was during the school summer holidays that there was plenty of altar overtime to be had.

There was a surfeit of priests in those days and many of them took their holidays in Tramore. The priests all had to say Mass every day, therefore, lots of extra work for altar boys. I use the term 'work', because the boys usually received remuneration in varying amounts from the visiting priests. It added up to sufficient pocket money for eight to twelve year olds. As the saying goes, "A nice little earner."

The altar boys would wait in the Sacristy from before first Mass until a visiting priest arrived and needed a server. It was all strictly regulated by the boys themselves, being done on a seniority basis, with the older more experienced boys first in line to serve priests who were regulars from year to year and who would be known as good "tippers."

Sometimes there were priests who would "forget" the altar boys after Mass. These forgetful men would be left to the boys lowest in the pecking order.

The priests, some of whom came from other parts of Ireland and some home on a break from the Missions, were known locally as "Strange Priests." This meant nothing more than the fact that they were strangers.There could be many of them in the town at the same time and so there would be lots of extra Masses.

Tramore Church in those days had four side altars, so that on a busy day, including the main altar, there could be five

Masses going on at once. The Masses would be all at different stages, some starting, some ending and some in the middle. It was very disconcerting and distracting, like watching five TV programmes at the same time. You would not know which one to follow.

Sometimes on a Sunday, I'd be late for Mass, running out the door at two minutes to eleven. When I got home, my mother would be waiting with the dreaded question,

"Were you on time for Mass?"

I'd reply, "There was a side-altar starting and I got that."

She would say, "That's not a real Mass. Get back up to that church and you'll be just in time for the twelve o'clock."

And of course I did. If I had not, that would have been the one time that the church roof fell in, and I would have been in trouble for not having been under it.

Apart from the "strange priests," Tramore was invaded every summer by another large group of "men in black." In July, the town would be black with Christian Brothers.

A few large houses in the town were taken over by the Brothers and their minders. While on holiday, they would be chaperoned by older Brothers. This was deemed necessary because many of them were only teenagers who had joined the Order from the age of twelve.

Like any young people, they enjoyed the beach and the amusement arcades but always under supervision, lest any of the local girls would put their eye on these attractive young men. Anyway, after a week, they would be gone and a new lot would arrive. They could be seen strolling along the Prom, carrying black swimsuits in rolled up towels, their bodyguards scanning the crowd.

So, who is missing from the story so far? Yes, the women in black— the nuns. Many of them came to Tramore to holiday in the local convent, but unlike their male counterparts, they were rarely visible around the town. No beach or amusement arcades for them. A group of giggling young nuns could not have been allowed to come face to face with a group of bashful young Christian Brothers. It would have been unthinkable.

The nuns' holiday was little more than an exchange from one convent to another. They had to make do with a great view of the sea from the convent windows and sedate strolls around the grounds in pairs, maybe to the grotto and back. Still, a change is as good as a rest, and I'm sure they were grateful for it.

During August, the visiting clergy gradually vacated the town. We went back to having one Mass at a time. My brothers went back to being unpaid altar boys to our own not very strange priests, and we did not give their invading brethren a second thought until they reappeared the following summer.

Aunty May, The Grocer

A Memory from Claire Moloney
Knocknacarra, Galway

*The local shop was the hub of village life around which
everything revovlved*

My aunt passed away on the tenth day of the tenth month in the year 2000. It was a very symmetric date, a symmetry that was totally lacking in her small grocery shop in a rural village in Co Clare. May stocked everything in her shop: from flour to paraffin oil; from nails of every length and dimension to onion sets; from wellingtons to funeral habits. She sold bottled gas, rat poison, door locks, pitch forks, brush handles, rope and briquettes. Piled high on the shop counter was bread, next to sweets, next to newspapers, next to fruit, next to the ham slicer. Hanging on overhead rails on two sides of the shop were shirts and jumpers, socks and baby clothes. People came to her from far and wide – a publican from Westport came to buy yellow ochre paint that was available nowhere else. As Westport was a two and a half hour drive away, it was a mystery as to how he had even heard of May and her magical shop.

May was a widow and ran the grocery shop since her husband's death over thirty years before. They had no children. After his death, she shared her house with both her own mother and his mother for many years. It was an unlikely mix but it was a very harmonious house. After they passed away, she lived on her own, but was never alone as she did not close the shop till after 11 every night. She never minded serving her customers regardless of the lateness of the hour as she welcomed the company. She was a warm, welcoming, sociable woman who loved to talk to people. Her sitting room was just off the shop and people would come in and have a chat by the fire, in addition to getting the small thing that they needed. Hours were spent in that sitting room reminiscing about past times and 'tracing' while the turf fire burned in the grate.

But May's shop was more than just a place to buy goods; it was a focal point for the village. Buying your 'messages' was almost a social outing; this was a time when people generally were not in a hurry and could stay to chat and swap news. There was a high stool outside the counter for people to sit on and chat. You certainly do not see that in convenience shops today. One elderly customer came every other day at around 12 and did not leave again till about 3. May provided him with his dinner, which he would eat very contentedly on his chair in the shop. Many customers had account books, where they bought their groceries on credit, and they would settle up every now and then. Many others who did not have books would regularly come in without money and request that the item would be put "on the file" for them to pay at a later date.

May worked right up to the end which was the way she wanted it. She had moved her bed down to the sitting-room as she could no longer mount the stairs with her bad knee. She died in the sitting room on a Tuesday morning as she was dressing for the day ahead, prior to opening her shop and serving her customers as she had done every day for the previous 60 odd years. The idea of 'serving' your customer is one that seems not to be in vogue any more – it has sadly passed on, along with this unique kind of shop and this unique kind of shop-keeper.

In the days after May's death, the children in the local national school painted pictures of May and her shop and what she and it meant to them. The pictures were hung up on the walls of the shop for all the mourners to see as they passed in to pay their last respects. It was a simple but moving tribute to this extraordinary woman who touched so many people on her simple journey through life. On her kitchen wall hung a frame with these words:

We shall pass this through this world but once. If therefore there be any kindness I can show, or any good thing that I can do to any fellow human being, let me do it now; let me not defer it or neglect it, for I shall not pass this way again.

It was a creed that my aunt lived and died by. Ar Dheis De a anam dilis.